FOR DUMMIES™

COMPUTER
BOOK SERIES
FROM IDG

Macintosh System 7.5 For Dummies

Cheat Sheet

Top Six Things You Should Never Do

6. Shut off your Mac by pulling the plug or flipping the power switch. Always use the Shut Down command in the Special menu or the •Shut Down DA in the Apple menu.

5. Pay attention to anyone who says that Windows is just like the Mac. Yeah, right. And Yugo is the Eastern-European cousin of Mercedes.

4. Bump, drop, shake, wobble, dribble, drop kick, or play catch with a hard disk while it's running. Don't forget that your Mac (unless it's ancient) has a hard disk inside it too.

3. Pay list price for any hardware or software. What lists for $499 at Pierre's Chrome and Glass Computer Boutique may only cost $275 at Bubba's Mail-Order Warehouse and Chili Emporium.

2. Get up from your Mac without saving your work. Just before your butt leaves the chair, your fingers should be pressing Command-S. Make it a habit.

1. Keep only one copy of your work. Make at least two backups and keep one of them in a safe place. Period.

Finder Keyboard Shortcuts

Learn these shortcuts. The less time you spend working, the more time you have to waste.

Command	Keyboard Shortcut
Close All	Command-Option-W
Close Window	Command-W
Copy	Command-C
Cut	Command-X
Duplicate	Command-D
Eject Disk	Command-E
Find	Command-F
Find Again	Command-G
Get Info	Command-I
Make Alias	Command-M
New Folder	Command-N
Open	Command-O
Paste	Command-V
Print	Command-P
Put Away	Command-Y
Select All	Command-A
Undo	Command-Z

D1299352

IDG
BOOKS

® Copyright © 1994 IDG Books Worldwide.
All rights reserved.

Cheat Sheet $2.95 value. Item 197-3.

For more information about IDG Books, call
1-800-434-3422 or 415-312-0650

. . . For Dummies: #1 Computer Book Series for Beginners

Macintosh System 7.5 For Dummies

Cheat Sheet

Keyboard Shortcuts in Open and Save Dialog Boxes

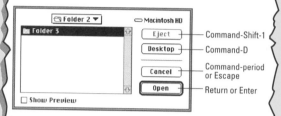

- Command-Shift-1 → Eject
- Command-D → Desktop
- Command-period or Escape → Cancel
- Return or Enter → Open

- ✔ Eject Disk: Command-Shift-1
- ✔ Desktop: Command-D
- ✔ Cancel: Command-period or Escape
- ✔ Open/Save: Return or Enter

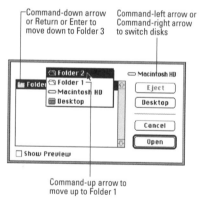

Command-down arrow or Return or Enter to move down to Folder 3

Command-left arrow or Command-right arrow to switch disks

Command-up arrow to move up to Folder 1

- ✔ Move up one folder: Command-up arrow
- ✔ Move down into the highlighted folder: Command-down arrow (also Return or Enter)
- ✔ Switch disks: Command-left arrow or Command-right arrow

Repeat after me: *The Open and Save dialog boxes are just another view of the Finder.*

Adjusting an Application's Preferred Size

1. Make sure that the application is not open.

2. Select the application's icon in the Finder.

3. Choose File➪Get Info or use the keyboard shortcut Command-I

4. At the bottom of the Info window, double-click the Preferred size text box.

5. With the number in the Preferred size text box highlighted, do one of the following:

   - If you want to give the application *more* RAM (to improve performance, enable it to open larger documents, or prevent out-of-memory errors), type a *higher* number in the Preferred size text box.

   - If you want to give the application *less* RAM (to make room to run more applications at once), type a *lower* number in the Preferred size text box. You shouldn't go below the application's Minimum size.

6. Close the Info window by clicking its close box (on the left side of the title bar) or by pressing the keyboard shortcut Command-W.

Close box

Change the application's preferred memory allocation here

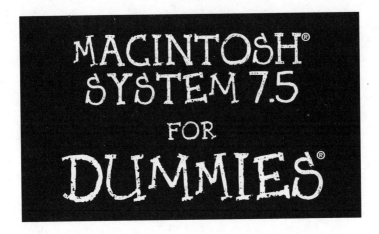

MACINTOSH® SYSTEM 7.5 FOR DUMMIES®

by Bob LeVitus

Foreword by Steven Bobker

IDG Books Worldwide, Inc.
An International Data Group Company

Foster City, CA ♦ Chicago, IL ♦ Indianapolis, IN ♦ Braintree, MA ♦ Dallas, TX

Macintosh® System 7.5 For Dummies®

Published by
IDG Books Worldwide, Inc.
An International Data Group Company
919 E. Hillsdale Blvd.
Suite 400
Foster City, CA 94404

Library of Congress Catalog Card No.: 94-77742

ISBN: 1-56884-197-3

Printed in the United States of America

10 9 8 7 6 5 4

1D/SZ/QW/ZV

Distributed in the United States by IDG Books Worldwide, Inc.

Distributed by Macmillan Canada for Canada; by Computer and Technical Books for the Caribbean Basin; by Contemporanea de Ediciones for Venezuela; by Distribuidora Cuspide for Argentina; by CITEC for Brazil; by Ediciones ZETA S.C.R. Ltda. for Peru; by Editorial Limusa SA for Mexico; by Transworld Publishers Limited in the United Kingdom and Europe; by Al-Maiman Publishers & Distributors for Saudi Arabia; by Simron Pty. Ltd. for South Africa; by IDG Communications (HK) Ltd. for Hong Kong; by Toppan Company Ltd. for Japan; by Addison Wesley Publishing Company for Korea; by Longman Singapore Publishers Ltd. for Singapore, Malaysia, Thailand, and Indonesia; by Unalis Corporation for Taiwan; by WS Computer Publishing Company, Inc. for the Philippines; by WoodsLane Pty. Ltd. for Australia; by WoodsLane Enterprises Ltd. for New Zealand.

For general information on IDG Books Worldwide's books in the U.S., please call our Consumer Customer Service department at 800-762-2974. For reseller information, including discounts and premium sales, please call our Reseller Customer Service department at 800-434-3422.

For information on where to purchase IDG Books Worldwide's books outside the U.S., contact IDG Books Worldwide at 415-655-3021 or fax 415-655-3295.

For information on translations, contact Marc Jeffrey Mikulich, Director, Foreign & Subsidiary Rights, at IDG Books Worldwide, 415-655-3018 or fax 415-655-3295.

For sales inquiries and special prices for bulk quantities, write to the address above or call IDG Books Worldwide at 415-655-3200.

For information on using IDG Books Worldwide's books in the classroom, or ordering examination copies, contact Jim Kelly at 800-434-2086.

For authorization to photocopy items for corporate, personal, or educational use, please contact Copyright Clearance Center, 222 Rosewood Drive, Danvers, MA 01923, or fax 508-750-4470.

 is a registered trademark under exclusive license to IDG Books Worldwide, Inc., from International Data Group, Inc.

About the Author

Bob LeVitus (pronounced Love-eye-tis) was the editor-in-chief of the wildly popular *MACazine* until its untimely demise in 1988. Since 1989, he has been a contributing editor/columnist for MacUser magazine, writing the "Help Folder," "Beating the System," and "Personal Best" columns at various times in his illustrious career. In his spare time, LeVitus has written 12 popular computer books, including *Dr. Macintosh, Second Edition*, a users guide on "How to Become a Macintosh Power User"; *Stupid Mac Tricks; Dr. Macintosh's Guide to the On-line Universe* (with Andy Ihnatko), a hip guide to using a Mac and modem; and his latest book before this one, *Guide to the Macintosh Underground*, a unique celebration of the Macintosh's 10th birthday.

Always a popular speaker at Macintosh user groups and trade shows, LeVitus has spoken at more than 100 international seminars, presented keynote addresses in several countries, and produced a series of seminars on How to Become a Macintosh Power User. He was also the host of Mac Today, a half-hour television show syndicated in over 100 markets, which aired in late 1992.

LeVitus has forgotten more about the Macintosh than most people know. He won the Macworld Expo MacJeopardy World Championship an unbelievable four times before retiring his crown. But most of all, LeVitus is known for his clear, understandable writing, his humorous style, and his ability to translate "techie" jargon into usable and fun advice for the rest of us.

He lives in Austin, Texas with his lovely wife Lisa, two adorable kids, Allison and Jacob, and Max and Sadie Vizsla.

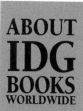

Welcome to the world of IDG Books Worldwide.

IDG Books Worldwide, Inc., is a subsidiary of International Data Group, the world's largest publisher of computer-related information and the leading global provider of information services on information technology. IDG was founded more than 25 years ago and now employs more than 7,500 people worldwide. IDG publishes more than 235 computer publications in 67 countries (see listing below). More than 60 million people read one or more IDG publications each month.

Launched in 1990, IDG Books Worldwide is today the #1 publisher of best-selling computer books in the United States. We are proud to have received 3 awards from the Computer Press Association in recognition of editorial excellence, and our best-selling ...*For Dummies*™ series has more than 17 million copies in print with translations in 25 languages. IDG Books Worldwide, through a recent joint venture with IDG's Hi-Tech Beijing, became the first U.S. publisher to publish a computer book in the People's Republic of China. In record time, IDG Books Worldwide has become the first choice for millions of readers around the world who want to learn how to better manage their businesses.

Our mission is simple: Every one of our books is designed to bring extra value and skill-building instructions to the reader. Our books are written by experts who understand and care about our readers. The knowledge base of our editorial staff comes from years of experience in publishing, education, and journalism — experience which we use to produce books for the '90s. In short, we care about books, so we attract the best people. We devote special attention to details such as audience, interior design, use of icons, and illustrations. And because we use an efficient process of authoring, editing, and desktop publishing our books electronically, we can spend more time ensuring superior content and spend less time on the technicalities of making books.

You can count on our commitment to deliver high-quality books at competitive prices on topics consumers want to read about. At IDG Books Worldwide, we value quality, and we have been delivering quality for more than 25 years. You'll find no better book on a subject than an IDG book.

John J. Kilcullen

John Kilcullen
President and CEO
IDG Books Worldwide, Inc.

IDG Books Worldwide, Inc., is a subsidiary of International Data Group, the world's largest publisher of computer-related information and the leading global provider of information services on information technology. International Data Group publishes over 235 computer publications in 67 countries. More than sixty million people read one or more International Data Group publications each month. The officers are Patrick J. McGovern, Founder and Board Chairman; Kelly Conlin, President; Jim Casella, Chief Operating Officer. International Data Group's publications include: **ARGENTINA'S** Computerworld Argentina, Infoworld Argentina; **AUSTRALIA'S** Computerworld Australia, Computer Living, Australian PC World, Australian Macworld, Network World, Mobile Business Australia, Publish!, Reseller, IDG Sources; **AUSTRIA'S** Computerwelt Oesterreich, PC Test; **BELGIUM'S** Data News (CW); **BOLIVIA'S** Computerworld; **BRAZIL'S** Computerworld, Connections, Game Power, Mundo Unix, PC World, Publish, Super Game; **BULGARIA'S** Computerworld Bulgaria, PC & Mac World Bulgaria, Network World Bulgaria; **CANADA'S** CIO Canada, Computerworld Canada, InfoCanada, Network World Canada, Reseller; **CHILE'S** Computerworld Chile, Informatica; **COLOMBIA'S** Computerworld Colombia, PC World; **COSTA RICA'S** PC World; **CZECH REPUBLIC'S** Computerworld, Elektronika, PC World; **DENMARK'S** Communications World, Computerworld Danmark, Computerworld Focus, Macintosh Produktkatalog, Macworld Danmark, PC World Danmark, PC Produktguide, Tech World, Windows World; **ECUADOR'S** PC World Ecuador; **EGYPT'S** Computerworld (CW) Middle East, PC World Middle East; **FINLAND'S** MikroPC, Tietoviikko, Tietoverkko; **FRANCE'S** Distributique, GOLDEN MAC, InfoPC, Le Guide du Monde Informatique, Le Monde Informatique, Telecoms & Reseaux; **GERMANY'S** Computerwoche, Computerwoche Focus, Computerwoche Extra, Electronic Entertainment, Gamepro, Information Management, Macwelt, Netzwelt, PC Welt, Publish, Publish; **GREECE'S** Publish & Macworld; **HONG KONG'S** Computerworld Hong Kong, PC World Hong Kong; **HUNGARY'S** Computerworld SZT, PC World; **INDIA'S** Computers & Communications; **INDONESIA'S** Info Komputer; **IRELAND'S** ComputerScope; **ISRAEL'S** Beyond Windows, Computerworld Israel, Multimedia, PC World Israel; **ITALY'S** Computerworld Italia, Lotus Magazine, Macworld Italia, Networking Italia, PC Shopping Italy, PC World Italia; **JAPAN'S** Computerworld Today, Information Systems World, Macworld Japan, Nikkei Personal Computing, SunWorld Japan, Windows World; **KENYA'S** East African Computer News; **KOREA'S** Computerworld Korea, Macworld Korea, PC World Korea; **LATIN AMERICA'S** GamePro; **MALAYSIA'S** Computerworld Malaysia, PC World Malaysia; **MEXICO'S** Compu Edicion, Compu Manufactura, Computacion/Punto de Venta, Computerworld Mexico, MacWorld, Mundo Unix, PC World, Windows; **THE NETHERLANDS'** Computer! Totaal, Computable (CW), LAN Magazine, Lotus Magazine, MacWorld; **NEW ZEALAND'S** Computer Buyer, Computerworld New Zealand, Network World, New Zealand PC World; **NIGERIA'S** PC World Africa; **NORWAY'S** Computerworld Norge, Lotusworld Norge, Macworld Norge, Maxi Data, Networld, PC World Ekspress, PC World Nettverk, PC World Norge, PC World's Produktguide, Publish& Multimedia World, Student Data, Unix World, Windowsworld; **PAKISTAN'S** PC World Pakistan; **PANAMA'S** PC World Panama; **PERU'S** Computerworld Peru, PC World; **PEOPLE'S REPUBLIC OF CHINA'S** China Computerworld, China Infoworld, China PC Info Magazine, Computer Fan, PC World China, Electronics International, Electronics Today/Multimedia World, Electronic Product World, China Network World, Software World Magazine, Telecom Product World; **PHILIPPINES'** Computerworld Philippines, PC Digest (PCW); **POLAND'S** Computerworld Poland, Computerworld Special Report, Networld, PC World/Komputer, Sunworld; **PORTUGAL'S** Cerebro/PC World, Correio Informatico/Computerworld, MacIn; **ROMANIA'S** Computerworld, PC World, Telecom Romania; **RUSSIA'S** Computerworld-Moscow, Mir - PK (PCW), Sety (Networks); **SINGAPORE'S** Computerworld Southeast Asia, PC World Singapore; **SLOVENIA'S** Monitor Magazine; **SOUTH AFRICA'S** Computer Mail (CIO),Computing S.A.,Network World S.A., Software World; **SPAIN'S** Advanced Systems, Amiga World, Computerworld Espana, Communicaciones World, Macworld Espana, NeXTWORLD, Super Juegos Magazine (GamePro), PC World Espana, Publish; **SWEDEN'S** Attack, ComputerSweden, Corporate Computing, Macworld, Mikrodatorn, Natverk & Kommunikation, PC World, CAP & Design, DataIngenjoren, Maxi Data,Windows World; **SWITZERLAND'S** Computerworld Schweiz, Macworld Schweiz, PC Tip; **TAIWAN'S** Computerworld Taiwan, PC World Taiwan; **THAILAND'S** Thai Computerworld; **TURKEY'S** Computerworld Monitor, Macworld Turkiye, PC World Turkiye; **UKRAINE'S** Computerworld, Computers+Software Magazine; **UNITED KINGDOM'S** Computing /Computerworld, Connexion/Network World, Lotus Magazine, Macworld, Open Computing/Sunworld; **UNITED STATES'** Advanced Systems, AmigaWorld, Cable in the Classroom, CD Review, CIO, Computerworld, Computerworld Client/Server Journal, Digital Video, DOS World, Electronic Entertainment Magazine (E2), Federal Computer Week, Game Hits, GamePro, IDG Books Worldwide, Infoworld, Laser Event, Macworld, Maximize, Multimedia World, Network World, PC Letter, PC World, Publish, SWATPro, Video Event; **URUGUAY'S** PC World Uruguay; **VENEZUELA'S** Computerworld Venezuela, PC World; **VIETNAM'S** PC World Vietnam.
05/11/95

Acknowledgments

Special thanks to my friends at Apple, who were there for me every step of the way: Bob Hagenau, Brian Lawley, Adam Samuels, Whitney Greer, Mary Devincenzi, Keri Walker, and Doedy Hunter, and everyone else on the System 7.5 development team. Thank you all. I couldn't have done it without your help.

Thanks also to superagent Carole "Swifty" McClendon of Waterside Productions, for putting this deal together. You're awesome.

Big-time thanks to the gang at IDG Books: Mary Breidenbach, Tyler Connor, Drew Moore, Gina Scott, Tricia Reynolds, Valery Bourke, Michael Simsic, Laura Schaible, Katherine Day, Mary Bednarek, Megg Bonar, Janna Custer, the pretty-big guy, David Solomon, and the big guy himself, John Kilcullen.

Extra special thanks to my editor, Tim "the Whipcracker" Gallan, who has been better than great.

Thanks to my family for putting up with my all-too-lengthy absences during this book's gestation.

And finally, thanks to you for buying it.

(The publisher would like to give special thanks to Patrick J. McGovern, without whom this book would not have been possible.)

Dedication

For Jodie, Andy, Robyn, Dad, Cousin Nancy, and all my other friends and relatives with new Macs. Now you can stop calling me at all hours.

Credits

Executive Vice President, Strategic Product Planning and Research
David Solomon

Senior Vice President and Publisher
Milissa L. Koloski

Editorial Director
Diane Graves Steele

Acquisitions Editor
Megg Bonar

Brand Manager
Judith A. Taylor

Editorial Manager
Kristin A. Cocks

Editorial Assistants
Stacey Holden Prince
Kevin Spencer

Acquisitions Assistant
Suki Gear

Production Director
Beth Jenkins

Supervisor of Project Coordination
Cindy L. Phipps

Pre-Press Coordinator
Steve Peake

Associate Pre-Press Coordinator
Tony Augsburger

Media/Archive Coordinator
Paul Belcastro

Project Editor
A. Timothy Gallan

Copy Editor
Michael Simsic

Technical Reviewer
Christopher J. Nalls

Project Coordinator
Valery Bourke

Production Staff
Gina Scott
Carla C. Radzikinas
Patricia R. Reynolds
Dwight Ramsey
Robert Springer
Theresa Sánchez-Baker
Kathie Schnorr
Mary Breidenbach
Linda M. Boyer
J. Tyler Connor
Dominique DeFelice
Drew R. Moore
Laura Puranen

Proofreader
Charles A. Hutchinson

Indexer
Sharon Hilgenberg

Book Design
University Graphics

Cover Design
Kavish + Kavish

Contents at a Glance

Cartoons at a Glance
By Rich Tennant

Table of Contents

· ·

Part IV: Beyond the Lunatic Fringe: The Infamous Part of Tens *353*

Chapter 16: Ten Optional Pieces of System Software You Might Someday Need 355

Foreword

● ●

*T*he name Bob LeVitus is a working definition for Not Dull. No matter where you run into Bob — in conversation, around the poker table, or in his writings about the Mac — you are not going to be bored. You will pay attention, not that he'll give you much of a choice. And that's good. His opinions tend to be provocative and well thought out, his poker playing is skilled enough to empty your wallet if you're not both good and lucky, and his knowledge of the Mac and his ability to communicate it to readers are unparalleled.

The release of System 7.5 is as important to Mac owners as System 7 was. Maybe even more so. The added functionality makes all Macs instantly far more powerful and at the same time, easier to use. I can't see any reasons, short of perversity or laziness, for System 7.1 owners not to upgrade.

When you do upgrade, you'll find a lot of new features worth mastering. Apple manuals are Apple manuals; don't expect a lot of help from them. You could hire a consultant, but that's expensive and not at all necessary. Just read this book. It's a wonderful guide to all of System 7.5.

This book, *Macintosh System 7.5 For Dummies*, might be better called *The Best Mac System Software Book Ever*. Bobby has gone past his usual really good writing level here and taken a dry subject (Who really gets excited about an operating system? A game, sure; and maybe even that exceptional productivity application, but the System software?) and created a book that makes you want to learn and use this important advance in Mac software.

He's also achieved the difficult trick of writing a book that works for first-time users as well as power users who have been using Macs since January 1984. That's no mean accomplishment. I've been writing for and editing Mac magazines since 1985 and know first hand the magnitude of Bobby's achievement here.

So why is this the book for you? Why not stick with the oh-so-pretty Apple manuals? Surely they have everything you're going find here? Well, no, that's not so. The Apple manuals are pretty, I have to give them that. But readable? I don't think so. They're so dry that they should be declared a fire hazard. They're very full of themselves and at the same time so carefully worded that it seems certain their final editing was at the hands of Apple's legal staff.

Their "avoid all risks, take no shortcuts because it might not be perfectly 110% safe" approach means that the Apple manuals are incomplete. They might tell you how to use your new software, but they never have and never will tell you how to use it most efficiently and productively. That's what *Macintosh System*

7.5 For Dummies does. It goes beyond the too-dry manuals and too-brief magazine articles and tells you everything about System 7.5. After you digest it, you have the choice of doing things the Apple manual way or really using and enjoying your Mac.

One example of dry manual versus Bob LeVitus is the coverage of the subject of backing up. Apple tells you to do it. Period. Bobby tells you why you must back up frequently. He covers the absolute best hardware and software tools, the tools to use if you can't afford the best tools, and the absolute need for multiple back up sets. And he doesn't bury this information toward the end of a long chapter where, odds are, most manual readers are asleep when they pass it by.

With wonderful and refreshing attitude for a person who didn't grow up (or even ever live) in New York, Bobby presents vital information, like his instructions on backing up, right in your face. He's never been shy, and if something is important, he makes sure you get it.

The greatest strength of *Macintosh System 7.5 For Dummies* is the breadth and depth of its content. System 7.5 opens a lot of new ground for Mac users, and this book covers it all. You're not going to find a better helper as you move into System 7.5.

The second greatest strength of *Macintosh System 7.5 For Dummies* is its solid dose of in-your-face attitude. This is a readable helper that cares. All too many computer books today are either chores to read or, in a couple of cases, simply unreadable because they seem to think dry seriousness is a business-like virtue. They're wrong. Readability counts big-time, and *Macintosh System 7.5 For Dummies* can be as hard to put down as the latest potboiler. You not only learn from it, but you enjoy the process.

Macintosh System 7.5 For Dummies jumps right to the top of the class in Mac System software books, easily surpassing all the others I've read (and that's just about all them; it's part of my job). Any book that surpasses it is going to have to be awfully good. And it wouldn't surprise me if Bob LeVitus is the author.

Steven Bobker

Introduction

. . . .

You made the right choice twice: System 7.5 and this book.

Take a deep breath and get ready to have some fun. That's right. This is a computer book and it's going to be fun. Whether you're new to the Mac or a grizzled old veteran, I guarantee that learning System 7.5 my way will be easy and fun. It says so right on the cover.

The 5th Wave   By Rich Tennant

"It's been reported that we went a little crazy trying to bring System 7.5 to market on time..."

Why a Book for Dummies?

Because there wasn't already a Dummies book about the Mac operating system (though *DOS For Dummies* and *Windows For Dummies* are huge hits), the nice folks at IDG Books asked me if I wanted to write one.

The thought of joining the ranks of *Dummies* authors, famous guys like Dan Gookin and Andy Rathbone, was more than I could bear. The deal was struck, and you're holding the result in your hands.

System 7.5 is a big, complicated, personal computer operating system. *Macintosh System 7.5 For Dummies* is a not-so-big (about 9" x 7" and not all that thick), not-very-complicated book that teaches you about System 7.5 without boring you, confusing you, or otherwise making you uncomfortable.

In fact, you'll be so comfortable that I wanted to call the book *Macintosh System 7.5 without the Discomfort*. But, as you'll find out when you get to the Part of Tens, there are some rules we *Dummies* authors must follow. Using the word *Dummies* in the title is one of them.

And speaking of dummies, it's just a word. I don't think you're dumb. Quite the opposite. I think you're very smart for buying this book. (If you're still standing in the aisle at the bookstore, approach the cashier with wallet in hand now, and I'll think you're even smarter.)

The book is chock full of information and advice, explaining every facet of what you're doing and why you're doing it, in language that you can understand.

This reference is supplemented with tips, tricks, techniques, and steps in generous quantities.

The tips, tricks, and so on are supplemented by rants and raves.

It all adds up to the only book in the world that makes learning System 7.5 both painless and fun. Can your beer do that?

How to Use This Book

We start off real slow. The first few chapters are where we get to know each other and discuss the basic everyday things you need to know to operate your Macintosh effectively.

This first part is so basic that it may bore you old-timers to tears. But hey, it's my sworn duty to teach you all there is to know about System 7.5 in the most painless manner possible. So we start at the very beginning. Skip the stuff you know already.

But here's a warning: If you skip over something important, like why you absolutely must back up your hard disk, don't come crying to me later when your life is made miserable by a horrendous hard disk crash.

In other words, it's probably best to read every word, though not necessarily in one sitting.

Another thing: We learn by doing, so it's best to go through the hands-on tutorials while sitting at your Mac. Sometimes things are easier to do than to read about, so sit at your Mac and try each step when you see the hands-on icon.

Finally, there are cross-references throughout the book and a very good index at the end.

Icons Used in This Book

Put on your propeller beanie and pocket protector. This is the truly nerdy stuff. It's not required reading, but it must be interesting or informative or I wouldn't have bothered.

Read these notes very, very carefully. They contain important information. The publisher and author will not be responsible if your Mac explodes, spewing flaming electronic parts, because you ignored a Caution icon.

I was just kidding. Your Mac won't explode or spew. But it's still a good idea to read Caution notes carefully.

This is where you'll find the juiciest morsels: shortcuts, tips, and undocumented secrets. In my humble opinion, the Tips are the best part, the soul of the book.

This icon warns you that a hands-on tutorial is coming. It's best to be at your Mac when you read these.

Me, ranting and raving about something. Imagine foam coming out of my mouth. Rants are usually irreverent or irrelevant and often both.

How This Book Is Organized

Macintosh System 7.5 For Dummies is divided into four logical parts. I suggest you read them in order, but you don't have to if you don't want to.

Part I: In the Beginning (The Hassle-Free Way to Get Started with System 7.5)

The first part of Part I is Very Basic Training. From the mouse to the Desktop, from the Menus (including the deliciously configurable Apple menu) to the tricky Open and Save dialog boxes, it's all here. Everything you need to know to use a Macintosh properly. Old-timers can skim it; newbies should read every word at least once.

Part II: Making It Purr (The Lazy Person's How-To Guide)

We'll start out with a rip-roaring tour of System 7.5's more than 50 improvements and enhancements. Then it's back to hands-on stuff, with chapters on organizing, printing, sharing (files, that is), and memory management. By the time you finish this part, your System will be running like a champ.

Part III: U 2 Can B A Guru

Now we're cooking. This part is about how things work and how you can make them work better.

Tips, tricks, techniques, control panels, scripts, and much more, plus the most useful chapter in the book, Chapter 15, "What Can Stay and What Can Go," which details every single gosh darn file in your System Folder and why you need it (or don't). If your Mac ran well after Part II, it'll run great after Part III.

Part IV: Beyond the Lunatic Fringe: The Infamous Part of Tens

Last but not least, it's the Part of Tens, a Letterman-like look at ten optional System software items, ten great things to throw money at, and the top ten troubleshooting tips for the times when good System software goes bad.

And that retires the side . . . almost.

One Last Thing

I'm thrilled at how this book turned out — I think it's the best thing I've ever written. But I didn't write it for me, I wrote it for you. So please drop me a line and let me know how you liked it.

Did it work for you? What did you like best? Least? What questions did I leave unanswered? What did you want to know more about? Less?

Send snail mail care of IDG Books (they'll see that I get it), or send electronic mail to me:

CompuServe: 76004,2076

America Online: LeVitus

Internet: 76004.2076@compuserve.com

If you have questions, I'll do my best to answer them. I do appreciate your feedback.

Bob LeVitus
Late Summer 1994

P.S. What are you waiting for? Go enjoy the book.

One More Thing after the Last Thing

Before you dive into a chapter, here are a couple of conventions I use in this book:

- ✔ When I refer to an item in a menu, I use something like File⇨Edit, which means pull down the File menu and choose the Edit command.
- ✔ For keyboard shortcuts, something like Command-A means hold down the Command key (it has a pretzel-like symbol on it) and press the letter A. Command-Shift-A means hold down the Command and Shift keys and press A.

Part I
In the Beginning (The Hassle-Free Way to Get Started with System 7.5)

In this part...

System 7.5 sports more new features than any Macintosh System Software upgrade in recent history. And I'll get to the hot new goodies soon enough, but you have to learn to crawl before you walk.

In this part, you'll learn the most basic of basics, such as the de rigueur-for-books-with-*Dummies*-in-the-title section on how to turn your Mac on (it's very short). Next I'll acquaint you with the System 7.5 desktop: icons, windows, menus, disks, and trash — the whole shmear.

So get comfortable, roll up your sleeves, fire up your Mac if you like, and settle down with Part I, a delightful little ditty I like to think of as "The Hassle-Free Way to Get Started with System 7.5."

Chapter 1

System 7.5 101
(Prerequisites: None)

● ●

In This Chapter

▶ What is System 7.5?

▶ A safety net for beginners

▶ The startup process revealed

▶ Installing System 7.5

▶ Back up now or regret it later

● ●

Choosing System 7.5 was a good move. It's more than just a System software upgrade; System 7.5 includes dozens of new or improved features that make using your Mac easier, and dozens more that help you do more work in less time. In other words, it'll make you more productive, give you fewer headaches, reduce your cholesterol level, and make you fall in love with your Mac all over again.

I know you're chomping at the bit, but we're going to start at the very beginning. This chapter mostly talks about System 7.5 in abstract terms. Don't bother to turn your Mac on yet, as there's no hands-on stuff here either (except the section on installing System 7.5, which many of you can skip 'cause it's already installed on your Mac). What you'll find is a bunch of very important stuff that will save the beginner from a lot of headaches.

If you already know what System software is and does, how to avoid disasters, what a startup disk is, how the startup process works, how to install System 7.5, and why you must back up your hard disk, then read those sections anyway — to refresh your memory — and skim the rest.

Everyone else: Read every word.

What is System Software?

Along with the code in its read-only memory (ROM), the System software, or *operating system,* is what makes a Mac a Mac. Without it, your Mac is a pile of silicon and circuits, no smarter than a toaster. It's got a brain (ROM), and it's got memory (RAM), and it's got ten fingers and toes (other stuff), but it doesn't know what to do with itself. Think of System software as an education, and System 7.5 is an Ivy League education. (A PC clone with DOS and Windows dropped outta high school in the 10th grade and flips burgers for a living.)

With System 7.5, your Mac becomes an elegant, powerful tool that's the envy of the rest of the computer industry.

Most of the world's personal computers use either DOS alone or DOS and Windows together. Poor schmucks. You're among the lucky few with a computer whose operating system is intuitive, easy to use, and, dare I say, fun. Windows is a cheap imitation of the Macintosh System software. Try it sometime. Go ahead. You probably won't suffer any permanent damage. In fact, you'll really begin to appreciate how good you've got it. Feel free to hug your Mac or give it a peck on the floppy drive opening. Just don't get your tongue caught.

What Does System Software Do?

Good question. It controls the basic (and most important operations) of your computer. In the case of System 7.5 and your Mac, the System software manages memory, controls how windows, icons, and menus work, keeps track of files, and does lots of other housekeeping chores. Other forms of software, such as a word processor, rely on the System software to create and maintain the environment in which this application software does its work.

When you create a memo, for example, the word processor provides the tools for you to type and format the information. The System software provides the mechanism for drawing and moving the window in which you write the memo; it keeps track of the file when you save it; it helps the word processor create drop-down menus and dialog boxes and communicate with other programs, and much, much more.

Now you have a little background in System software. Before you do anything else with your Mac, take a gander at the next section.

A Safety Net for the Absolute Beginner — or Any User

If you're a first-time Mac user, please, please read this section of the book very carefully. It could save your life. Well, now I'm just being overly dramatic. *It could save your Mac* is what I meant to say. I deal with the stuff that the manual that came with your Mac doesn't cover in nearly enough detail, if at all. If you're an experienced Mac user, read this section anyway. Chances are, you need a few reminders.

✔ **If you don't know how to turn your Mac on, get help.** Don't feel bad. Apple, in its infinite wisdom, has manufactured Macs with power-on switches on every conceivable surface: the front, side, back, and even the keyboard. Some Macs (most PowerBooks) even hide the power-on button behind a little plastic door.

In his bestseller, *Macs For Dummies*, David Pogue devotes several pages to locating the on switch for every current model of Macintosh. If you're having trouble, it'll be worth your while to check out the latest edition of his book. Or you can always look in the manual that came with your Mac.

Like personal fouls in the NBA, authors are only allowed so many weasel-outs per book. I hate to use one so early, but in this case, I think it's worth it for both of us. I promise this is the first and only time I'll say, "Look in the manual." Maybe.

✔ **Always use the Special⇨Shut Down command before turning your Mac off.** Turning the power off without choosing Special⇨Shut Down first is one of the worst things you can do to your poor Mac. It can screw up your hard disk real bad or scramble the contents of your most important files, or both.

Of course, most of us have broken this rule several times without anything horrible happening. Don't be lulled into a false sense of security. Do it one time too many and your most important file will be toasted.

System 7.5 is the first version of System software that actually scolds you if you don't shut down properly. If you break this rule, the next time your Mac is turned on, it will politely inform you that your Mac was shut down improperly, as shown in Figure 1-1.

If you find the little "this Mac was shut down improperly" reminder annoying, you can turn it off in the General Controls control panel. I actually like it and leave the warning enabled. You should too.

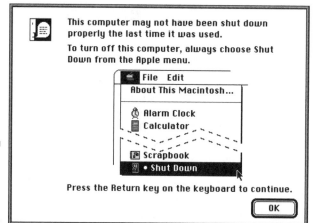

This computer may not have been shut down properly the last time it was used.

To turn off this computer, always choose Shut Down from the Apple menu.

File   Edit
About This Macintosh...

⚬ Alarm Clock
▤ Calculator

▣ Scrapbook
▨ • Shut Down

Press the Return key on the keyboard to continue.

OK

Figure 1-1:
Polite little
machines,
aren't they?

A pop quiz on mousing

For those of you who need to hone your mousing skills, here's a little quiz.

1. How do you select an icon on the Desktop?

A. Stare at it intently for five seconds.

B. Point to it with your finger, slap the side of your monitor, and say, "That one, stupid!"

C. Move the mouse pointer on top of the icon and click once.

2. When do you need to double-click?

A. Whenever you find yourself saying, "There's no place like home."

B. When you're using both hands to control the mouse.

C. When you want to open a file or folder.

3. How do you select multiple items or blocks of text?

A. Get several people to stare intently at the items you want to select.

B. You need to attach multiple mice to your Mac.

C. By sliding the mouse on your desk, move the on-screen pointer to the location where you want to begin selecting. Press and hold down the mouse button. Drag the pointer across the items or text that you want to select. Then let go of the mouse button.

4. How do you move a selected item?

A. Call U-Haul.

B. Pick up and tilt your monitor until the item slides to the proper location.

C. Click the item and hold down the mouse button. With the mouse button still held down, drag the pointer to the new location and let go of the mouse button.

If you haven't figured it out by now, the correct answer to each of these questions is C. If any other answer sounded remotely plausible for you, sit down with your Mac and just play with it for a while. If you have kids at your disposal, watch them play with your Mac. They'll be showing you how to use it in no time.

✔ **Don't unplug your Mac when it's turned on.** See my blurb in the preceding bullet.

✔ **Don't use your Mac when lightning is near.** Lightning strike = dead Mac. 'Nuff said. Oh, and don't place much faith in inexpensive surge protectors. A good jolt of lightning will fry the surge protector right along with your computer. There *are* surge protectors that can withstand most lightning strikes, but they're not the cheapies you buy at your local computer emporium. Unplugging is safer and less expensive.

✔ **Don't jostle, bump, shake, kick, throw, dribble, or punt your Mac, especially while it's running.** Unless your Mac is ancient, it contains within it a hard disk drive that spins at 3600+ r.p.m. A jolt to a hard disk while it's reading or writing a file can cause a head crash, which can render many or all the files on the disk totally and irreversibly unrecoverable.

✔ **Turn off your Mac before plugging or unplugging any cables.** This advice may be overkill, as even Apple seems to say that you can safely plug cables into the serial ports — the modem or printer ports — while your Mac is turned on. But other cables, specifically SCSI cables and ADB cables, should never under any circumstances be plugged or unplugged without first shutting down your Mac.

OK, that about does it for bad stuff that can happen. If something bad has already happened to you, see Chapter 18.

SCSI, ADB, and other conversation topics for parties

SCSI is the acronym for Small Computer System Interface, the relatively high-speed bus chosen by Apple to connect peripheral devices such as hard disks, tape drives, scanners, and even some printers, to your Macintosh. SCSI is pronounced "scuzzy" and is fun to say aloud. Try it:

"I got a 1 gigabyte hard disk, a pair of big SyQuests, a 4mm DAT, and a 24-bit scanner on my scuzzy bus."

A movement to pronounce SCSI as "sexy" instead of "scuzzy" never really got off the ground.

Bus, of course, is nerd-speak for the hardware, cabling, and protocols used to connect peripherals to the computer. The Mac has other busses, most notably its expansion slots (the NuBus bus) and the Apple Desktop Bus (ADB) bus.

A Mac can have up to 7 SCSI devices connected simultaneously in a daisy-chain. One device is connected to the next, and so on, until the last device.

Every Macintosh since the Mac Plus has a SCSI port; internal hard disks are a part of the SCSI chain.

ADB is the TLA (three-letter acronym) for Apple Desktop Bus, another Apple bus scheme for keyboards and pointing devices (and sometimes drawing tablets and modems). It's slower than the SCSI bus but fast enough for mice, trackballs, and tablets. Every Macintosh since the Macintosh SE has an ADB port, and many Macs have two. A Mac can have several ADB devices connected simultaneously to each ADB port in a daisy chain. Though in theory you can connect a bunch of devices — like 12 or 16 — to each ADB port, in practice you should limit yourself to two or three per ADB port. More than that can cause your Mac to behave erratically.

What You Should See after Turning the Power On

After a small bit of whirring, buzzing, and flashing (the System software is loading) you should see a cheerful little happy Mac in the middle of your screen like the one in Figure 1-2.

Figure 1-2:
The Mac startup icon. Cute as puke, isn't it?

Soon thereafter come those soothing words we all know and love, "Welcome to Macintosh." Makes you feel kind of warm and fuzzy, doesn't it? The message indicates that System 7.5 is loading properly.

This might be a good time to take a moment to think good thoughts about whoever convinced you that you wanted a Mac. They were right. If you had bought an IBM PC or clone, you would be cursing at a blinking C prompt right about now instead of gazing at a soothing welcome message and a smiling Mac.

Anyway, in a few more seconds, the familiar Macintosh Desktop will materialize before your eyes. If you haven't customized, configured, or done any other tinkering, your Desktop should look something like Figure 1-3.

In the unlikely event you didn't see the smiling Mac, soothing message, and familiar Desktop, read the next section — "What's Happening Here" — very carefully. If this section doesn't set things right, skip to Chapter 18.

What's Happening Here? (The Startup Process Revealed)

When you turn on your Macintosh, you set in motion a sophisticated and complex series of events that culminates in the loading of System 7.5 and the appearance of the familiar Mac Desktop. Fortunately, the mechanics of the

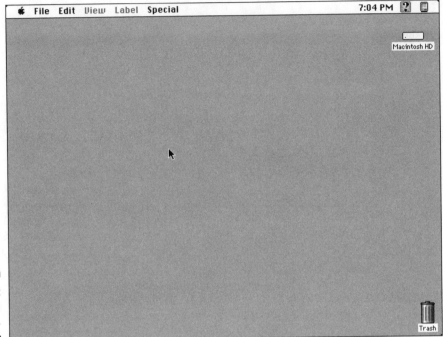

File Edit View Label Special	7:04 PM

Macintosh HD

Trash

Figure 1-3:
The Mac
Desktop.

process are unimportant. In brief, your Mac tests all your hardware — slots, ports, disks, memory (RAM), and so on. If everything passes, you hear a pleasing chord and see the happy Mac and "Welcome to Macintosh" on your monitor as your Mac loads the System software it needs from disk to RAM.

You're not a failure

If any of your hardware fails when tested, you'll see a black screen with the dreaded Sad Mac icon (see Figure 1-4) and hear a far less pleasing musical chord known by Mac aficionados as the Chimes of Doom. The fact that something went wrong is no reflection on your prowess as a Macintosh user. Something inside your Mac is broken, and it probably needs to go in for repairs (usually to an Apple dealer). If it's under warranty, dial 1-800-SOS-APPL and they'll tell you what to do.

Before you do anything, though, skip ahead to Chapter 18. It's entirely possible that one of the suggestions there will get you back on track without spending even a moment on hold.

Figure 1-4:
The Sad
Mac icon:
Look upon
this face, ye
mighty, and
despair!

Question Mark and the Mysterions

Although it's unlikely that you'll see a sad Mac, all users eventually encounter the flashing question mark (shown in Figure 1-5) in place of the usual happy Mac at some time in their lives. Don't worry. This one is a breeze. This icon means that your Mac can't find a *startup disk*, a floppy or hard disk containing valid System software.

Figure 1-5:
Your Mac is
having an
identity
crisis when
you see this
icon.

When you turn on your Mac, the first thing it does (after the aforementioned hardware tests) is check the floppy disk drive for a startup disk (something with System 7.5 on it). If it doesn't find one there, it scans the SCSI bus. At this point, your Mac usually finds your hard disk, which contains a System Folder, and the startup process continues on its merry way with the happy Mac and all the rest.

Think of the flashing question mark as your Mac's way of saying, "Please provide me with System software."

If Apple can figure out a way to put a flashing question mark on the screen, why the heck can't the software engineers find a way to put the words, "Please insert a startup disk" on the screen as well. The curtness of the flashing question mark is one of my pet peeves about the Macintosh.

I know, you're clever and smart (you're reading *Macintosh System 7.5 For Dummies*, aren't you?), so you know that a flashing question mark means that you should insert a startup disk. But what about everyone else?

Get with the program, Apple.

The ultimate startup disk

Chances are you have a copy of the ultimate startup disk right there on your computer table. It's called Disk Tools, and it's one of the disks that you get with all versions of System 7. If you've got a flashing question mark, pop Disk Tools into your floppy drive and your Mac will boot, just like magic.

Disk Tools is the ultimate startup disk because, in addition to a System and Finder, the two files that must be present on a startup disk, it also has copies of Disk First Aid and Apple HD SC Setup, two programs that you may need if you see a flashing question mark. Disk First Aid can repair hidden damage to your hard disk; HD SC Setup can install new hard disk drivers. Both Disk First Aid and Apple HD SC Setup are described more completely in Chapter 18.

Now what?

OK, so you've gotten your Mac to boot from the Disk Tools disk, but there's still this little problem. Like you'd prefer that your Mac boot from your (much faster) hard disk than that piddly little Disk Tools floppy. Not to worry. All you need to do is install System 7.5. Read on.

The legend of the boot

Boot this. Boot that. "I booted my Mac and . . .," "Did it boot?" It seems nearly impossible to talk about computers for long without hearing the word.

But why boot? Why not shoe or shirt or even shazam?

It all began in the very olden days, maybe the 1970s or a little earlier, when starting up a computer required you to toggle little manual switches on the front panel, which began an internal process that loaded the operating system. The process became known as "bootstrapping" be-

cause if you toggled the right switches, the computer would "pull itself up by the bootstraps." It didn't take long for the phrase to transmogrify into "booting" and "boot."

Over the years, booting has come to mean turning on almost any computer or even a peripheral device like a printer. Some people also use it to refer to launching an application: "I booted Excel."

So the next time one of your gear-head friends says the B word, ask if he or she knows where the term comes from. Then dazzle your friend with the depth and breadth of your knowledge.

Those of you who are going to upgrade from System 7.x to System 7.5 may want to read along, too. The rest of you, the ones whose Macs booted from a hard drive with System 7.5 installed, can breathe a sigh of relief and skip ahead to the next section.

Anyone Can Install System 7.5

The System 7.5 disks that came with your Mac can install more than just System software. I'll just discuss a plain vanilla installation here. QuickDraw GX and PowerTalk, which require separate installation, are covered in their own section later in the book. There are several other optional pieces of System software — MacTCP, TokenTalk, Easy Access, and Close View — that also require a separate installation process. I'll cover all of those things in due time.

In Chapter 15, you'll learn more about Custom Installation and Custom Removals. For now, I'm going to talk about the Easy Install option, the most foolproof choice.

The procedure is the same regardless of whether you're upgrading from an earlier version of System software or installing System 7.5 on an empty hard disk.

The first thing to do is look for a "Read Me" file. There may or may not be one, and it may not be called "Read Me." It might be called something like "Read Me First" or "System 7.5 Read Me." If there is such a file, read it before you proceed. It may have information that was discovered after this book went to press (such as the Safe Install utility).

Ready? Take a deep breath.

Installing from floppies

Read this section if you are installing System 7.5 from floppy disks.

Shut down your Macintosh if it's turned on. Insert the floppy disk called Install Disk 1 and turn on your Mac. Your Mac will start up and the Installer program will launch automatically. You'll see a comforting welcome screen like the one in Figure 1-6.

(Are you beginning to detect a pattern? Macs are warmer and fuzzier than other personal computers?)

Click the Continue button. The Installer window will appear in the middle of your screen (see Figure 1-7).

Figure 1-6:
The
welcome
screen of
the System
software
installer.

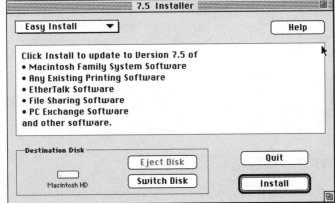

Figure 1-7:
The Installer
window.

If you have more than one hard disk, you may have to click the Switch Disk button one or more times. When your hard disk's icon appears in the Destination Disk area, click the Install button or press the Return or Enter key.

Notice how the Install button has an outline and the Switch Disk, Quit, and Help buttons do not. The outline indicates that Install is the *default button*. You can click on the default button, but it's also activated when you press the Return or Enter key on your keyboard. It's a shortcut. But be careful: sometimes pressing the Enter or Return key too fast, before you read the dialog box carefully, can cause unwanted results.

After a minute or two, you'll see a progress box, which shows you which disks you'll need to perform the installation (see Figure 1-8).

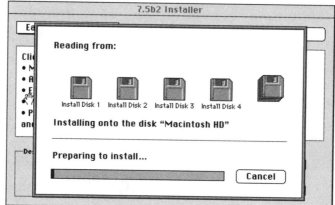

Figure 1-8:
The
Installer's
progress
box.

After a few more minutes your Mac will ask you to insert Install Disk 2. Do it. It will later ask for Install Disk 3, 4, 5, and so on. Eventually it will ask you to insert Install Disk 1 again. That's the signal that installation is almost over. After a little more whirring and clicking, your Mac will politely inform you that the installation was successful and that you must restart your Mac. Click the Restart button and away you go.

That's it. Your hard disk now has System 7.5 installed. Piece of cake. The hardest part is moving your arm.

Installing from the CD

If you've got the CD version of System 7.5, installation is an even tastier piece of cake.

If you have an Apple CD-ROM drive, you can boot directly from the System 7.5 CD. The Installer will launch just as if you had booted from a floppy.

You can also run the Installer from the Finder. You'll want to use this method if your Mac has a non-Apple CD-ROM drive.

With your Mac on and no other applications running, insert the System 7.5 CD into your drive. When its icon appears on the Desktop, double-click it. Next, double-click the Installation folder. Then double-click the System Install folder. Finally, double-click the Installer icon. Your Mac launches the Installer program.

When using the Installer, follow the instructions in the preceding section (but remember that you don't have to shuffle floppies), and you're all set.

Goodies on the CD

Oh, and here's one more thing I ought to mention about installation. The CD-ROM version of System 7.5 has a bunch of extra stuff you won't find on the floppies:

✔ PowerTalk Demos

- PowerTalk Demos

- QuickMail Gateway

- Internet Gateway

- CompuServe Gateway

- Fax Gateway

- PowerTalk Direct DialUp

- Notify! Pager Gateway

- PowerTalk Tour

✔ QuickDraw GX tools

- Peirce Paper Saver

- Peirce Water Mark

- GX Font Demonstration

✔ Miscellaneous

- eWorld

- Eric's Ultimate Solitaire Demo

- PlainTalk Update

- QuickTime Extras

- At Ease Patch

QuickDraw GX and Peirce Print Tools are discussed in Chapter 8. For info on PowerTalk and a little more on QuickDraw GX, see Chapter 15.

Back Up Now or Regret It Later

If the stuff on your hard disk means anything to you, you must back it up. Not maybe. You must. Unlike an earlier section in this chapter, this section is a safety net for everyone. Before you do any significant work on your Mac (or even if your most important file is your last saved game of Jump Raven), you need to realize how important it is to back up.

Dr. Macintosh sez, "There are only two kinds of Mac user — those who have never lost data, and those who will." Which kind will you be?

Although Macs are generally reliable beasts, some day your hard disk will die. I promise. They all do. And if you haven't backed up your hard disk, there's a good chance that you'll never see your files again. And if you do see them again, it'll only be after paying Scott at the DriveSavers data recovery service a king's ransom, with no guarantee of success. DriveSavers is the premier recoverer of lost data on hard disks. They do good work and can often recover stuff nobody else could. They charge accordingly.

I'm going to give you DriveSavers' phone number. It's 415-883-4232. Now pray you never need it. Back up often and you won't. If somehow, none of this sinks in, tell Scott I say, "Hi."

In other words, you absolutely, positively, without question MUST BACK UP. Just as you've adopted the Shut Down command and made it a habit, you must learn to back up your hard disk often.

How often is often? That depends on you. How much work can you afford to lose? If the answer is that losing everything you did yesterday would put you out of business, you need to back up daily, or possibly twice a day. If you'd only lose a couple of unimportant letters, you can back up less frequently.

Backing up is (not) hard to do

There are lots of ways to back up your hard disk. Some are better than others.

The manual "brute force" method

Drag your files a few at a time to floppy disks.

Yuk. If it sounds pretty awful, trust me, it is. It takes forever; you can't really tell if you've copied every file; and there's no way to only copy files that have been modified since your last backup. Almost nobody sticks with this method for long.

Get some commercial backup software

There's nothing else in this book that I'm going to insist that you buy, but you must buy backup software if you don't already have some.

For some unfathomable reason, Apple has never seen fit to provide backup software with new Macintoshes or include it with System software releases. I know Performas have a passable backup program, but Apple has left the other 12 million Mac owners clueless.

Mac owners get nothing more than a brief passage regarding backing up in the *Macintosh User's Guide*. It ought to be in big red letters, in the first chapter, and include a warning from the Surgeon General or something. And it wouldn't kill them to provide a backup utility either. Sheesh, even DOS has a backup command, albeit a lousy one.

C'mon, Apple, give Mac owners a fair shake. At least include the Apple Backup program Performa owners get.

Fortunately, there is plenty of very good backup software available for well under $100, including DiskFit Pro, DiskFit Direct, and Redux Deluxe. If you want the best, most flexible, most powerful, top-of-the-line backup software, spend a little more and pop for Retrospect.

Backup software automates the task of backing up. The backup software remembers what is on each backup disk and only backs up files that have been modified since the last backup. Your first backup with commercial software should take no more than 90 minutes and a couple of dozen 1.4MB floppy disks. Subsequent backups, called *incremental backups* in backup software parlance, should only take a few minutes.

Be sure to label the floppy disks that you use for your backups because during incremental backups, the backup software is going to ask you to "Please insert backup disk 7." If you haven't labeled your floppies clearly, you have a problem.

Why you should probably make two sets of back up disks

You're a good soldier. You back up regularly. You think you're immune.

Now picture this: One day you take a floppy disk to QuicKopyLazerPrintz to print your resume on their laser printer. You make a few changes while at QuicKopyLazerPrintz and take the floppy home and stick it into your Mac.

Unbeknownst to you, the floppy became infected with a computer virus at QuicKopyLazerPrintz. (I discuss viruses in the "Virus trivia" sidebar.) When you inserted the disk into your Mac, the infection spread to your hard disk like wildfire.

Then you backed up. Your backup software, believing that all the infected files have been recently modified (well, they had — they'd been infected with a virus!), proceeds to back them up. You notice that the backup takes a little longer than usual, but otherwise, things seem to be OK.

A few days later your Mac starts acting strangely. You borrow a copy of that excellent virus detection software, Disinfectant, and discover that your hard disk is infected. "Ah ha," you exclaim. "I've been a good little boy/girl, backing up regularly. I'll just restore everything from my backup disks."

Not so fast, bucko. The files on your backup disks are also infected.

This scenario demonstrates why you need multiple backups. If you had several sets of backup disks, chances are pretty good that one of the sets would be clean.

I keep three backup sets. I use one on even-numbered days, one on odd numbered days, and the third I update once a week and store in my bank's vault. This scheme ensures that no matter what happens, even if my office burns, floods, is destroyed by a tornado or hurricane, or is robbed, I won't lose more than a few days worth of work. I can live with that.

Virus trivia

A computer virus, in case you missed it in *Time* or *Newsweek,* is a nasty little piece of computer code that replicates and spreads from disk to disk. Most viruses cause your Mac to misbehave; some viruses can destroy files or erase disks with no warning.

If you use disks that have been inserted in other computers, you need some form of virus detection software. If you download and use files from some BBSes, you need some form of virus detection as well.

Don't worry much if your BBS is run by a Mac user group or is a commercial on-line service like America Online, CompuServe, or eWorld. They are very conscientious about viral infections. Do worry about that BBS called Pirates Den that an unsavory friend told you about.

John Norstad's excellent virus detection and eradication software, Disinfectant, is widely available and is freeware. Just make sure that you have the latest version, as new viruses appear on the scene every so often and Disinfectant (and all antivirus software) requires updating to detect and fight them.

On the commercial front, Virex, SAM (Symantec Anti-Virus for Macintosh), and Central Point Anti-Virus all have their fans. I'm using Virex right now but have used the others at one time or another and have never gotten a virus.

The big advantage of a commercial antivirus program is that the publisher will contact you each time a virus is discovered and provide you with a code that you can type into the software to update it to protect you against the new strain. Or, for a fee, the publisher will send you a new version of the software every time a new virus is found.

If you only use commercial software and don't download files from bulletin boards with strange names, you have a very low risk of infection. On the other hand, if you swap disks with friends regularly, shuttle disks back and forth to other Macs, use your disks at service bureaus or copy shops, or download files from bulletin boards with strange names, you are at risk.

If you're at risk, either download a new copy of Disinfectant each time a new virus is discovered or buy a commercial antivirus program.

Chapter 2

Meet the Desktop

- -

- -

This is where we get down to the nitty-gritty; this is the chapter about the Macintosh desktop. Your Desktop is the center of your Macintosh universe. Just about everything you do on your Mac begins and ends with the desktop. The Desktop is where you manage files, store documents, launch programs, adjust the way your Mac works, and much more. If you ever expect to master your Mac, the first step is to master the desktop.

Once again, those of you who have been using System 7 for a while may find some of the information presented in this chapter repetitive; many of the features discussed in this chapter are unchanged from earlier versions of System 7. Still, you'd be foolish to skip it completely. If you do, I assure you you'll miss sarcasm, clever word play, shortcuts, awesome techniques, a bad pun or two, and lots of good advice on making the Desktop an easier place to be. If that's not enough to convince you, there's also a bunch of stuff Apple didn't bother to tell you.

Tantalized? Let's do it.

I Think ICON, I Think ICON

Icons, those funny little pictures on your Desktop and in your windows, represent containers, and these containers hold things that you work with on your Mac, like programs, documents, System software items, discarded files (the Trash icon), and more. All icons appear on your screen as little pictures with their names attached.

The first icon you should become familiar with is the icon for your hard disk. It's in the upper-right corner and is named "Macintosh HD" unless you've renamed it (see Figure 2-1).

Figure 2-1:
A plain-vanilla hard disk icon.

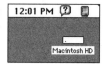

The look you want to know better

Icons come in all shapes and sizes. After you've been around the Macintosh for a while, you get a kind of sixth sense about what an icon contains just by looking at it. For example, application (that is, program) icons are often diamond shaped. Unless, of course, they're rectangular or square or oddly shaped (see Figures 2-2, 2-3, and 2-4).

Figures 2-2, 2-3, 2-4:
Application icons come in many different shapes.

Generic Application Icon   SimpleText   Microsoft Word   Aldus PageMaker

ClarisWorks   Retrospect   Now Contact   Adobe Photoshop

Microsoft Excel   Inspiration   FontChameleon   MacroMind Director

OK, so application icons are all over the place. Document icons, on the other hand, are almost always reminiscent of a piece of paper (as shown in Figure 2-5).

Figure 2-5:
Typical document icons.

Word Document   Excel Document   Photoshop Document   Simple Text Document

See? You're already acquiring that sixth sense. Application icons are all over the place; document icons look like paper.

Now let's talk about the four kinds of icons: application, document, folder, and System software. (OK, there are actually five kinds of icons. Aliases are an icon type in their own right.)

Applications are programs, the software that you use to accomplish tasks on your Mac. Your word processor is an application. So is America Online and Prodigy. MYST and Spectre Supreme are applications (they're also great games).

Documents are files created by applications. "Letter to Mom," which you created in ClarisWorks, is a document. So are "Bob's Calendar" and "Expense Report."

Folders are the Mac's organizational containers. You put icons, usually application or document icons, into folders. You can also put folders inside other folders. Folders look like, well, folders. Some folder icons have pictures; most don't (see Figure 2-6).

Figure 2-6:
Typical
folder icons.

System software is the stuff in your System Folder — the System, the Finder, control panels, extensions, and almost everything else. The files that make up your System software have many purposes, most of which will be second nature to you by the end of this book. For now, I'll just talk about the icons, though.

System software icons usually have a distinctive look as well. For example, the System and Finder have distinctive Mac-flavored icons (see Figure 2-7).

Figure 2-7:
The System
file and
Finder icons.

Control panel icons usually have a slider bar at the bottom or on one side (as illustrated in Figure 2-8).

Figure 2-8:
Control
panel icons
have a
slider bar.

Keyboard   Easy Access   Map   Numbers

Extension icons usually look like jigsaw puzzle parts (see Figure 2-9).

Figure 2-9:
Common
extension
icons
display a
puzzled look.

Macintosh Easy Open   File System Extensions   Network Extension

But that's where the metaphor breaks down. The rest of your System software icons may look like just about anything (see Figure 2-10).

Figure 2-10:
Miscellaneous
System
software
icons.

AppleShare   AppleTalk Service   Foreign File Access

There's lots more to be said about all of these kinds of icons, and I'll do so in upcoming chapters. But that's enough about what icons look like. I'm sure you're anxious to do something with icons already.

Open sesame

There are three ways to open any icon. (OK, there are four ways, but I'm saving aliases for later. You don't need to know just yet.) Anyway, here are the ways:

✔ Click once on the icon to select it; then point to the File menu (it's the one that says File) and press on the word File. Remember, a press is half a click. Don't release the mouse button yet. A menu will drop down. Move the pointer downward until the word Open is highlighted (see Figure 2-11).

(I probably could have saved a whole paragraph by simply saying "Choose File⇨Open." But you may have been pulling down a menu for the first time. I wanted to be safe.) The icon will open.

By the way, in case you hadn't noticed, you just learned how to choose an item from a menu. Don't go hog-wild. There's lots more to know about menus, but it's in the next chapter. In fact, all of Chapter 3 is about menus.

✔ Double-click the icon by clicking directly on it twice in rapid succession. If it doesn't open, you double-clicked too slowly.

✔ Select the icon and then use the keyboard shortcut, Command-O. That means you press the Command key, the one with the pretzel and the apple on most keyboards, and then press the O key while continuing to hold down the Command key.

Figure 2-11:
The Open
command in
the File
menu.

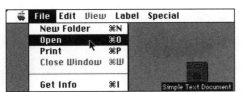

If you look at Figure 2-11, you'll see that the keyboard shortcut appears on the menu after the word Open. Pretzel-O. Any menu item with one of these pretzel-letter combinations after its name can be executed with that keyboard shortcut. Just press the pretzel (Command) key and the letter shown in the menu — Command-N for New Folder, Command-F for Find, and so on — and the appropriate command will be executed.

It's never too soon to learn good habits, so I'll mention here that experienced Macintosh users use the keyboard shortcuts as often as possible. Keyboard shortcuts let you get things done without opening the menu, which means that you don't have to reach for the mouse, which means that you get more done in less time. It's a good idea to memorize shortcuts for menu items you use frequently.

Although the letters next to the Command key symbol (I'm done calling it a pretzel now) in the Finder's menus are capital letters, you don't have to press the Shift key to use the keyboard shortcut. Command-P means hold down the Command key and press P. Some programs have keyboard combinations that require the use of Command-Shift, but these programs let you know by calling the key combination something like Command-Shift-S or Command-Shift-O. You don't have to worry about the capitalization of the letter.

The name game

Icon, icon, bo-bicon, banana fanna fo ficon. Bet that you can change the name of any old icon. Here are two ways:

- ✔ Click directly on the icon's name. Don't forget to release the mouse button.
- ✔ Click the icon and then press the Return or Enter key on your keyboard.

Either of these ways will select the icon's name and put a box around it, waiting for you to type (see Figure 2-12).

In addition to selecting the name, the cursor changes from a pointer to a text-editing I-beam. An I-beam cursor is your Mac's way of telling you that it's OK to type now. At this point, if you click the I-beam cursor anywhere within the name box, you can edit the icon's original name. If you don't click and just begin typing, the icon's original name will be completely replaced by what you type.

If you've never changed an icon's name, give it a try.

Other various and sundry icons

Before I get off the subject of icons completely, and because this is the chapter where you meet your Desktop, I'd be remiss if I didn't mention a couple of other icons that you'll probably find there. The most important of these is . . .

The Trash

The Trash is a special container where you put the icons you no longer want on your hard or floppy disk. Got four copies of TeachText on your hard disk? Drag three of them to the Trash. Old letters that you don't want to keep? Drag them to the Trash as well. To put an icon in the Trash, drag it on top of the Trash icon. When the tip (cool people call it the *hot spot*) of the pointer is directly over the Trash icon, it will invert (as shown in Figure 2-13).

When the Trash inverts, release the mouse button and, voilà, whatever you dragged to the Trash is trashed. But it's not gone forever until . . .

. . . you choose Special⇨Empty Trash. You know how the garbage in the can in your kitchen sits there until the sanitation engineers come by and pick it up each Thursday? The Macintosh Trash works the same. When you put something in the Trash, it sits there until you choose the Special⇨Empty Trash command.

Figure 2-13:
The Trash.

Think twice before you Empty Trash. Once the Trash has been emptied, the files it contained are gone forever. (Of course, you read Chapter 1 and you've backed up your hard disk several times, right? So even though the files are gone forever from your hard disk, *you* can get them back if you like, right?)

What the heck's the Finder, anyway?

You may have noticed that I use the words *Finder* and *Desktop* interchangeably. As you probably know, the Finder is one of the files in your System Folder. The Finder is superprogram. Among other things, it creates the desktop metaphor — the icons, windows, and menus that make up the Macintosh Desktop. Unlike ordinary programs, you can never quit the Finder. Like Katz's Deli, the Finder never closes. And unlike ordinary programs, you don't have to open the Finder to use it. The Finder is always open; it opens automatically when you turn on your Mac.

Because the Finder is, among other things, responsible for creating the Desktop and its menus, many people, myself included, use the words *Finder* and *Desktop* interchangeably. You can too.

The only time it gets confusing is when you are talking about the Finder icon in your System Folder. Just say "the Finder icon" instead of "the Finder" and you'll sound just like the pros. It can also be confusing when you're talking about the gray Desktop.

By the way, you *can* quit the Finder if you really want to and you're handy with ResEdit, Apple's resource editing utility. But that's power-user voo-doo and you'll have to buy a different book, preferably one from IDG Books such as *Macworld Mac and PowerMac SECRETS* (he says, scoring massive brownie points with his publisher), if that kind of hacking turns you on.

Like all icons, you can open the Trash (you know at least three ways to open an icon) to see what's in there. You can tell there's something in the Trash because the Trash icon bulges when it's full (as shown in Figure 2-14).

Figure 2-14:
The bulging
Trash icon.

There are utility programs available that allow you to retrieve a trashed file after you empty the Trash. Norton Utilities and Central Point MacTools are the two most popular. They don't have a 100-percent success rate, so you should still consider the Empty Trash command fatal to files.

If you drag an icon that's *locked* to the Trash, you'll see a message telling you to hold down the Option key when you choose Special⇨Empty Trash to delete locked items.

Close encounters of the icon kind

If you've used System 7.5 for very long, you've probably encountered a couple of other icons. You've probably got an icon for a Desktop Printer on your Desktop, which Figure 2-15 illustrates.

Figure 2-15:
A Desktop
Printer icon.

Each Desktop Printer icon represents one printer available to your Mac. If you're on a network, you may have more than one Desktop Printer icon. If you don't have one, don't fret. You'll make one soon (in Chapter 8).

If you use PowerTalk, you'll probably have one or more Catalog icons as well as an In Tray icon on your desktop (see Figure 2-16).

If you have any or all of these icons on your Desktop, ignore them for now. They won't hurt anything. You'll learn in good time how to make them appear on *your* Desktop, what they are, and what they do. (That would be in Chapter 16.)

Figure 2-16:
The Catalog
and In Tray
icons —
two compo-
nents of
PowerTalk.

Figure 2-16:
The Catalog
and In Tray
icons —
two compo-
nents of
PowerTalk.

Windows (Definitely Not the Microsoft Kind)

Windows are such a fundamental part of the Macintosh experience that Microsoft blatently ripped off the name for their operating system add-on.

Do your friends a favor. Before they buy a personal computer, make sure they know that Windows is not a Mac, regardless of what the lousy salesperson at the computer store says.

If you're relatively new to the Mac, you might want to read this section while sitting at your computer, trying the techniques as you read them. I've always found it easier to remember something that I read if I actually do it. If you've been abusing your Mac for long, you've probably figured out how windows work by now, but there's still some stuff in here you may not have tried. Your mileage may vary.

Doin' windows

Windows are an ubiquitous part of Macintosh computing. Windows on the Desktop show you the contents of disk and folder icons; windows in applications usually show you the contents of your documents.

You've already learned three different ways to open an icon, so you know how to open a window. When you open a window, its icon turns fuzzy gray (see Figure 2-17), which is your Mac's way of letting you know that that icon's window is open. Clever, eh?

Figure 2-17:
A fuzzy
gray icon.

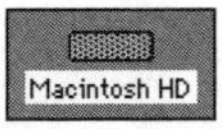

Zooming right along...

Notice how the Macintosh HD window in Figure 2-18 says "4 Items" near the top, but only one item seems to be showing. That's easily remedied. To make a window larger, click the *zoom box* in the upper-right corner (see Figures 2-19 and 2-20). This action will cause the window to grow, which should reveal the rest of its contents.

I say "should" because if a window contains more icons than the window can display, it will grow as large as it can and still leave room for your disk and Trash icons on the right side of the screen when you click the *zoom box*.

Click the zoom box again to return the window to its original size.

Figure 2-18:
This window
says that it
contains
four items,
but you only
see one.
What gives?

**Figures 2-19
and 2-20:**
By clicking
the zoom
box in the
upper-right
corner of
the window,
the window
expands to
show all of
the items it
contains.

Cutting windows down to size

Another way to see more of what's in a window is by using the *size box* in the lower-right corner. It's shown in Figure 2-21. Click on the size box and drag downward and to the right to make the window larger (see Figure 2-22). You use the size box to make a window whatever size you like.

Figures 2-21 and 2-22:
Click on and drag the size box to make a window larger or smaller.

A scroll new world

Yet another way to see more of what is in a window is to *scroll*. You scroll using *scroll bars*, which appear on the bottom and right sides of any window that contains more icons than those that you can see in the window (see Figure 2-23).

Figure 2-23:
Scroll bars.

There are four ways to scroll:

Way #1: Click on a *scroll box* and drag, as shown in Figure 2-24.

Figure 2-24:
You can scroll by clicking on and dragging a scroll box.

Way #2: Press on a *scroll arrow* (see Figure 2-25).

Figure 2-25:
You can scroll by pressing on a scroll arrow.

Way #3: Click in the gray *scroll bar* area, as shown in Figure 2-26.

If the scroll bar is white, then there are no items to scroll to — everything that the window contains is visible.

Figure 2-26:
By clicking to the right of the scroll box in the gray area, the window will scroll to the right.

Clicking in the gray scroll *bar* scrolls the window a lot; clicking a scroll *arrow* scrolls the window a little; and pressing and dragging the scroll *box* scrolls the window an amount that corresponds to how far you drag it.

Way #4: Use the keyboard. Select an icon in the window first and then use the arrow keys to move up, down, left, or right. Using an arrow key will select the next icon in that direction and automatically scroll the window if necessary.

You can also press the Tab key on the keyboard to select the next icon alphabetically. So if I clicked on SimpleText and then pressed the Tab key, the System Folder, the icon that comes next alphabetically, would be selected. If the System Folder wasn't showing when I selected SimpleText, the Macintosh HD window would scroll automatically to reveal the System Folder after I press the Tab key.

Transportable windows

To move a window, click anywhere in the *title bar* (shown in Figure 2-27) and drag the window to its new location. Figure 2-28 shows an example of moving a window. The title bar is the striped bar at the top of the active window. It contains the window's name, as well as the close box and the zoom box.

The window will move to its new position as soon as you release the mouse button.

Just below the title bar is the window's *status line,* which tells you the number of items the window contains (4), the amount of used space on your hard disk (22.1MB), and the amount of space available on your hard disk (132MB).

Figure 2-27:
The title bar.

Figure 2-28:
Click and drag on the title bar to move a window.

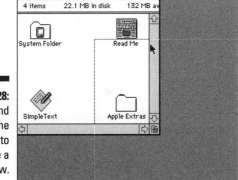

Ladies and gentlemen, activate your windows

In order to work with a window, the window must be active. Only one window at a time may be the *active window.* To make a window active, click anywhere on it — in the middle, on the title bar, on a scroll bar. It doesn't matter where.

The active window is always the frontmost window, and inactive windows always appear behind the active window. The active window's title bar has black lines; its size, zoom, and close boxes are defined, as are its scroll bars. Inactive windows show the window's name but none of these other distinctive window features. See Figure 2-29 for an illustration of active and inactive windows.

Figure 2-29:
An active
window
appears in
front of
inactive
windows; all
of an active
window's
features are
clearly
defined.

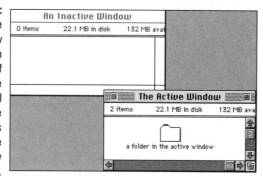

Shut yo' windows

Now that you know just about all there is to know about windows, I suppose I ought to tell you how to close them. Here we go again with the ways. There are three ways to close an active window:

Way #1: Click the *close box* in the upper-left corner of the title bar (see Figure 2-30).

Figure 2-30:
You can
click on the
close box to
close a
window.

Way #2: Choose File⇨Close Window (see Figure 2-31).

Figure 2-31:
You can use
the Close
Window
command in
the File
menu to
close an
active
window.

Way #3: Use the keyboard shortcut Command-W. Note that in Figure 2-31, the Close Window command in the File menu has this keyboard shortcut listed next to it.

If you're like me, by the end of the day you've got windows open all over your Desktop, sometimes a dozen or more. Wouldn't it be nice if there were a way to close them all at once with a single "close all windows" command? But you don't see a Close All command in the menus, do you?

You will in a second. There is one, but Apple, in its infinite wisdom, has hidden it from mere mortals. To make this useful command come out and play, merely hold down the Option key as you close the active window using Ways #1, #2, or #3. In other words, hold down the Option key when you click the active window's close box, hold down the Option key when you choose File⇨Close Window, or hold down the Option key and the Command key while you press the W key (Command-Option-W).

Apple didn't hide the Close All command very well. As Figure 2-32 illustrates, if you press the Option key before pulling down the File menu, Close Window is magically transformed into Close All.

Figure 2-32:
Hold down the Option key while pulling down the File menu and you'll see the Close All command.

The remarkable WindowShade effect

System 7.5 introduces a new wrinkle to windows, the *WindowShade* effect. The WindowShade effect doesn't actually close windows; it rolls them up. To see it, double-click the title bar of a window. Figure 2-33 shows an example.

Figure 2-33:
Double-click
the title bar
of a window
to see it
roll up.

The window "rolls up" and only the title bar remains. To unroll the window, double-click the title bar again.

You can control WindowShade's behavior — turn the WindowShade effect or its associated whooshing sound on or off, or change the trigger keys — with the WindowShade control panel, which I'll talk about in Chapter 13.

Congrats: you now do windows

That retires the side. You now posess a massive, all-encompassing, thoroughly pervasive knowledge of windows and how they work. You can do windows with the best of them.

And I have good news for you: Windows in 99 percent of all applications (programs) that you will ever encounter work the same as windows in the Finder. Just about every application has active and inactive windows with title bars, close boxes, zoom boxes, scroll bars, scroll arrows, and scroll boxes.

Windows are windows, for the most part. As you use different programs, you'll probably notice that some of them (Microsoft Word, for example) take liberties with windows by adding features such as page counters and style indicators to the scroll bar area. Don't worry. You know how to do windows. That stuff is just window dressing.

When a disk is unlocked, you can't see through the hole because there's a little tab of plastic blocking it (see Figure 2-36).

Disk Could Be the Start of a Beautiful Friendship

Groan. I apologize but assure you that you don't want to hear the alternatives. While I don't think there's such a thing as a good pun, in retrospect, this one *is* particularly odious. Sorry.

For all the low-down on what floppy disks are and where they came from, you ought to see Poguerama's *Macs For Dummies*. I'm going to limit my discussion to stuff you do with disks when they're on the Desktop.

You should think of the disk icons that appear on your Desktop as if they were folders. When you double-click them, their windows open. You can drag stuff in and out of a disk's window, and you can manipulate the disk's window in all the usual ways.

Initialization and erasure

Brand new disks usually need to be *initialized*, prepared to receive Macintosh files, before they can be used. I say usually because you can buy new disks that are *preformatted* and are already initialized. It only takes a couple of minutes to initialize a disk, so don't pay a whole lot more for preformatted disks unless you really believe that time is money.

When you pop an uninitialized disk into your Mac, it will walk you through all the steps necessary to initialize it. If you need extra help, see *Macs For Dummies*.

Surprise: PC disks work as well!

One of System 7.5's most welcome new features is the fact that it reads both Mac and DOS floppy disks without any user intervention. DOS disks are formatted for use with personal computers running DOS or Windows. If a friend has a Windows computer, you can now read his or her disks by just sticking them in your floppy drive. Your unfortunate friend, on the other hand, can't do diddly squat with your Mac formatted disks — yet another reason why Macs are better.

There are two other formats that you might run into: ProDOS is the Apple II format, rarely used any more, and Macintosh HFS Interchange Format is a weirdo format nobody I know uses for anything.

When you insert a disk formatted for the DOS, you'll see a distinctive PC disk icon like the one in Figure 2-34. PC files on the disk sport distinctive PC icons as well (shown in Figure 2-35).

Figure 2-34:
A PC-
formatted
disk on your
Mac
Desktop.

Figure 2-35:
PC files also
have special
icons in the
Finder.

Getting disks out of your Mac

You know about everything there is to know about disks except one important thing: How to eject a disk. Piece of cake, actually.

And, of course, there are four ways.

Way #1: Click the disk's icon to select it. Then choose Special⇨Eject Disk. Notice how even though the disk has been ejected and is probably in your right hand, its icon still appears on the Desktop, albeit with an unusual ghostly gray pattern (see Figure 2-36).

Figure 2-36:
The icon of
a disk
ejected with
the
Special⇨Eject
Disk
command.

The ghostly gray indicates that the disk is not currently mounted (inserted). Note that a dismounted disk's icon is not that same as a disk with its window open. The icon of a disk with its window open is shown in Figure 2-37.

Figure 2-37:
The icon of
a disk with
it's window
open.

Why would you want the icon for an ejected disk on your Desktop? So you can copy files from one floppy disk to another even though you have only one floppy disk drive. There's a whole section on copying files coming up in a few pages.

Way #2: Use the keyboard shortcut Command-Shift-1. This action way will also eject the disk but leave its icon on the Desktop.

Way #3: Drag the disk's icon onto the Trash. The disk's icon will *not* remain on the Desktop after you trash it. (see Figure 2-38).

Figure 2-38:
You can
drag a disk's
icon to the
Trash to
eject the
disk.

Way #4: Select the disk then choose File⇨Put Away (or use its Command-key shortcut, Command-Y).

If you drag a disk's icon onto the Trash or use the Put Away command, the disk's ghost icon is *not* left on the Desktop. If you used Way #1 or Way #2 to eject your disk, you can get rid of its ghost image by dragging the ghost icon to the Trash or selecting it and choosing File⇨Put Away. Unless you plan to copy files from one floppy to another, you don't want floppy disk icons on your Desktop after you eject the disks. Ways #3 and #4 or the most commonly used methods of ejecting disk.

If you insist on leaving ghost icons of long-ago ejected disks on your Desktop, it's only a matter of time before your Mac presents you with the dreaded "Please insert the disk" dialog box, which is shown in Figure 2-39.

Figure 2-39:
When you leave ghosted disk icons on the Desktop, your Mac may ask for them back.

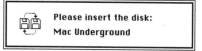

Please insert the disk:
Mac Underground

Notice that there is no OK or Cancel button in the dialog box in Figure 2-39. There's no way out but to insert the disk your Mac is asking for.

OK, I lied. There is a way out. Press Command-period. This keyboard shortcut will cancel the dialog box and allow you to drag the ghost disk icon to the Trash. Command-period is a good shortcut to remember. In most dialog boxes, Command-period is the same as clicking the Cancel button.

The dreaded "Please insert the disk" dialog box usually appears if you try to open the icon for an unmounted disk or try to open any of the files in the unmounted disk's window.

Get in the habit of dragging disks to the Trash or using the Put Away command to get disks off your Desktop. Both techniques eject the disk and get rid of its pesky ghost icon. Unless you plan to copy files from one floppy to another, which you don't do all that often, these methods are the best ways to eject a disk.

Up the Organization: Copying and Moving Files and Folders

Now that you know icons and windows and disks, it's time to get serious and learn something useful, like how to work with folders and how to move and copy icons from folder to folder and from disk to disk.

Know when to hold 'er, know when to folder

If your hard disk is a filing cabinet, folders are its folders. Duh. You use folders to organize your icons.

Makin' folders

To create a new folder, first decide which window you want the new folder to appear in. Make that window active by clicking anywhere on it. Now either choose File⇨New Folder or use the shortcut Command-N. A new, untitled folder appears in the active window with its name box already highlighted and ready for you to type a new name for it (see Figure 2-40).

Figure 2-40:
Use the
New Folder
command to
get a new,
untitled
folder like
the one
highlighted
in this
window.

Name your folders with relevant names. Folders called "sfdghb" or "stuff," or worst of all, "Untitled" won't make it any easier to find something six months from now.

Usin' 'em

Folders are icons; icons are containers. Folders icons (like disks icons) can contain just about any other icon.

You use folders to organize your stuff. There's no limit to how many folders you can have, so don't be afraid to create new ones and put stuff in them.

At the very least, you should have a System Folder (if you don't, go back and read Chapter 1 again). Until you get a *lot* of stuff, may I suggest that you start out with Application and Document folders, at the very least. You can even have the Mac create these two folders automatically by using the General Controls control panel (more about that in Chapter 13).

Later, when you get more files, you can subdivide the Documents folder into meaningful subfolders like those shown in Figure 2-41.

As your subfolders get fuller, create subfolders within them. The idea is to have enough folders so that no one folder ever has hundreds of items in it while simultaneously avoiding folders with only one or two items in them. Strive for balance. And try not to go deeper than 4 or 5 levels. If you find yourself creating subfolders that you have to open 8 folders to get to, consider reorganizing the stuff in levels 5 through 8 so that your folder hierarchy is no more than 4 levels deep. Trust me, you'll save a lot of time if you don't stash stuff 10 folders deep.

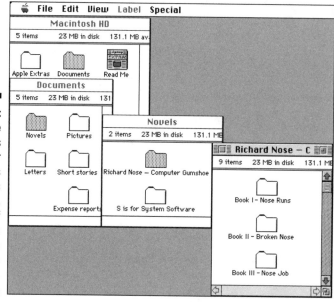

Figure 2-41:
The
Documents
folder
contains
numerous
subfolders,
each of
which
contains
more
subfolders.

Moving and copying and folders

You can move icons around within windows to your heart's content. Just click and drag within the window.

Now let's look at how you move an item into a folder. For example, let's see how you move One Folder into Another. As you might expect from me, the king of ways, there are two ways to do it.

✔ As shown in Figure 2-42, drag the icon for One Folder onto the icon for Another and release when Another folder is highlighted. This technique works regardless of whether Another folder's window is open. If its window is open, you can use the second way.

✔ Drag the icon for One Folder into the open window for Another folder (or disk), as shown in Figure 2-43.

Figure 2-42:
Placing one
folder on
another.

Figure 2-43:
You can
also move a
folder by
dragging its
icon into
the open
window of
another
folder.

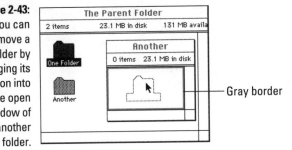

Gray border

Notice the little gray border that appears around Another folder's window in Figure 2-43. This is your Mac telling you that if you release the mouse button right this second, the One Folder icon will be moved into Another folder. If you move the pointer out of the Another folder window, the gray border will disappear.

You use these two techniques to move any icon — folder, document, System software, or program icons — into folders or disks.

But what if you don't want to move something? What if instead you want to copy it, leaving the icon in its original location and an identical copy in the destination window?

You might be thinking, why would I want to do that? Trust me, someday you will. Say you've got a file called "Long Letter to Mom" in a folder called "1987 Correspondence." You figure Mom's forgotten it by now, so you want to send the letter again. But before you do, you want to change the date and delete the reference to Clarence, her pit bull, who passed away last year. So you want a copy of "Long Letter to Mom" in your "1995 Correspondence" folder.

There are three ways to copy, but the first two are the same as you saw in the One Folder and Another example, with one small difference — you must hold down the Option key during the dragging portion of the move. In the Finder, Option-dragging an icon to any folder icon or window copies it instead of moving it. So you Option-drag the Letter to Mom icon onto either a folder icon or an open window to deposit a copy.

Now you have two copies of the file "Long Letter to Mom," one in the "1987 Correspondence" folder and another copy in the "1995 Correspondence" folder. Open the one in the 1995 folder and make your changes. Don't forget to Save. (There's more about saving in Chapter 5.)

If I were you, I'd change the name of the 1995 copy, as it's not a good idea to have more than one file on your hard disk with the same name, even if the files are in different folders. Trust me, having ten files called "expense report" or 15 files named "Gelson's Invoice" can be confusing no matter how well organized your folder structure is. Add something distinguishing to file and folder names — something like "expense report 10/95" or "Gelson's Invoice 10/30/95." You'll be glad you did.

The third way to copy a file is to use the File⇨Duplicate command, which is covered in the very next chapter.

Moving and copying and disks

Moving an icon from one disk to another works the same as moving folders in the previous example. Because you're moving the icons from one disk to another disk, the "copy" part is automatic; you don't need the Option key. When you move a file from one disk to another, you're automatically making a copy of it. The original is left untouched and unmoved. If you want to move a file from one disk to another, copy it. You can then delete the original by dragging it to the Trash.

Copying the entire contents of a floppy disk to your hard disk works a little differently. To do this task, select the floppy disk's icon and drag it onto your hard disk's icon or onto your hard disk's window, as shown in Figure 2-44 and 2-45. A progress bar appears (see Figure 2-46).

Figure 2-44:
To copy the entire contents of a floppy disk to your hard drive, you can drag the floppy disk's icon onto your hard drive's icon.

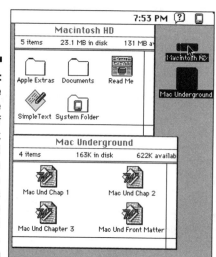

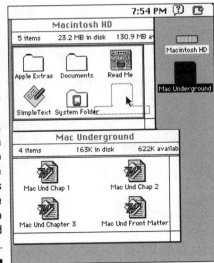

Figure 2-45:
You can
also drag a
floppy disk's
icon onto a
hard disk's
open
window to
copy the
floppy's
entire
contents to
the hard
disk.

Figure 2-46:
When you
copy items,
a progress
bar shows
you what's
happening.

When the progress bar disappears, a folder bearing the same name as the floppy disk will appear on your hard disk, as Figure 2-47 shows.

Figure 2-47:
The entire
contents of
the floppy
disk named
Mac Under-
ground have
been copied
to a folder of
the same
name on the
hard disk.

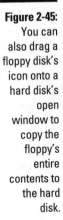

The folder on your hard disk now contains each and every file that was on the floppy disk of the same name.

By the way: You can drag a floppy disk icon onto any folder icon or window on your hard disk if you like, not just onto the first level of your hard disk (that first level is sometimes called the *root level*). Just substitute the folder's icon or window for the Macintosh HD icon and window in the previous example.

Be careful copying disks containing System Folders to your hard disk. You never want to use the above technique to copy a floppy to your hard disk if the floppy has a System Folder. One hard and fast rule of the Mac is that there should never be more than one System Folder on your hard disk.

If a floppy disk contains a System Folder and you want to copy everything else to your hard disk, do the following: Create a new folder on your hard disk. Then select every icon in the floppy disk's window *except* the System Folder and drag them all onto the new folder's icon or window.

To select more than one icon, click once and drag. You'll see an outline of a box around the icons as you drag, and icons within the box will highlight (see Figure 2-48).

Figure 2-48:
To select
more than
one item,
click and
drag with
the mouse.

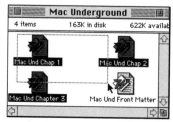

Another way to select multiple icons is to click one and then hold down the Shift key as you click on others. As long as you hold the Shift key, each new icon you click is added to the selection. Click an icon a second time while still holding the Shift key down to deselect it.

Be careful with multiple selections, especially when you drag icons to the Trash. It's easy to accidentally select more than one icon, so it's possible to put an icon in the Trash by accident if you're not paying close attention. So pay close attention.

Meet the Desktop

Earlier I said that Finder and Desktop were used interchangeably, referring to the total Macintosh environment you see — icons, windows, menus, and all the other cool stuff. Well, just to make things confusing, the background you see on your screen, the gray or patterned backdrop behind your hard disk icon and open windows, is also called the Desktop.

Any icon can reside on the Desktop. Just move icons to the Desktop from any window. It's not a window, but it acts like one. You can move any icon there if you like; the Desktop is a great place for things you use a lot, like folders, applications, or documents that you use every day.

It's even better to use aliases of things you use often so that you can keep the originals tucked away in one of your perfectly organized folders. But I'm not going to talk about aliases until Chapter 3, so for now, just tuck that little tidbit away in the back of your mind.

In Figure 2-49, you see five items (six if you count the Macintosh HD window) on my Desktop: Macintosh HD (disk icon), Documents (folder icon), SimpleText (application icon), Read Me (document icon), and the Trash icon.

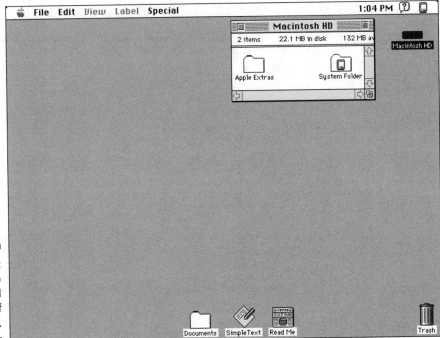

Figure 2-49:
My Desktop
with all
kinds of stuff
on it.

Disk icons always appear on the Desktop, as does the Trash icon. The other icons, a document, a folder, and an application, were moved from the root level of Macintosh HD to the Desktop by me to make them easier to use.

Items on the Desktop behave the same as they would in a window. You move them and copy them in the same way you would an icon in a window — except that they're not in a window; they're on the Desktop, which makes them more convenient to use.

Got it? It's convenient. It's fast. Put stuff there.

But not too much. If you keep putting stuff on the Desktop, eventually it gets very cluttered. That's the time to put infrequently used icons on the Desktop back in the folder or disk window they came from. Fortunately, your Mac makes this task easy, even if you've forgotten which folder they came out of. Select the icon or icons that you want moved back to where they came from and then choose File⇨Put Away. The icon will be magically transported back into the folder or disk icon from which it came and will no longer appear on the Desktop. Neat, eh?

Many users cover their Desktops with icons, sometimes dozens or more. That's because the Desktop is the most convenient place for things that you use often. You save time and effort because you don't have to open any windows to open an icon on the Desktop.

I'll talk more about convenience, the Desktop, and cool techniques for making life with your Mac easier and more productive in Chapter 7. For now, let's move on to the next chapter and look at something quite delicious, your Mac's menus.

Chapter 3

A Bevy of Delectable Menus

*L*ike icons and windows, menus are a quintessential part of the Macintosh experience. In this chapter, we'll take a brief look at each and every Finder menu item.

I'm trying to provide an appropriate level of detail based on the menu item's importance. On the other hand, I think the entire Label menu is dumb; you may think it's the best thing about System 7.5. (I hope not!)

Anyway, I'll start with a few menu basics and then move on to the menus in almost the order they appear on your screen, File, Edit, View, Label, Special, Help, and Application. Because it's so long, I'm going to give the Apple menu its own chapter, the very next one after this.

Menu Basics

Mac menus are often referred to as pull-down menus. That's because to use them, you press on their name to make the menu appear and then pull (drag) down to select an item. Piece of cake, eh?

Command performance

As noted previously, many menu items have Command key shortcuts after their names. These key combinations indicate that you can activate that menu item without using the mouse by pressing the Command (notice I refrained from calling it a pretzel) key and then pressing another key without releasing the Command key. And, as I've said before and will say again, it pays to memorize the shortcuts you use often.

It's elliptical

Another feature of Mac menus are ellipses after the menu item's name. Ellipses, in case your English teacher forgot to mention them, are the three little dots (...) that appear after certain menu items' names. According to the Bible (actually, the *Chicago Manual of Style*, but for writers it might as well be the Bible), "Any omission of a word or phrase, line or paragraph . . . must be indicated by ellipsis points (dots). . . ."

Apple is true to this definition. Ellipsis points in a menu item mean that choosing it will bring up a dialog box where you can make further choices. Choosing a menu item with an ellipsis never actually makes anything happen other than opening a dialog box, where you make further choices and then click a button to make things happen.

Dialog box featurettes

Dialog boxes may contain a number of standard Macintosh features like radio buttons, pop-up menus, text entry boxes, and check boxes. You'll see these features again and again, in dialog boxes, control panels, and elsewhere. So let's take a moment to look at each of these featurettes and I'll demonstrate how they're used.

Radio, radio (buttons)

Radio buttons are called radio buttons because, like the buttons on your car radio, only one can be pushed at a time. Radio buttons always appear in groups of two or more; when you push one, all the others are automatically unpushed. I think eggheads call this setup "mutually exclusive." Take a look at Figure 3-1 for an example of radio buttons.

In Figure 3-1, *Normal: print now* is currently selected. If you click on any of the other choices, *Normal: print now* will be deactivated.

Figure 3-1:
A group of
radio
buttons.
Only one
may be
selected at
a time.

Set the print time priority to:

⊙ Normal: print now
○ Urgent: print before other documents
○ Print at: 10:53 AM   5/22/94
○ Hold document in printer "Bob's Printer"

Menus redux: pop-up style

Pop-up menus are called pop-up menus because that's what they do — they pop up when you press on them. You can always tell a pop-up menu because it appears in a rectangle with a shadow and a down-pointing arrow. Figure 3-2 shows a pop-up menu before you click on it; Figure 3-3 shows the same menu after you click on it and hold the mouse button down.

Figure 3-2:
Pop-up
menus have
a distinctive
look, with a
shadow and
an arrow.

Destination:

Figure 3-3:
To pop a
pop-up
menu, click
on the
rectangle
and hold
down the
mouse
button.

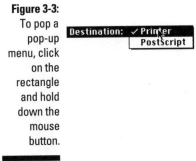

OK, so now you've looked at two features, radio buttons and pop-up menus, and they both do the exact same thing: allow you to make a single selection from a group of options. Sometimes a radio button is associated with a text entry box, which happens to be the feature I cover next.

Championship boxing: text entry style

Text entry boxes let you enter text (including numbers) from the keyboard. When a text entry box appears in conjunction with a radio button, the text entry box or boxes only matter if the associated radio button is pressed. Take a look at Figure 3-4. You can enter text in the two text entry boxes next to the From radio button, but if you click the All radio button, your text will disappear. Conversely, if you click in one of the text entry boxes and type, the From radio button will automatically become selected.

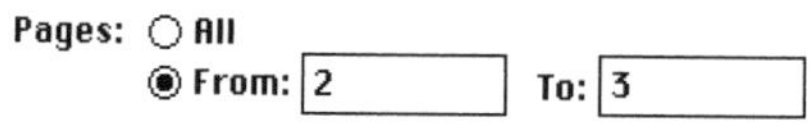

Figure 3-4:
Type letters
or numbers
into text
entry boxes.

Pages: ○ All
        ⦿ From: 2   To: 3

Had Apple chosen to use a pop-up menu instead of radio buttons in the Figure 3-4 example, the menu would have taken up more valuable screen real estate. So that's the reason for two featurettes that do the same thing.

And now you know how to use both.

Checkmate

The last featurette you'll see frequently is the check box. Check boxes are used to choose items that are not mutually exclusive. In a group of check boxes, you can turn each on or off individually. When you see check boxes, they are on when they contain an X and off when they're empty. Figure 3-5 shows two check boxes that are both on.

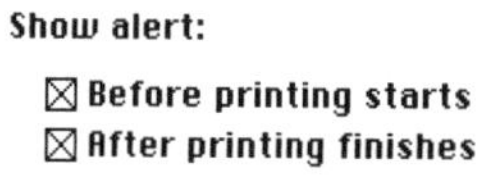

Figure 3-5:
In this
example,
both check
boxes are
checked.

Show alert:
   ⊠ Before printing starts
   ⊠ After printing finishes

Unlike radio buttons, which force you to choose one and only one item, check boxes are independent. Each one can either be on or off.

Here's a nifty and undocumented shortcut: Check boxes and radio buttons can usually be activated by clicking on their name (instead of clicking right on the button or box). Didn't know that, did you?

File Management and More: Meet the File Menu

The File menu (shown in Figure 3-6) contains commands that allow you to manipulate your files and folders.

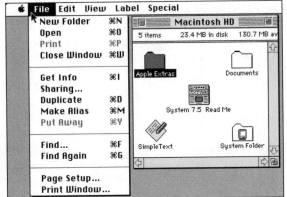

Figure 3-6:
The File
menu.

Menu items that can be used to act upon the item or items selected in the active window (or on the Desktop) appear in black and are currently available; menu items not available at the current time are displayed in gray. You cannot select a gray menu item.

In this example, only two items are disabled — Print and Put Away. That's because you can only print documents, not folders, and the selected item in the active window is a folder (Apple Extras). And the Put Away command is dimmed because you can only Put Away items that reside on the gray Desktop. The rest of the commands appear in black and are valid selections at this time.

New Folder (Command-N)

I talked about this command in the last chapter, but just for the record, New Folder creates a new untitled folder in the active window. If no window is active, it creates a new folder on the Desktop.

You'll probably do a lot of new-folder making, so it might be a good idea to memorize this command's keyboard shortcut, Command-N. It'll come in handy later as most software uses the shortcut Command-N to create a new document, another thing you'll do a lot of.

If your memory is bad, use this mnemonic device — N is for New.

Most menu items, or at least most common ones, have keyboard shortcuts that have a mnemonic relationship to their name. For example, New is Command-N, Open is Command-O, Get Info is Command-I, Make Alias is Command-M (which is good news because in earlier versions of System 7, there was no keyboard shortcut for Make Alias), and so on.

Open (Command-O)

This command opens the selected item. Not much more to say except to remind you that in addition to the menu command and its shortcut Command-O, a double-click also opens an icon.

Print (Command-P)

This command prints the selected item. This command is only active if the selected icon is a document. Furthermore, it will only work if you have the application that created the document on your hard disk. If you try to print (or Open) a document when you don't have the application that created it, you'll see a dialog box like the one shown in Figure 3-7.

Figure 3-7:
Try to print
or open a
document
when you
don't have
the program
that created
it and you
may see this.

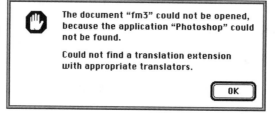

The document "fm3" could not be opened, because the application "Photoshop" could not be found.

Could not find a translation extension with appropriate translators.

OK

I'll talk about what translators are when I discuss Macintosh Easy Open in Chapter 13. For now, let's leave it at this: If you select a document icon and then use the Open or Print command, the command will only work if you have the application that created the document or another application that is capable of opening that type of document.

That's where the translator part comes in (refer to Figure 3-7 again). Many programs can open files created by another program, but only if the proper *translator* is available. I'll save the details for later.

Close Window (Command-W)

This command closes the active window. Duh. Don't forget, if you hold down the Option key before you click on the File menu, this command changes to Close All.

I talked about this command in Chapter 2, so I'll just move on.

Get Info (Command-I)

When you select any icon and choose the Get Info command (or use its keyboard shortcut Command-I), a Get Info window opens (see Figure 3-8).

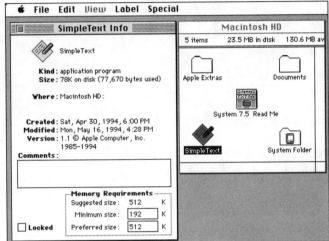

Figure 3-8:
A typical
Get Info
window
for an
application.

The top portion of the Get Info window provides details about the icon, such as what it is (application, document, disk, folder, etc.), how big it is, where it is on your disk, when it was created, when it was last modified, and its version number.

The middle section is called the Comments box because that's where you type your comments about the icon. Don't get too fond of comments. I don't recommend ever using this Comments box because the comments will disappear after you rebuild your desktop, and, as you'll learn in Chapter 18, you should rebuild your desktop on a regular basis.

The bottom section of an application's Get Info box deals with its memory requirements. This stuff gets a little complicated, so I won't go into it here. (If you just can't wait, skip ahead to my dandy and easy-to-understand explanation in Chapter 10.)

The last item in an application's Get Info box is the Locked check box. When an application is locked, its name can't be changed, and it can't be emptied from the Trash.

If you try to empty the Trash when there's a locked item in it, you'll see a message telling you to hold down the Option key before you choose Special⇨Empty Trash. Holding down the Option key when you choose Empty Trash empties the Trash even if there are locked items in it.

Artistic Icons

The Get Info box serves another more frivolous but fundamentally fun function—it lets you change any icon's icon to anything you like.

Don't like the Mac's folder icon? Give it a new one. Here's how. Find an icon you like—let's say it's an armadillo (hey, I'm a Texan!). Select it and select the Get Info command. Now select the folder that you want to give the 'dillo icon to and bring up the Get Info window. In the upper-left corner of the 'dillo's Get Info box, you'll see the 'dillo (see below).

Click on the 'dillo in its Get Info box. A box will appear around the 'dillo icon indicating that it's now selected. Choose Edit⇨Copy, as shown in the following figure.

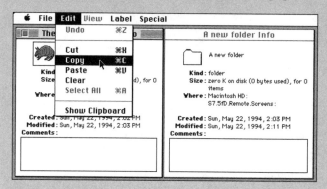

Now click on the folder icon in its Get Info window and choose Edit⇨Paste. The results of this last step are shown below.

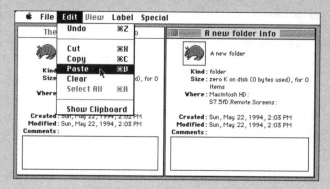

(continued)

(continued)

There you go! This technique works on any icon — disk, folder, application, or document. And if you can't find an icon you like, you can create a picture in any graphics program, select it, choose Edit⇨Copy, and then paste it into the Get Info box of any icon.

Furthermore, on-line services like CompuServe, America Online, and eWorld, as well as Macintosh user groups, offer humongous collections of icons for your pasting pleasure.

While I'm on the subject, do you hate the dialog box you see each time you try to empty the Trash (you know, the one that says: "The Trash contains X items. It uses X K of disk space. Are you sure you want to permanently remove it?")? If you never want to see this pain-in-the-bottom dialog box again, select the Trash icon, the Get Info command (Command-I), and uncheck the Warn before emptying check box.

Documents, folders, and disks each have slightly different Get Info boxes. Folders and disks can't be locked; documents can. And the Get Info box for documents includes an additional check box to make the document a Stationery pad. (Stationery pads are neat. They're also covered in Chapter 5.)

Sharing (sorry, it has no keyboard shortcut)

The Sharing command lets you decide who can share your files. There's so much to say about Macintosh File Sharing that I could write an entire chapter about it. And in fact, I have. If you're interested, take a look at Chapter 9.

Duplicate (Command-D)

Duplicate duplicates the selected icon. More precisely, it makes an exact copy of the selected icon, adds the word "copy" to its name, and places the copy in the same window as the original icon. Figure 3-9 shows the results of using the Duplicate command.

The Duplicate command can be used on any icon except a disk icon.

Figure 3-9:
The
Duplicate
command in
action.

Make Alias (Command-M)

Aliases are a wonderful, fabulous organizational tool introduced with System 7.0. An alias is a tiny file that automatically opens its *parent* file. To create an alias for any icon, select the icon (the parent) and then choose File⇨Make Alias or press Command-M.

When you Open an alias, the parent Opens.

An alias is different from a Duplicated file. For example, my word processor, Microsoft Word 5.1a, uses 891K of disk space. If I duplicated it, I would have two files, each using 891K of disk space. An alias of Microsoft Word uses a mere 3K.

When you make an alias, it has the same icon as its parent, but its name appears in *italic* type and the suffix "alias" is tacked onto its name. Figure 3-10 shows an alias and its parent icon.

Figure 3-10:
An alias
icon looks
identical to
its parent.

You can put aliases in convenient places like the Desktop or the Apple Menu Items folder (so that they appear in your Apple menu).

There must be at least a dozen ways aliases can help organize your Macintosh existence, and I'll talk about all of them in Chapter 7.

Put Away (Command-Y)

Choose Put Away to move the selected icon from your Desktop to the window it was in before you moved it to the Desktop. This command even works if it's been years since the icon was moved to the Desktop and you don't remember which folder it came out of.

The Put Away command is only active when an icon on the Desktop is selected; it is dimmed whenever any icon in a window is selected. Put Away is also dimmed when the Trash icon is selected.

And, as mentioned previously, the Put Away command will eject a floppy disk and remove its ghost icon from the Desktop. In other words, Put Away has the same effect on a floppy disk as dragging its icon to the Trash.

Find (Command-F)

Use this command when you need to find an icon on your hard disk and you can't remember where you put it. This is a System 7.5 feature that really kicks earlier versions' butts. The new Find command is awesome.

There are three different ways to invoke the Find dialog box (here I go again with the ways).

  ✔ Choose File⇨Find.

  ✔ Use the keyboard shortcut Command-F.

  ✔ Choose Find File from the Apple menu.

Whichever way you choose, the next thing you'll see is the Find dialog box (shown in Figure 3-11).

Figure 3-11:
The Find
dialog box.

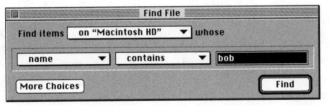

Just type in the name of the file that you're looking for and then click the Find button or press the Return key. In a flash (System 7.5's Find is about a zillion times faster than earlier incarnations), you'll see the Find File Results window (see Figure 3-12) showing every file on the disk you searched that matches the word you typed in the text entry box.

In Figure 3-12, the file "Letter to Bob" is in the Letters folder, which is in the Documents folder, which is on the Macintosh HD.

At this point there are three ways to open the file:

  ✔ Choose File⇨Open Item.

  ✔ Use the keyboard shortcut Command-O.

  ✔ Double-click the file in the top or bottom part of the Find File Results window.

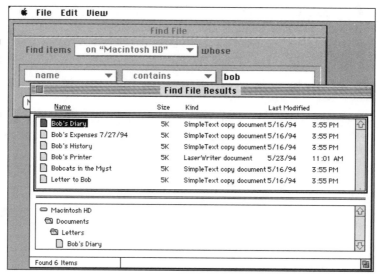

If you prefer to open the folder that contains the item, there are three ways to do that:

- ✔ Choose File⇨Open Enclosing Folder.
- ✔ Use the keyboard shortcut Command-E.
- ✔ Double-click the folder in the bottom part of the Find File Results window.

If searching by name alone finds too many files, you can narrow your search by clicking the More Choices button in the Find dialog box and adding one or more additional criteria for the search. These criteria include the following:

- ✔ Size of file
- ✔ Kind of file (application, alias, and so on)
- ✔ Label (see the Label menu section later in this chapter)
- ✔ Creation Date (date the file was created)
- ✔ Modification Date (date the file was last Saved)
- ✔ Version Number (is or is not)
- ✔ Lock Attribute (file is locked or not)
- ✔ Folder Attribute (empty, shared, or mounted)
- ✔ File Type code
- ✔ Creator Type code

Figure 3-13 shows what the Find dialog box looks like after you click the More Choices button.

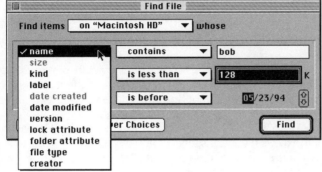

Figure 3-13:
This search
will find only
files whose
name
includes the
word "bob,"
are smaller
than 128K,
and were
created be-
fore 5/23/94.

Find Again (Command-G)

I dunno. This seems pretty dumb to me. As far as I can tell, it does the exact
same thing as the Find command — opens the Find dialog box. I think it's a relic
from earlier versions of System 7. With any luck, it will be gone before the
software ships, but it's in the prerelease version I'm using now, so I've got to
mention it.

Page Setup (no keyboard shortcut)

Choosing Page Setup brings up the Page Setup dialog box (shown in Figure 3-14),
which is where you specify the type of paper in your printer (letter, legal,
envelope, and so on), page orientation (longways or wideways), and scaling
(100% = full size).

In addition to the one here in the Finder, there will be a Page Setup command in
almost every program that you use. There's a whole chapter on printing coming
up in a little while (Chapter 8, to be exact), so I'll leave this topic alone for now.

Figure 3-14:
The Page
Setup dialog
box lets you
specify stuff
about the
document
that you're
about to
print.

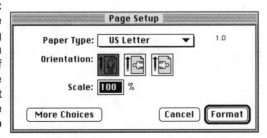

Print (no keyboard shortcut)

This command is a little tricky. If no windows are open, the command is called Print Desktop. If a window is open, the command's name changes to Print Window.

If you choose Print Desktop, your Mac will print a picture of your Desktop, its icons and Trash (but not the menu bar), exactly as you see them on the screen. If you have anything but a 9" built-in monitor, this image will take two pieces of paper.

If you choose Print Window, your Mac will print a picture of the active window, showing all the icons it contains, even if you would have to scroll to see the icons on the screen. If the window contains a lot of icons, printing this document may require more than one sheet of paper.

And if a document is selected when you choose the Print command, the application that created the document will launch automatically and you'll see a Print dialog box. (Printing is covered in full and loving detail in Chapter 8.)

The Print dialog box, which appears when you select the Print command, is show in Figure 3-15.

Again, Chapter 8 covers printing, so let's move on.

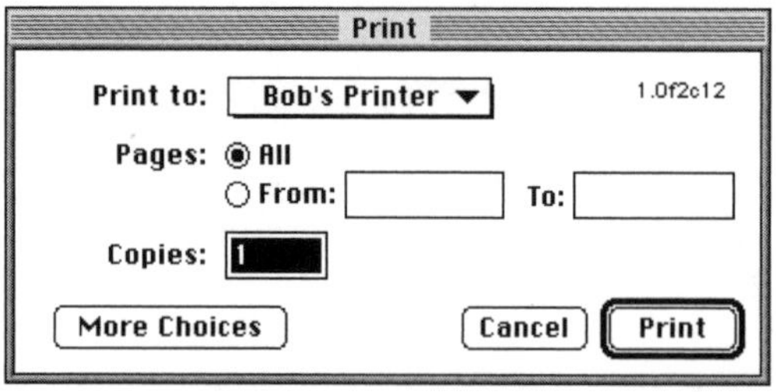

Figure 3-15:
The Print
dialog box.

The Edit Menu (Which Shoulda Been Called the Clipboard Menu)

In contrast to the File menu, which has commands that mostly deal with file management and are exclusive to the Finder, the Edit menu's commands and functions are available in almost every Macintosh program ever made (see Figure 3-16).

Because almost every program has an Edit menu, and because almost every program uses the same keyboard shortcuts on its Edit menu, it will behoove you to learn these keyboard shortcuts by heart, even if you learn no others.

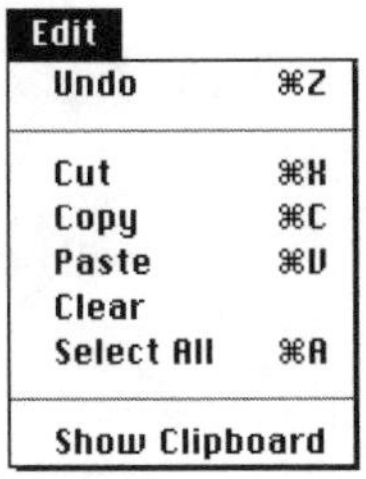

Figure 3-16:
The Edit menu.
Memorize
these
keyboard
shortcuts even
if you never
memorize any
others.

Edit	
Undo	⌘Z
Cut	⌘H
Copy	⌘C
Paste	⌘U
Clear	
Select All	⌘A
Show Clipboard	

The Edit menu should probably have been called the *Clipboard* menu because most of its commands deal with the Macintosh Clipboard.

If you read the little sidebar about the Clipboard, you'll learn 75 percent of what you need to know about the Edit menu. Still, because IDG's paying me to be thorough, and because the Finder's Edit menu has a couple of commands that aren't Clipboard-related, I'll go through the Edit menu's commands one by one.

The Clipboard

Essential to your understanding of the Mac and essential to your understanding of the Edit menu is an understanding of the concept of the Macintosh Clipboard. In a sentence, the Clipboard is a holding area for the last thing that you cut or copied. A thing can be text, a picture, a portion of a picture, an object in a drawing program, a column of numbers in a spreadsheet, or just about anything that can be selected. In other words, the Clipboard is the Mac's temporary storage area.

As a storage area, the Clipboard is ephemeral, which means that its contents are temporary. Very temporary. When you cut or copy an item, that item remains on the Clipboard only until you cut or copy something else. Then the Clipboard's contents are replaced by the new item, which remains on the Clipboard until you cut or copy something else. And so it goes.

To place the item that's on the Clipboard somewhere else, click where you want the item to go and then paste. Pasting does not remove the item from the Clipboard; the item remains there until another item is cut or copied.

Almost all programs have an Edit menu and use the Macintosh clipboard properly, which means that you can usually cut or copy something in a document in one program and paste it into a document from another program. Usually.

The Clipboard commands in the Edit menu are relatively intelligent. If the currently selected item *can* be cut or copied, then the Cut and Copy commands in the Edit menu will be enabled; if the item can't be cut or copied, the commands will be unavailable and grayed out. And when nothing at all is selected, the Cut, Copy, Paste, and Clear commands are grayed out.

The contents of the Clipboard don't survive a restart, shut down, or a system error or crash. The Clipboard is ephemeral in the sense that any of these events purges its contents, so when your Mac comes back to life, the Clipboard will be empty.

Undo (Command-Z)

This is a great command! You're gonna love it. Undo undoes the last thing you did. Try it.

1. Create a new folder in any window or on the Desktop. (It will be called "untitled folder.")

2. Change the name "untitled folder" to "undo me."

3. Without clicking anywhere else or doing anything else, choose Edit⇨Undo or use the keyboard shortcut Command-Z.

The folder's name should magically undo itself and change back to "untitled folder."

Neat, huh? Don't forget about this command 'cause it can be a lifesaver. Almost every program has it.

Now for the bad news: The Undo command is ephemeral, like the Clipboard. It only undoes your last action and as soon as you do something else, you lose the ability to undo the original action. To see what I mean, repeat the exercise and change "untitled folder" to "undo me." But this time, click on another icon before you undo. What's that you say? The Undo command is grayed out and not available any more? I told you. When you clicked the other icon, you forfeited your chance to use Undo.

Unfortunately, Undo doesn't work with things like moving icons or copying files. In fact, as you learn more about using your Mac, you'll discover lots of actions that can't be undone. Still, it's a great command when it's available, and I urge you to get in the habit of trying it often.

Incidentally, the Undo command *toggles* between the new and old states as long as you don't do anything else. So in the first example, if you Choose Edit⇨Undo again without clicking anywhere else, the name would transform back to "undo me." And if you choose Edit⇨Undo again, it will change back to "untitled folder." You can continue to undo and redo until you click somewhere else.

You can use the Undo toggle to compare two versions of a document — a letter, a picture, and so on. Here's how: Say I'm writing a letter and I conclude it with "Very truly yours, Robert A. LeVitus." I decide that sounds a bit too formal, so I select "Very truly yours, Robert A. LeVitus" and replace it with "Sincerely, Bobby." Now I can use the toggle. As long as I don't click or type anywhere else before I undo, I can toggle between the two versions, "Very truly yours, Robert A. LeVitus" and "Sincerely, Bobby." I can repeat this process, looking at the closing one way and then the other, until I decide which version I like best. As long as I don't do anything else — click, use menus, save, or other stuff — the toggle continues.

Cut (Command-X)

The Cut command removes the selected item and places it on the Clipboard. Let's see this command in action:

1. Create an untitled folder.

2. Select only the word "untitled" ("untitled" should be black with white letters; "folder" should be white with black letters).

3. Choose Edit⇨Cut or use the keyboard shortcut Command-X.

The word "untitled" disappears from the folder's name. Where did it go? You cut it! It's removed from the folder and is now waiting on the Clipboard.

(You could, of course, use the Undo command at this point to make "untitled" reappear as long as you haven't clicked anything else.)

Show Clipboard (no keyboard shortcut)

I know I'm not covering the commands in the order that they appear on the Edit menu, but there's a method to my madness. If you don't believe that the word "untitled," which you cut in the previous section, is on the Clipboard, choose Edit⇨Show Clipboard. A window will appear, telling you the type of item (text, picture, sound, and so on) on the Clipboard and displaying it if it can be displayed (see Figure 3-17).

Figure 3-17:
The Show Clipboard command displays the current contents of the Clipboard.

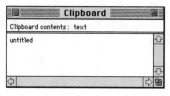

There is another way to display the Clipboard's contents — open the Clipboard icon in your System Folder. Because some programs don't have a Show Clipboard command, it's convenient to make an alias of the Clipboard file and put the alias in your Apple Menu Items folder so that it appears in your Apple menu. (Don't panic. I'm going to talk about the Apple menu in the very next chapter.) Then, even if you're in a program that doesn't have a Show Clipboard command, you can select the Clipboard alias from the Apple menu. This technique saves you two steps; without it you'd have to first go back to the Finder and then choose Edit⇨Show Clipboard. Choosing the Clipboard alias from the Apple menu does both steps automatically.

Copy (Command-C)

Copy makes a copy of the selected item and places it on the Clipboard. The original is not removed as it is when you cut. Try it. Select your System Folder and choose Edit⇨Copy or use the keyboard shortcut Command-C. Now choose Edit⇨Show Clipboard. The Clipboard contains the text "System Folder."

It's that simple.

Paste (Command-V)

We've been cutting and copying but not doing much with the stuff on the Clipboard except looking at it to make sure it's really there. Now let's learn to use what we've cut or copied. Do this:

1. Create a new folder.

2. Change the folder's name to "Elvis Costello."

3. Copy the word "Elvis" to the Clipboard. (C'mon, you know how.)

4. Create another new folder and select its name (which should be "untitled folder" if you've been following my instructions).

5. Choose Edit⇨Paste.

The new folder is now called "Elvis." Pasting doesn't purge the contents of the Clipboard. Don't believe me? Choose Edit⇨Show Clipboard to confirm that Elvis is still alive and well and on the Clipboard.

Which is where he'll stay until you: cut, copy, crash (the three C's of Macintosh computing), or restart or shut down.

Clear (no keyboard shortcut)

Clear deletes the selected item without involving the Clipboard. It works the same as pressing the Delete key on your keyboard. Use it when you want to make something disappear forever.

Clear can be undone as long as you haven't done anything else like click, type, save, or use a menu.

Select All (Command-A)

Select All selects all. If a window is active, Select All selects every icon in the window, regardless of whether you can see them. If no window is active, Select All selects every icon on the Desktop.

Go ahead and try it a couple of times. I'll wait.

Select All has nothing whatsoever to do with the Clipboard. So why is it on the Edit menu? Who knows? It just is.

A View from a Window: The View Menu

The View menu offers seven ways to look at icons in a window. Choosing a command in the View menu changes what the icons look like in the active window. If no window is active, the View menu is unavailable, grayed out.

Although there are seven commands in the View menu, there are really only two ways to view the contents of windows: Icon views and list views. Icon views include both small icons and big icons. The rest are list views: by Name, by Size, by Kind, by Label, and by Date.

by Icon

Viewing by icon is the "Macintosh" view, the one most closely associated with the Macintosh experience. It's also, in my humble opinion, the least useful view, as those big horsy icons take up far too much valuable screen real estate. And, as you'll see in a minute, the list views offer a nifty navigational extra. The window in Figure 3-18 uses the Icon view.

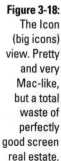

Figure 3-18: The Icon (big icons) view. Pretty and very Mac-like, but a total waste of perfectly good screen real estate.

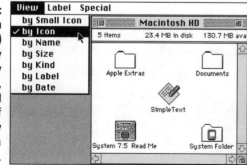

In all fairness I must say that there are many perfectly happy Mac users who love the Icon view and refuse to even consider anything else. Fine. But as the number of files on your hard disk increases (as every Mac user's does), screen real estate becomes more and more valuable.

By the way, if you like the big icon view, they now make monitors as big as 21 inches.

by Small Icon

The Small Icon view (shown in Figure 3-19) is better and wastes less screen space than those blocky big icons, but I still say that the list views are better.

The only thing the icon views have over list views is the ability to move icons anywhere you like. Big deal.

Figure 3-19:
Viewing by
Small Icon.

The list views

The list views are lumped together because they all look the same with one small exception — the order that the icons appear varies.

View by Name

Displays the icons in alphabetical order (see Figure 3-20).

View by Size

Displays the icons in descending order by size, with document and applications sorted together by size, followed by folders in alphabetical order (see Figure 3-21).

If you have the Calculate Folder Sizes option turned on in the Views control panel (I recommend that you keep it turned off — it seems to make the Finder feel a bit sluggish), the icons, including folders, will be sorted in descending order from biggest to smallest (see Figure 3-22).

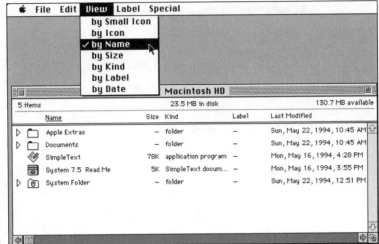

Figure 3-20:
View by
Name.

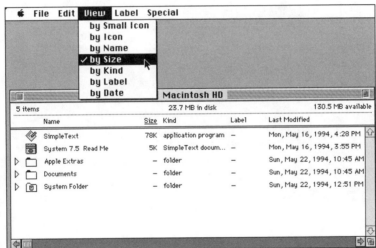

Figure 3-21:
View by
Size.

View by Kind

Displays the icons in this order: applications, documents, folders. Not usually very useful.

View by Label

See the section on the Label menu.

View by Date

View by Date displays the icons by modification date, with the most recently modified icon first (see Figure 3-23).

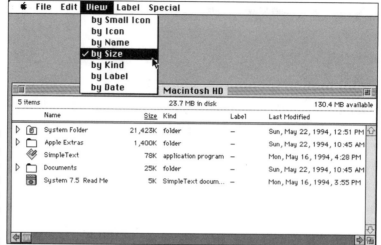

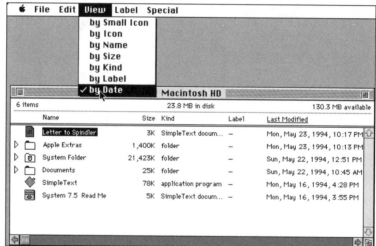

Use this view for folders with lots of documents in them. That way, the ones you used most recently will be listed first. If that gets confusing, you can easily switch to the by Name view for a second to find things alphabetically.

Another way to switch between list views

Notice how the appropriate column title is underlined in Figures 3-20 through 3-23 — how "Name" is underlined in Figure 3-20, "Size" is underlined in Figure 3-21, and so on. This underline tells you which of the list views is in use.

Now for the shortcut: You don't need to use the View menu to switch between list views. Instead, just click directly on the column title, and the window's view will change. Go ahead, give it a try. The only proviso is that you must be in a list view in the first place (the column titles don't appear in icon views).

The triangles

In list views, folder icons have a little triangle to the left of their name. This is the outline metaphor, and it's only available in the list views. You click on the triangle to reveal the folder's contents right there in the same window.

In my humble opinion, this is a much better way to get to an icon buried three or four folders deep. Figure 3-24 shows the slow and tedious way of getting to the icon; Figure 3-25 shows the cool, savvy, and efficient way of getting to the same icon.

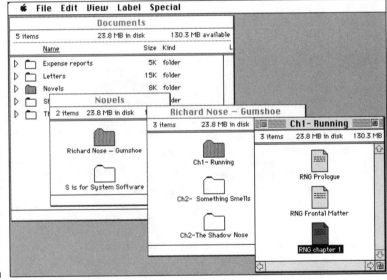

Figure 3-24: Getting to the document "RNG chapter 1" the usual way, by opening windows.

In Figure 3-24, I had to double-click three folders to get to "RNG chapter 1." When I got to it, I had four windows open on the Desktop.

In Figure 3-25, I had to single-click three triangles to get to "RNG chapter 1." When I got to it, only one small window was open, keeping my Desktop neat and tidy.

There are other advantages to the triangle/outline metaphor. First and foremost, you can copy or move items from separate folders in one move, as Figure 3-26 illustrates.

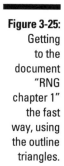

Figure 3-25:
Getting
to the
document
"RNG
chapter 1"
the fast
way, using
the outline
triangles.

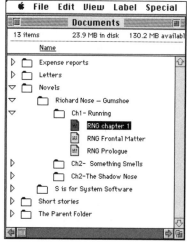

Figure 3-26:
Moving or
copying files
from two
separate
folders is
easy if
you're using
one of the
list/outline
views.

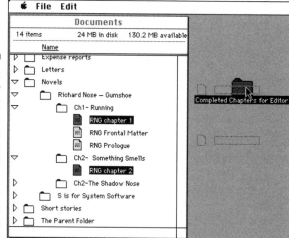

In the list view, you can copy or move items from different folders with a single motion, without opening multiple windows. In either of the icon views, on the other hand, moving files from two separate folders requires opening several windows and two separate drags.

Another feature of the triangles appears when you hold down the Option key and click a triangle. This action reveals *all* subfolders to the deepest level (see Figures 3-27 and 3-28).

Figure 3-27:
A regular click on the Novels triangle reveals only the next level of folders.

Figure 3-28:
An Option-click on the Novels triangle expands all of its subfolders.

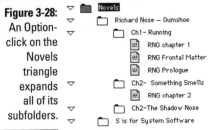

The bottom line is that I have almost all of my windows displayed in the list view by name. If I want to switch to a different list view, I always click the column name and never use the View menu. Finally, I almost always use the triangles to reveal the contents of folders and rarely have more than one or two windows open at a time.

The Views control panel, which I'll talk about in Chapter 13, offers additional controls. You choose options such as the size of the icons and the columns that appear in list views. You can also change the font used in all views. If you feel adventurous, go ahead and play with it a little now.

You can move among icons using the keyboard. If a window is active, make sure that no icons are selected and then type the first letter of a file's name. Regardless of which view you chose, the first icon that starts with that letter will be selected. To move to the next icon alphabetically, press the Tab key. To move to the previous icon alphabetically, press the Shift and Tab keys at the same time.

If no window is active, typing a letter will select the first icon on the Desktop that starts with that letter. The Tab and Shift-Tab commands work the same with Desktop icons as they do with icons in a window.

If you have many icons that start with the same letter, you can type more than one letter (that is, type **sys** to select the System Folder, even if you've got folders called "Stuff" and "Slime" in the same window).

Don't Label Me: Introducing The (Near-Worthless) Label Menu

Maybe it's just me, but I've never really gotten the hang of the Label menu. And I hardly know anyone who uses it diligently, which is the only way it's useful. Anyway, the Label menu, which looks a lot neater in color than it does in Figure 3-29, lets you organize your files yet another way, by label.

Figure 3-29: The Label menu lets you assign labels to icons.

To apply a label to an icon, select it and then choose the appropriate label from the Label menu. Again, labels are more useful on a color screen, as they tint the icon the appropriate color. On black-and-white or gray scale monitors, the only way you know a label has been applied to an icon is by looking in the Label column of a list view (see Figure 3-30).

Figure 3-30: In list views, labels show up in the Label column.

	Name	Size	Kind	Label	Last Modified
Apple Extras	—	folder	Essential	Mon, May 23, 1994, 10:13 PM
Documents	—	folder	Personal	Tue, May 24, 1994, 7:47 AM
Letter to Spindler	3K	SimpleText docum...	Hot	Mon, May 23, 1994, 10:17 PM
SimpleText	78K	application program	Cool	Mon, May 16, 1994, 4:28 PM
System 7.5 Read Me	5K	SimpleText docum...	In Progress	Mon, May 16, 1994, 3:55 PM
System Folder	—	folder	Essential	Sun, May 22, 1994, 12:51 PM

Macintosh HD — 6 items — 24.1 MB in disk — 130 MB available

Because the Find command can search by Label, you have reason to use labels. Still, unless you're very organized and remember to label every file (which, unfortunately, has to be done in the Finder, not when you save from within an application, when it might actually be useful), labels won't be much use.

On the other hand, if you're severely obsessive, compulsive, or retentive, you can have hours of fun assigning labels to your icons. It's your call.

You can change the names and colors of your labels in the aptly named Labels control panel, which is discussed in Chapter 13.

Something Special in the Menu Bar: The Special Menu

The Special menu is a repository for a group of unrelated functions that don't really fit in any of the other menus: cleaning up (rearranging) icons, emptying trash, erasing and ejecting disks, some PowerTalk stuff, and the Restart and Shut Down commands, to be precise. Figure 3-31 shows the Special menu.

Figure 3-31:
The all-
over-the-
board
Special
menu.

Special
Clean Up Desktop
Empty Trash...
Eject Disk   ⌘E
Erase Disk...
I'm at...
Unlock Key Chain...
Restart
Shut Down

Interestingly, only the Eject Disk command has a keyboard shortcut. One explanation might be that you wouldn't want to accidentally erase a disk or restart or shut down your Mac with something as easy to do as pressing the wrong key combination.

Clean Up

The Clean Up command aligns icons to an invisible grid; it is used to keep your windows and Desktop neat and tidy. (If you like this invisible grid, don't forget that you can turn it on or off in the Views control panel.) Clean Up is only available in icon views or when no windows are active. If no windows are active, the command's name changes to Clean Up Desktop.

If you're like me, you have taken great pains to place icons carefully in specific places on your Desktop. Clean Up Desktop will destroy all your beautiful work and move all your perfectly arranged icons around.

Here's how the Clean Up command works. Figure 3-32 shows a window before and after cleanup.

 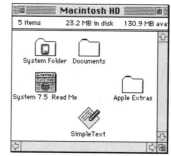

Figure 3-32:
A window before (left) and after (right) cleanup.

You can force the Clean Up command to use one of the list view criteria (name, size, type, and so on) to determine the order of the icons. It's easier to show than to explain, so:

1. Open a window and choose the list view that you want to use as the criteria for cleaning up. In this example, we'll use "by Name."

2. Switch to either icon view — by Icon or by Small Icon.

3. Hold down the Option key and choose Special⇨Clean Up by Name. Figure 3-33 shows what happens.

Figure 3-33:
Cleaning up by Name. Don't forget that Option key!

Notice that the command changes from Clean Up to Clean Up by Name when you hold down the Option key. And notice how the icons are now in alphabetical order in the window.

Had you chosen another list view in Step 1 (by Size, by Date, and so on), the command would change accordingly to Clean Up by Size, Clean Up by Date, or whatever, and the order of the cleaned-up icons would reflect that command.

Empty Trash

I've already talked about the Trash (just last chapter, as a matter of fact). And I talked about it earlier in this chapter when I showed you the Get Info box.

I've said it before and I'll say it again: use this command with a modicum of caution. Once a file is trashed and emptied, it's gone. (OK, maybe Norton Utilities or MacTools can bring it back, but don't bet the farm on it.)

Eject Disk and Erase Disk

See Chapter 2 for more information than you need on ejecting and erasing disks.

I'm at and Unlock Key Chain

Both of these commands deal with PowerTalk, the built-in set of features for collaboration. If you didn't install PowerTalk (or you've turned it off), you won't even see these commands in the Special menu. Because there's information on PowerTalk and collaborative computing coming up later, I'll skip this pair of optional commands for now.

Feel free to look at them if you like, but don't change anything or you may have to go read Chapter 16 right this second. And I've still got things to talk about, such as . . .

Restart

The Restart command shuts down your Mac briefly and then starts it back up. Why do you need such a thing? Every so often, your Mac will act wonky. By wonky I mean things don't seem to work right. You can't launch a program that used to launch fine. You can't rename an icon. You can't use the keyboard. Or something. That's when to use Restart.

You see, computer problems often disappear when you clear the computer's memory, which is one of the things that occurs when you restart.

One of the best pieces of advice I give people when they call me in a panic is to restart their Mac and try it again. At least half the time the problem goes away and never comes back after restarting. I'm a little paranoid about things going wrong, so I often restart my computer in the middle of the day, just in case something is *about* to go wrong. It couldn't hurt.

Sometimes when your Mac gets really wonky, you'll be unable to choose Special⇨Restart for one reason or another. If you can't, because the cursor won't move, or for any other reason, try pressing the Command and Option keys while you press the Escape (Esc) key. If things aren't too messed up, you should see a dialog box asking if you're sure you want to force the current application to quit. You do. Your Mac is so wonked that you had to resort to the Command-Option-Escape technique, so click the Force Quit button. If it works, the current application (or the Finder) will quit. If you're in the Finder, it will restart automatically. You'll lose any unsaved changes in the application that you quit, but you may regain the use of your Mac. If you do, immediately save any documents you have open in other applications and restart. *The Force Quit command leaves your Mac in an unstable state, and you should always restart as soon as possible after using it.* After, of course, saving any unsaved documents.

If that trick doesn't work, try pressing both the Command and Control keys while you press the Power On key (the one with the little left-pointing triangle on it). This technique will force your Mac to restart. Unfortunately, it doesn't work all the time or on all Macintosh models.

If Command-Control-Power On doesn't work for you, look for the reset and interrupt switches on the front or side of your Mac and press the reset switch, which is the one with a triangle. This technique will also force your Mac to restart. Unfortunately, not all Macs have these switches.

If you're still having problems and still can't choose Special⇨Restart, turn the power off using the power switch and leave it off for at least 10 seconds before you try to start up again.

Shut Down

Shutting down is the last thing you do at the end of every session at your Mac. When you're all done using it, choose Special⇨Shut Down.

Because I ragged on endlessly in the last chapter about how important the Shut Down command is, I'm not going to do it again.

Use it or lose it.

Not Just a Beatle Movie: Help and the Help Menu

One of System 7.5's niftiest new features is Macintosh Guide, the new interactive assistance system that is built in. You'll find it in the Help menu, which doesn't actually say "Help." It's easy to find, though; it's the one with the question mark (see Figure 3-34).

Figure 3-34:
The Help
Menu is the
one with the
question
mark
instead of
a name.

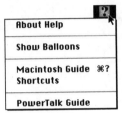

About Help

Show Balloons

Macintosh Guide ⌘?
Shortcuts

PowerTalk Guide

For what it's worth, Balloon Help is still available, but Macintosh Guide goes it one (actually, a few) better.

About Help (no keyboard shortcut)

Choose the About Help command to read about the Help menu. You probably never need to do so because you're reading *Macintosh System 7.5 For Dummies*, and my text is better than theirs.

If you insist, you'll see a single little screen that doesn't say much.

Show Balloons (no keyboard shortcut)

The Show Balloons command turns on Balloon Help. When Balloon Help is on, pointing at almost any item on the screen causes a little help balloon to pop up and explain it (as illustrated in Figure 3-35).

After you choose Show Balloons, the command in the Help menu changes to Hide Balloons until you choose it again, at which time the command changes back to Show Balloons. And so on.

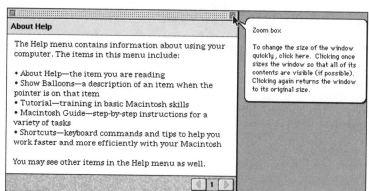

Figure 3-35:
Balloon Help
in action.

I rarely use Balloon Help myself, but if you're relatively new to the Mac, you may find it helpful. Some (but not enough) applications include excellent Balloon Help, so don't forget that you can turn balloons on in programs as well as the Finder.

Macintosh Guide (Command-?)

In the beginning, there wasn't much help built into your Mac. In fact, before System 7.0, there was none. System 7 introduced Balloon Help, and it was good. Well, actually, it was kind of lame, and not that many developers implemented it at first, but it was better than nothing.

Now that most software does include Balloon Help, Apple is raising the bar with Macintosh Guide, a totally new, interactive step-by-step guidance system for accomplishing tasks on your Mac. It's hot. Apple calls it an electronic assistant, and for once I don't think it's oversell. Macintosh Guide is neat.

It's like having a consultant at your side. But there's nothing to open your eyes like a demonstration, so here's how to have your new assistant, Macintosh Guide, answer a question for you. I'll use this demonstration to reinforce the good habit I've taught you about shutting down. Follow along if you like.

1. Choose Macintosh Guide from the Help menu (or use the keyboard shortcut Command-?)

2. When the Macintosh Guide window appears (see Figure 3-36), click the Topics button at the top of the window. Then click "Reviewing the Basics" in the topic list on the left and click "turn off the computer" in the list on the right. Click OK.

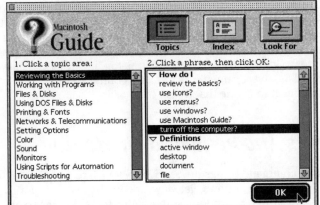

Figure 3-36:
The
Macintosh
Guide —
your new
assistant.

3. Read what the Guide has to say in this first screen and then click the right-arrow button at the bottom right of the windoid to receive further instructions.

4. When windoid 2 appears (look between the arrows to see the windoid number), your assistant will tell you what to do and even draw a circle around where you should do it (see Figure 3-37).

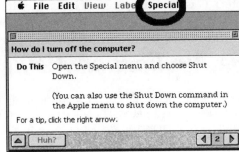

Figure 3-37:
Your
assistant,
telling you
what to do
next.

5. For another tip, click the right arrow again.

Macintosh Guide has circles, arrows, and a whole arsenal of other visual cues to help you figure out how to do things on your Mac. There's even a Huh? button in case you don't understand (unfortunately, it's not active in all screens). Still, Macintosh Guide is an excellent resource, especially for those of you who are new to the Mac. I urge you to explore it further at your leisure.

Incidentally, the Macintosh Guide engine is built into the System software. That means your word processor, spreadsheet, or graphics program can use it as easily as Apple uses it in the Finder. Although it may be a while before third-party developers (that is, the folks who publish application software) implement Macintosh Guide in their programs, look for "Includes Macintosh Guide" on the box and in advertisements as a selling point. I know I'd rather buy a program that has it than one that doesn't.

Shortcuts (no keyboard shortcut)

The Shortcuts command brings up a series of help screens that teach you shortcuts about icons, windows, list views, dialog boxes, and more. It wouldn't be a bad idea for you to take a look at these shortcuts. There are only a few screens for each category, and even though I've already taught you many of the shortcuts, you may learn something that you didn't know.

I doubt it, but you might.

PowerTalk Guide (no keyboard shortcut)

The PowerTalk Guide command brings up a Macintosh Guide window specifically about PowerTalk. If you haven't installed PowerTalk or have it turned off, you won't see this menu item. PowerTalk is discussed in Chapter 16.

Apply Yourself: The Application Menu

Last but not least is the Application menu. It's the one in upper-right corner. Because all of this menu's functions are related, I'm going to skip describing its commands one at a time and try to convey the gestalt of the Application menu instead.

If the Finder is the active application, the Application menu displays a little Mac icon like the one shown in Figure 3-38.

If another application is currently active, a little version of that application's icon represents the Application menu instead (see Figure 3-39).

The Application menu allows you to choose which program you want to use. Like windows, only one application is active at a time. Because System 7.5 allows you to open more than one application at a time (if you have enough RAM), the Application menu is one of the ways to switch between all currently running applications and the Finder (I discuss the other methods near the end of this section.)

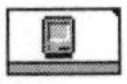

Figure 3-38:
The Application menu in the Finder.

Figure 3-39:
The Application menu uses the icon of the active application, in this case, SimpleText.

If a program is running, its name appears in the Application menu; the Finder's name always appears in it.

For illustration purposes, imagine that two programs, the Finder and SimpleText, are running. If the Finder is currently active and you want to switch to SimpleText, choose its name in the Application menu. SimpleText's menus appear in the menu bar and, if there's a document open (or an untitled new document), its window becomes the active window.

To switch back to the Finder, you choose Finder in the Application menu. Piece of cake, right?

Wrong. When you switch back to the Finder, SimpleText's document window may obscure items on the Desktop. Finder windows aren't a problem — they float to the front. But icons on the Desktop may be covered. Figure 3-40 illustrates what happened.

This is where the Hide and Show commands come into play. You could switch back to SimpleText and quit it, but there's an easier way to free up Desktop real estate. Choose Hide Others from the Application menu, and the SimpleText window (called Brief Bio in Figure 3-40) will be hidden from view (see Figure 3-41). SimpleText is still running, but its window or windows are hidden from view.

To make Brief Bio visible again, choose Show All from the Application menu.

Open any application and play around with the Hide and Show commands on the Application menu. They're easier to understand after you play with them a little.

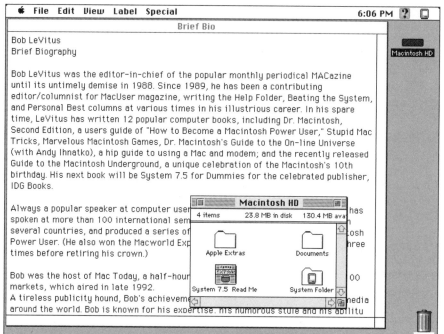

Figure 3-40:
The Finder is active, but some of the icons on my Desktop are hidden by the Brief Bio document in the inactive window.

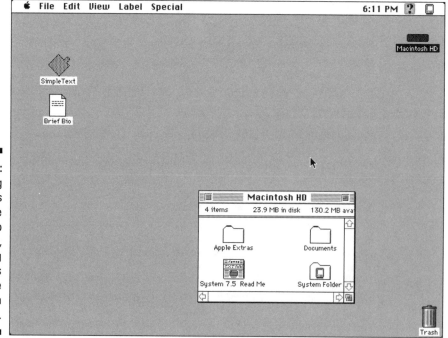

Figure 3-41:
Choosing Hide Others hides the Brief Bio window, revealing some icons that were hidden on the Desktop.

Chapter 4

Polishing the Apple (Menu)

· ·

In This Chapter

▶ About This Macintosh (yours)

▶ Desk accessories

▶ Those interestingly named folders in the Apple menu

▶ Customizing your Apple menu

▶ And a deep, dark secret

· ·

*T*he Apple menu is beneath the little Apple logo, an apple with a bite taken out of it, that graces the upper-left corner of your screen. It gets its own chapter because, unlike the menus I discussed previously, it's entirely configurable by you, the user. This is one of the finest features of the Mac — the ability to create your own customized file-launching and folder-accessing environment.

System 7.5's Apple menu breaks new ground. Most significant is the addition of hierarchical submenus, which power users have loved in the form of Now Software's NowMenus and other, similar programs for years. Finally everyone else can see what the power-user elite have been raving about for so long. Submenus in the Apple menu are fantastic!

The rumor is that Apple had submenus ready to go as far back as System 7.0. But some mucky-muck high up the Apple organization decreed submenus too *complicated* for normal users. So they were put into mothballs. The overwhelming popularity of NowMenus, H.A.M., MenuChoice, and every other utility that provides submenus must have convinced Apple to put it in System 7.5. I'm very glad they did. You'll like them and the price is right.

So I'll teach you the basics of configuring *your* Apple menu in this chapter, but I'm telling you in advance: I'm saving the really cool tricks for Chapter 12.

Before I talk about how to customize your Apple menu, I'll describe the stuff that's already in it: *desk accessories*, the little mini-programs (Jigsaw Puzzle, Calculator, and so on) that Apple thoughtfully stuck in your Apple menu along with several special folders. In all fairness, I'll also show you how to use the essential and useful desk accessories such as the Scrapbook and the Chooser, so don't that think all desk accessories are lame. Only most of them are.

Oh, and one last thing: At the end of this chapter, I'll let you in on a deep, dark secret that you probably figured out already.

About This Macintosh (Yours)

Before we do anything, let me tell you a bit about the Apple menu's only permanent item, About This Macintosh.

The first item on each and every Apple menu (at least if the Finder is the active application) is the About This Macintosh command. Take a peek at it every now and then — it lets you know how much of your memory (RAM) is currently being used, which programs are using it, and how much is left for programs yet to be launched. Those are good things to know. It also tells you what version of the System software is running.

In Figure 4-1 you can see that my System software is using 5,248K of RAM.

Figure 4-1:
About This
Macintosh
is chock full
of useful
information.

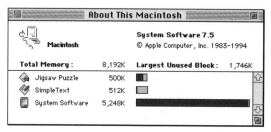

```
▒▒▒▒▒▒▒▒▒▒▒▒▒▒  About This Macintosh  ▒▒▒▒▒▒▒▒▒▒
                          System Software 7.5
       Macintosh         © Apple Computer, Inc. 1983-1994

Total Memory :    8,192K   Largest Unused Block:   1,746K

  Jigsaw Puzzle       500K   ▐█▌
  SimpleText          512K   ▐▒▌
  System Software   5,248K   ▐███████████████▌
```

5,248K of RAM is a lot for System software. But I'm running all the options System 7.5 has to offer — PowerTalk, QuickDraw GX, File Sharing, AppleScript, QuickTime — the whole shebang. In Chapter 15, I'll show you how to turn this stuff off (or get rid of it completely), as well as give you advice on when it's safe for you to do so. For now, let's just say that your System software will probably use somewhat less RAM than mine.

In Figure 4-1, the Jigsaw Puzzle application is using 500K, and SimpleText is using 512K. The bars to the right of the programs' names and numbers are especially meaningful. The light gray part of each bar reflects the amount of memory the program has grabbed (the number just to the left of the bar). The dark gray part shows how much of that memory the program is actually using at the moment. My System software looks like it's using almost all of its allocation; SimpleText looks like it's using almost none. Jigsaw Puzzle seems to be using a little more than half.

What? You aren't willing to accept "a little more than half" as an answer? Sigh. OK. To find out *exactly* how much RAM Jigsaw Puzzle is using, choose Help⇨Show Balloons and then point at the bar for Jigsaw Puzzle. What you ought to see is shown in Figure 4-2.

Figure 4-2:
Jigsaw
Puzzle is
using
exactly 325K
of the 500K
it requested
when I
opened it.

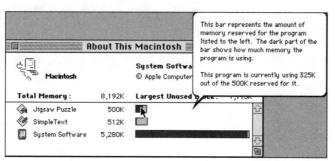

Why is the information in the About This Macintosh window important? I'll tell you why. First, you can see how much RAM is left (the Largest Unused Block) for launching additional programs. If I launched a program that requires 2MB of RAM, the Mac will politely inform me that there's not enough memory to launch this program (I only have 1,746K). So the Largest Unused Block is a good thing to know.

The other thing that's important is that I can see that SimpleText gobbled up 512K when I launched it, but it's only using 58K of its allocation at this time. (I found that out using the Balloon Help trick.) So it's grabbing over 400K of precious RAM and not using it.

What can I do about it? Well, I can tell SimpleText to grab less RAM next time I launch it. Here's how:

Oops. Almost forgot. If SimpleText is open, quit before performing this following procedure. An application cannot be running when you adjust its Preferred Memory Size.

1. Select the SimpleText icon.

2. Choose File⇨Get Info or use the keyboard shortcut Command-I.

   The SimpleText Info window appears (as shown in Figure 4-3).

3. In the lower portion of the SimpleText Info window, change the Preferred size from 512K to a smaller number, somewhere between the Minimum and Suggested size.

4. Close the Get Info window.

The change doesn't take effect until the Get Info window is closed.

Figure 4-3:
Reduce the
Preferred
size from
512K to a
smaller
number.

SimpleText Info

SimpleText

Kind : application program
Size : 78K on disk (77,670 bytes used)

Where : Macintosh HD :

Created : Sat, Apr 30, 1994, 6 :00 PM
Modified : Mon, May 16, 1994, 4 :28 PM
Version : 1.1 © Apple Computer, Inc.
1985–1994

Comments :

┌──── **Memory Requirements** ────
| Suggested size : 512 K
| Minimum size : 192 K
☐ **Locked** | Preferred size : 512 K

When I say "a smaller number," it's not because I don't want to tell you what number to use. But it's not a precise science. I don't know how big the documents you open with SimpleText are, and that's what determines how much RAM it needs. Try 256K. If you someday discover that you can't open a document due to low memory (your Mac will tell you so), increase this number a bit — to 384K or even 450K. It still saves you a little over the old setting of 512K.

Don't perform the preceding procedure haphazardly. Most programs run better with their Preferred memory set *higher* than the Suggested size. But (and it's a big but) if you're short on RAM for other programs and you can see that a program is only using a fraction of the RAM that it requests, you can probably reduce its Preferred size at least a little and maybe a lot.

Easter egg hunt

This sidebar has nothing to do with anything, but bear with me for a moment. You're about to discover your first Mac Easter egg. In the Finder, hold down the Option key and choose Apple Menu⇨About The Finder (that's what you should see instead of About This Macintosh when you hold down the Option key). The result of this action is shown in Figure 4-4.

This little display is a re-creation of the About The Finder dialog box from the original 128K Mac's Finder, version 1.0. Click anywhere on the picture to dismiss it.

Wanna see another Easter egg? Hold down both the Command and the Option keys and choose Apple Menu⇨About the Finder. Hint: Look at the cursor.

I have to say that these Easter eggs were in earlier versions of System 7. Still, it's nice to see that the System software engineers at Apple have a sense of humor.

Are there more Easter eggs in System 7.5? We'll see. . . .

By the way, these Easter eggs appeared in my beta (prerelease) copy of System 7.5. There's a slight possibility that someone at Apple with no sense of humor at all will remove them before the official release. That's the breaks in big-time book publishing. This book has to be at the printer before Apple releases System 7.5 to the adoring public. So I have to write about this beta copy (which is supposed to be "feature frozen" and is working flawlessly so far) and hope that Apple doesn't change anything between now and then. Feature frozen means, at least in theory, that this version works exactly the same as the final version will. I just don't know if Apple considers Easter eggs a feature.

Note to Apple (if you're reading this): LEAVE THE EASTER EGGS IN.

Figure 4-4:
Your first
Easter egg.

From the Desk (Accessories) of...

You use items in the Apple menu the same way that you use any menu item — click on the Apple and drag down to the item. When you release the mouse button, the item opens. If the item is a folder, it will have a submenu; you can see its contents by dragging down until the folder is highlighted and stopping. Don't release the mouse button, or the folder will pop open. To choose an item in the submenu, drag to the right.

If you haven't modified your Apple menu, it probably looks something like Figure 4-5.

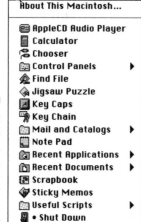

Figure 4-5:
A standard issue, unconfigured, fresh-from-the-installer Apple menu.

Ignoring the folders for now (I'll talk about them after I ridicule a few desk accessories), let's take a look at each desk accessory in turn.

Technically, only a few of the items in the Apple menu are *desk accessories* (known affectionately as DAs), special types of mini-programs that are a little different from regular applications and are a holdover from System 6 and earlier. The rest are regular old applications. Even so, most people refer to the programs Apple sticks under the Apple menu as desk accessories, and so will I. Desk accessories are basically mini-applications, and they're discussed along with control panels and extensions in Chapter 15.

Sounds good to me: AppleCD Audio Player

First on the Apple menu is the CD Audio Player. It's a little program you use to play regular old stereo CDs on your CD-ROM drive (see Figure 4-6). Just pop your *Brutal Youth* CD into the CD-ROM drive, select AppleCD Audio Player from the Apple menu, and then click the Play button. Your room will be filled with the mellow tones of Elvis Costello and the Attractions.

Figure 4-6:
AppleCD
Audio
Player is a
slick remote
control
program for
playing
audio CDs
in your
CD-ROM
drive.

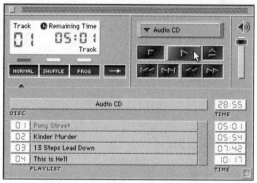

You must plug a pair of amplified stereo speakers into the stereo output jacks on most CD-ROM drives to hear audio CDs. They won't play through your Mac speaker. A good pair of multimedia speakers will shake the walls when you slap an Elvis CD in your drive. And you must have the Audio CD Access extension in the Extension folder within your System Folder for the AppleCD Audio Player to function.

There's a whole chapter (Chapter 15) about every item in your System Folder and whether you need it. It also explains what an extension is, in case you're wondering. In any event, it should be obvious to you even now that this program isn't much use if you don't have a CD-ROM drive.

Listen. I'm a big fan of CD-ROM technology, so instead of getting rid of it, consider AppleCD Audio Player justification to get a CD-ROM drive today. You wouldn't want to waste this perfectly good piece of software, would you?

A calculated risk: Calculator

The Calculator has been in the Apple menu as long as I can remember, and it hasn't changed one iota since it was introduced. (Alright, it got a spiffy new icon when System 7 first arrived, but that's the extent of it.) Figure 4-7 shows what the ol' Calculator looks like.

Figure 4-7:
The ancient-
yet-
venerable
Calculator
DA.

The Calculator DA is the pixel (for PIcture ELement, the little dots that make up your screen) equivalent of the cheesy calculators that cheap companies give away — or the kind you see at the grocery store for $1.99. The Apple Calculator does have one feature that makes it different from all those Taiwan specials — cheap calculators don't require a four-figure investment in computer equipment.

I'm kidding of course. Even though it's looking a little long in the tooth (Hey, Apple ... how about a facelift for the old fellow? Maybe some pastel colors? More graceful-looking buttons? A paper tape? And a Clear Entry button instead of only Clear All?), it still comes in handy more often than you might expect. For example, my wife used it to balance our checkbook for years ('til we discovered Quicken).

If you're lucky enough to own one of the Power Macs, with the blazing fast PowerPC chip inside, then you've probably already run across the awesome new Graphing Calculator that crunches equations into graphs in real time. It's too cool for words (especially if you have a use for its features — if you need to cheat to pass Algebra this semester), but it would run like a snail on Quaaludes on a non-Power Mac. So the rest of us have to make do with the antiquated Calculator DA.

The Calculator DA works just like a real calculator. Use the numeric keypad on your keyboard; the keys correlate to their on-screen counterparts.

Unfortunately, the Calculator lacks all but the most basic features. It doesn't have a paper tape, a Clear Entry key, or even a single memory recall. There are shareware and commercial calculators galore, with features galore. If you need a calculator DA, almost anything you can buy or download will be better than the Calculator DA that comes with System 7.5.

Be choosy: use the Chooser

The Chooser is a desk accessory that lets you choose two things: which printer to use and which computer(s) to share files with.

If you click on a printer icon on the left side of the window, all the printers available on the network appear in a list on the right side of the window (see Figure 4-8).

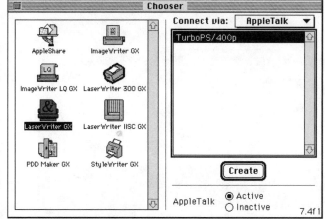

Figure 4-8:
The Chooser lets you choose a printer and/ or choose another computer to share files with.

You don't need to choose a printer every time you print, only the first time. After that, you only have to choose a printer again if you want to print to a different printer. If, like many people, you only have one printer, choose it once and forget about it evermore.

The Chooser is also where you choose other Macs to share files with. If you click on the AppleShare icon on the left side of the Chooser, every Mac on your network that has File Sharing turned on will appear in the list on the right.

There's an entire chapter on printing and yet another one about File Sharing. I think you know enough about the Chooser to hold you till you get to them.

Finder of lost files: Find File (again)

Choosing Find File from the Apple menu is the same as choosing File⇨Find in the Finder (try saying that fast three times). The only advantage this DA has is that, because it is in the Apple menu, you can choose it even if the Finder isn't currently the active application. If you've forgotten how Find File works, reread Chapter 3.

Better than the old puzzle, it's Jigsaw Puzzle

Better than the old 15-numbers-in-16-squares puzzle of System software of old, the Jigsaw Puzzle is only a little less lame. It's a jigsaw puzzle. Click on the pieces to move them around (see Figure 4-9).

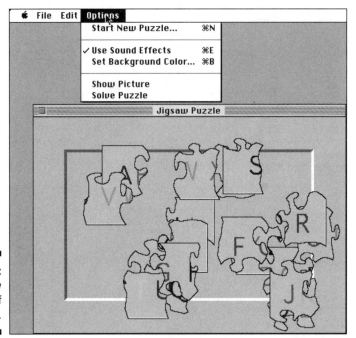

Figure 4-9:
It's a jigsaw
puzzle, of
course.

Figure 4-9 pretty much explains all its features. One cool thing is that you can Paste another picture onto the puzzle and that picture becomes the jigsaw puzzle. It's kind of fun. Here's how to do it with any icon:

1. Select any icon and choose File⇨Get Info or use the keyboard shortcut Command-I.

2. Click on the icon's picture at the top of the Info window to select it.

3. Choose Edit⇨Copy.

4. Open Jigsaw Puzzle and choose Edit⇨Paste.

   In Figure 4-10, I've pasted an application's icon into Jigsaw Puzzle.

Figure 4-10:
Paste a new
picture, get
a new
puzzle.

And there you have it — a new puzzle for you to solve. If you thought that was fun, open the Map control panel and choose Edit⇨Copy. Then open the Jigsaw Puzzle and choose Edit⇨Paste, and voilá, a map jigsaw puzzle for your solving pleasure.

The key to your fonts: Key Caps

Want to know what every character in a font looks like? Or where the funny optional characters like ™, ®, ©, ¢, and • are hidden on your keyboard? Sounds like a job for Key Caps, a modest little desk accessory that shows you a lot about your installed fonts.

If you're not sure what a font is, choose Apple menu⇨Key Caps. After Key Caps opens, pull down the Key Caps menu (see Figure 4-11).

The items in the Key Caps menu are your fonts. If you haven't installed any fonts yourself, your Key Caps menu should look like mine in Figure 4-11.

To see what a font looks like, choose it in the Key Caps menu and type a few words. They appear in the white text entry box at the top of the Key Caps window. If you want to see what those words look like in another font, choose that font from the Key Caps menu.

Of course, you could do the same thing in any program that has a font menu. In fact, you can do more because Key Caps only displays the font in a single size, 12 point; other programs will let you change the size as well as the font, and you can also apply character styles such as bold, italic, and outline.

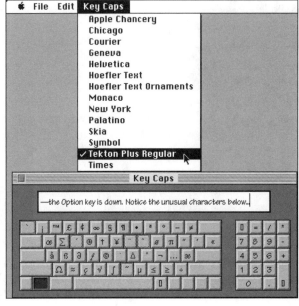

Figure 4-11:
The Key
Caps DA
shows you
all of the
cute
characters
in your
fonts.

So what good is Key Caps? It's the easiest way to find special symbols like ™, ®, ©, ¢, and •, or ß, √, ₤, °, and ¿. Just open Key Caps, choose a font, and hold down the Option key. Key Caps will display the special symbols and characters on the keyboard. For example, to type ™ in your document, hold down the Option key and press the 2 key on your keyboard. Instant ™.

What Key Caps doesn't show you is how to create diacritical marks such as acute accents and umlauts. To type them, follow these instructions:

✔ To type a grave accent (`) , type Option-` and then type the character. So to accent an *e,* you type **Option-`** and then type **e**. It will come out looking like this: è. (The ` key is usually in the top row to the left of the "1" key.)

✔ To type an acute accent (´), type Option-e and then type the character. So to accent an *e,* you type **Option-e** and then type **e**. It will come out looking like this: é.

✔ To type a circumflex (^), type Option-i and then type the character. So to put a circumflex over an *i,* you type **Option-i** and then type **i**. It will come out looking like this: î.

✔ To type a tilde (˜), type Option-n and then type the character. So to put a tilde over an *n,* you type **Option-n** and then type **n**. It will come out looking like this: ñ. I'm pretty sure that the *n* is the only character you can put a tilde over; I tried to put it over other characters, but they came out looking like this: ˜b.

✔ To type an umlaut (¨), type Option-u and then type the character. So to put an umlaut over a *u*, you type **Option-u** and then type **u**. It will come out looking like this: ü, as in Motley Crüe.

I'd like to take a moment to thank Apple for adding a few new fonts to the core collection that comes with every Mac. It's been a long time since they added any fonts to the mix. The new guys are Apple Chancery, Hoefler, Hoefler Ornaments, Skia, and Tekton. They're nice fonts and a welcome change from the old faithfuls like Times, Helvetica, and Courier. I'm particularly pleased about the addition of Tekton, one of my very favorite Mac fonts and one I got from Adobe years ago. (These fonts are installed when you install QuickDraw GX, not when you install System 7.5.)

The key to your PowerTalk chain: Key Chain

Choosing Key Chain from the Apple menu shows the services included in your Key Chain. It's also where you change your Key Chain password. See Chapter 16 for the gory details.

Take note of the Note Pad

Note Pad is a handy, dandy little note-taking utility that lets you store gobs of unrelated text items without saving a zillion different files all over your hard disk. Everything that you type into Note Pad is automatically saved in the Note Pad File, which is in your System Folder. Figure 4-12 shows Note Pad in action.

Figure 4-12: Note Pad is a handy little program for jotting random thoughts and phone numbers.

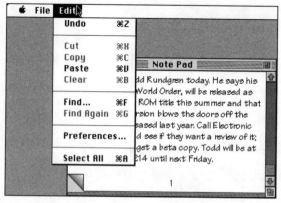

Note Pad uses a page metaphor. Click the dog-ear corner at bottom-left to change the page or choose File⇨Go to Note and type in the page number of the note that you want to go to.

The Note Pad in System 7.5 has several improvements over Note Pads of old. Most welcome is the Find command. And at last, its window is resizable and it has scroll bars. (Can you believe it took Apple this long to add scroll bars and make its window resizable?) Finally, the pages seem to hold a lot more text than older versions. Oh, and you can choose a font in the Preferences dialog box; the old Note Pad gave a choice of Geneva or Geneva.

You can print notes, and Note Pad (like almost every Mac application ever made) includes full support of Cut, Copy, or Paste, so you can easily get text in and out of Note Pad by using the Clipboard.

For a freebie, Note Pad is relatively well-equipped. If you have a lot of random thoughts that you'd like to type, you might want to leave it open all day (it only uses a little RAM).

Not scrappy at all: the Scrapbook

The Scrapbook is like the Note Pad, but you use it to store graphics and sounds. Instead of pages, the Scrapbook uses an item metaphor. You move from item to item by using the scroll bar in the lower part of the Scrapbook window (see Figure 4-13).

Figure 4-13:
The
Scrapbook
is a storage
repository
for graphics,
sounds, and
text.

To put something into the Scrapbook, copy it to the Clipboard; then open the Scrapbook and choose Edit⇨Paste or use the keyboard shortcut Command-V. The pasted item will become the item before the current item. So if you're looking at item 1 when you paste, the pasted item becomes item 1 and the former item 1 becomes item 2, and so on.

Here are the various ways to use the Scrapbook:

✔ To remove an item from the Scrapbook and use it elsewhere, choose Edit⇨Cut or use the keyboard shortcut Command-X. This action will remove the current item from the Scrapbook and place it on the Clipboard for pasting into another document.

✔ To use a Scrapbook item in another document without deleting it, choose Edit⇨Copy or the keyboard shortcut Command-C. Then open a document and choose Edit⇨Paste.

✔ To delete a Scrapbook item forever, choose Edit⇨Clear or use the keyboard shortcut Command-B. Doing so will delete the item from the Scrapbook without placing it on the Clipboard.

You can't always paste a picture or sound into a document. The determining factor is the kind of document that you're trying to paste into. For example, you can't paste a picture into cells in spreadsheets or most fields in databases. And you can't usually paste a sound into a graphics file.

If you try to paste an inappropriate item into a document, your Mac will either beep at you or do nothing. If nothing happens when you paste, assume that the document can't accept the picture or sound you're trying to paste.

You can paste text into the Scrapbook, but it's probably easier to paste it into the Note Pad where you can select only a portion of it or edit it. After text is pasted into the Scrapbook, it can't be selected or edited, so if you want to change it, you'll have to copy and paste the entire chunk of text into an application that supports text editing (such as Note Pad, SimpleText, or a word processor).

If you want to replace the old version of an item in the Scrapbook with a changed version, you'll have to copy the new version to the Clipboard and then paste it into the Scrapbook. Don't forget to delete the old version by scrolling until it appears and choosing Edit⇨Clear (Command-B) to delete it.

Don't get stuck: use Stickies

Stickies, new in System 7.5, are electronic Post-It Notes™ for your Mac. They are akin to the Note Pad; a slightly different but no less convenient place to jot notes or phone numbers. Stickies are shown in Figure 4-14.

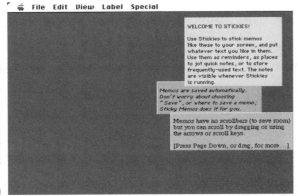

Figure 4-14:
Stickies are the electronic equivalent of Post-It Notes™.

Stickies are nothing if not flexible. They can be moved around on-screen by dragging them by the title bar. They can display text in any font you desire. They can be collapsed by Option-clicking their grow boxes. They can be any color you like (if you have a color monitor, of course). You can import and export text files. And, of course, you can print Stickies.

Like the Note Pad, anything that you type on a Sticky is saved automatically as long as you keep that note open. But when you close a note (by clicking its close box, choosing File⇨Close, or using the keyboard shortcut Command-W), you lose its contents forever. Fortunately, Stickies gives you a warning (shown in Figure 4-15) and a second chance to save the note in a separate file on your hard disk.

Figure 4-15:
Stickies warns you to save before closing and losing your text.

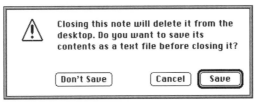

If you like to live dangerously, you can turn the warning off by choosing Edit⇨Preferences and unchecking the Confirm Window-Closing option. In the Preferences dialog box, you can also tell Stickies to save all notes every time you switch to another application (safer), set the zoom box so that it collapses the window without the Option key, and set whether Stickies should launch automatically at startup (if you check this item, Stickies creates an alias of itself and puts it in your Startup Items folder).

Another way to shut down

The Shut Down desk accessory does the same thing as the Shut Down command in the Finder's Special menu. Like the Finder's Shut Down command (in case you've forgotten already), the Shut Down DA performs an orderly shut down of your Macintosh, closing all files and then killing the juice.

The only advantage the DA has over the Shut Down command in the Finder's Special menu is that it can be invoked when you're not in the Finder. So you can Shut Down without first quitting ClarisWorks (or whatever). Your Mac will always give you the opportunity to save any files that need saving when you use either Shut Down command.

Those Interestingly Named Folders in the Apple Menu

There are a handful of folders you will see in your Apple menu spread out amongst the desk accessories. You may see little triangles to the right of their names (if you don't, I'll show you how to turn them on in a minute). The triangles indicate that these folders have hierarchical submenus and will reveal their contents when you pull down the Apple menu and drag the cursor onto them. Submenus are a new feature, introduced with System 7.5, though commercial programs like NowMenus and shareware programs like MenuChoice have provided this functionality since the early days of System 7.0.

To select an item in the submenu, drag to the right and highlight it, as shown in Figure 4-16.

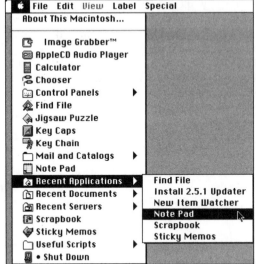

Figure 4-16:
A hier-
archical
submenu.

To choose Note Pad in the Recent Applications folder (see Figure 4-16), click on the Apple, drag down until the Recent Applications folder is highlighted, drag to the right and down until Note Pad is highlighted, and then release the mouse button.

If you don't see little triangles on your folders, here's how to turn them on:

1. Choose Apple menu⇨Control Panels.

2. Open the Apple Menu Options control panel.

3. Click the On radio button, as shown if Figure 4-17.

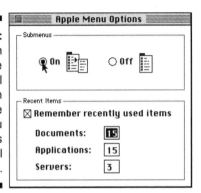

Figure 4-17:
Turning on
the
hierarchical
submenus in
the Apple
Menu
Options
control
panel.

What is a control panel anyway?

Control panels are little programs that you use to adjust and configure your Mac. Each one has one or two specific functions — set the Mac clock (Date & Time), change menu blinking (General Controls), configure memory (Memory), adjust the mouse (Mouse) and keyboard (Keyboard), and so on.

Control panels go in the Control Panels folder inside your System Folder. The Installer automatically creates an alias of the Control Panels folder and puts it in your Apple menu for you when you install System 7.5.

If you get a new control panel (many screen savers and other utilities are control panels), simply drag it onto the System Folder icon and System 7.5 will automatically put it in its proper place, the Control Panels folder. (Incidentally, System 7.5 is smart about extensions, fonts, and sounds as well. If you drag an extension, font, or sound onto the System Folder, System 7.5 will put it in its proper place automatically.)

There's a whole chapter on control panels and how to configure them (Chapter 13), so I'll leave it at that for now.

Now that you know how submenus work, let's talk about the five or six folders you may see in your Apple menu.

The Control Panels folder

As previously noted, the Installer creates an alias of the Control Panels folder and puts it in your Apple menu that so you always have access to your control panels, even when you're using an application other than the Finder. Before System 7.5's submenus, you would have to choose the Control Panels folder from the Apple menu. That action would automatically switch you to the Finder (if you were in another application) and open the Control Panels folder's window. Then you had to open the icon for the control panel manually. Ugh. System 7.5, with its marvelous submenus, is much nicer.

Mail & Catalogs

You may or may not have this folder in your Apple menu, depending on whether you've installed PowerTalk (which is discussed in Chapter 16). If you have, the installer puts this folder in the Apple menu when it installs PowerTalk.

If you see it in your Apple menu even though you don't use PowerTalk, check out Chapter 15 to find out the proper way to get rid of it (it may not be as easy as you think).

If you don't even know what PowerTalk is (hint: the official definition is "support for collaborative computing at the System software level"), don't feel bad. Just read Chapter 16 to get the scoop. If you've got a modem or you're on a network, take a look at PowerTalk. It's still a young technology, and there's not a lot of support for it yet, but it's pretty interesting. If it catches on, it could make collaboration — email, file transfer, document control, and so on — much more convenient.

Recent Applications, Recent Documents, and Recent Servers

I'll discuss these three Apple menu items together because they're related and all work the same way.

If you don't see them in your Apple menu, open the Apple Menu Options control panel (choose Apple menu⇨Control Panels⇨Apple Menu Options) and check the Remember recently used items check box. This action will create the folders in your Apple Menu Items folder as soon as you open an application, document, or server. If you never open a server (access another Macintosh over a network), the Recent Servers folder will never be created.

Even if you do see these items in your Apple menu, you may want to use the Apple Menu Options control panel to change the number of applications, documents, and servers that the folders will remember. I find that fifteen is a good number — enough to ensure that the application or document (I rarely use the server folder) that I am looking for is still there, but not so many that the submenu scrolls off the screen.

These three folders track the last *x-many* applications, documents, and servers that you opened. Each time you open one of these three types of icons, the System makes a mental note of it and then creates an alias of that application, document, or server and pops it into the appropriate folder in your Apple Menu Items folder. The system also limits the number of items in each folder based on the Apple Menu Options control panel's settings. So when you open your 16th application, the oldest application alias in the Recent Applications folder disappears.

Why are these folders useful? Often the document or application that you're looking for is one you had open earlier in the day or yesterday. These special folders in the Apple menu keep recently used items handy. Chances are, if you used it recently, you'll want to use it again soon. If so, look in one of these folders (hint: use the submenu — it's faster).

Automated Tasks

The Automated Tasks folder contains collection of useful AppleScript scripts. AppleScript is the Mac's internal scripting language. Scripts can perform many Macintosh tasks that would take several steps to perform manually, such as turning File Sharing on and off, changing the number of colors that you see on your monitor, and adjusting the speaker's volume. Many people refer to what a script does as a *macro*.

AppleScript is kind of neat and it's included with System 7.5 at absolutely no charge. If you're the kind of person that likes to climb under the hood and get your fingers dirty, there's a whole chapter (Chapter 14) about AppleScript, the scriptable Finder, and tips on creating your own scripts. Don't miss it.

Roll Your Own: Customizing Your Apple Menu

Do you remember Figure 4-1, way back there in the beginning of the chapter? Can you say "Boooorrring." The Apple menu is fully configurable. Whatever is in the Apple Menu Items folder appears in the Apple menu. It's that simple.

So let's start to transform your Apple menu from a dull repository for barely useful software to a turbocharged powerhouse that lets you open any file in seconds. (You'll finish the transformation in Chapter 12.)

So open your Apple Menu Items folder (it's in your System Folder) and get ready to rock.

Before you do anything else, choose View⇨by Name. Now the Apple Menu Items folder's contents reflect the order that they appear in the Apple menu.

Doing the right thing with your desk accessories

As you've seen, most of the desk accessories are pretty lame. You probably won't use most of them very often. We're going to rearrange your Apple menu now so that they don't take up as much space while preserving your ability to open them quickly. Here's how:

1. Open the System Folder by double-clicking its icon (or by single-clicking its icon to select it and then choosing File⇨Open or pressing its keyboard shortcut Command-O).

2. Open the Apple Menu Items folder (it's in the System Folder) and create a new folder inside it. (To create a new folder, choose File⇨New Folder or press Command-N.) Name the new folder Desk Accessories.

3. Choose View⇨by Size, or, if you're already in a list view, simply click on the word Size at the top of the Apple Menu Items folder window to change the view to by Size.

4. Click just to the left of the first icon in the list (Find File in Figure 4-18) and drag to the right and down until everything but folders and aliases of folders are selected (see Figure 4-18).

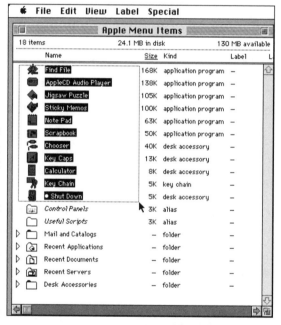

Figure 4-18:
Select everything from Find File to •Shut Down and drag them to the Desk Accessories folder at the bottom.

5. Release the mouse button and then click on any of the highlighted icons and drag it onto the Desk Accessories folder that you created in Step 2. The rest of the highlighted icons should follow the icon that you click and drag; when you release the mouse button, all the desk accessories, applications, and key chains will move into the Desk Accessories folder.

6. Click the word Name in the column header to change to the Name view. This folder's contents are a preview of what your Apple menu will look like.

7. Pull down your Apple menu and revel in your handiwork. It should look like Figure 4-19.

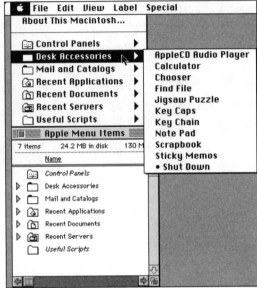

Figure 4-19:
Your Apple menu is now a lean, mean, file-launching machine.

Placing applications in the Apple menu

OK, that last trick was pretty easy, wasn't it? Try one more thing before you move on. Why not add your favorite applications — the programs you use most often — to the Apple menu.

1. Find a favorite application on your hard disk, select it, and make an alias of it (File⇨Make Alias or Command-M).

2. Move the alias to the Apple Menu Items folder.

3. Repeat Steps 1 and 2 for the any additional applications that you wish to appear in your Apple menu.

If you have a lot of programs that you use often, you can create a folder called Favorite Programs in the Apple Menu Items folder and put all the application aliases there instead, which keeps your Apple menu short and sweet (see Figure 4-20).

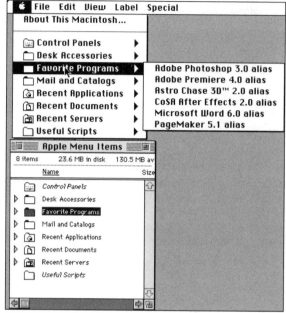

Figure 4-20:
My short
and sweet,
do-it-
yourself file
launcher.

My Deep, Dark Secret

I can't go on with this charade any longer. The figure caption for that last picture did it. "*My* short and sweet . . ."my butt. I confess: the screen pictures you've been looking at aren't my Mac. They're from a Mac I borrowed to create the screen shots for this book. My Mac looks *totally* different.

I'm a power user. I've got my Mac souped up and tricked out to the max. I've got strange icons in the menu bar. My menus are in Geneva 9 font so that they take up less space. I've got Trash alias icons everywhere.

I didn't want to confuse you, so I borrowed a Mac that has nothing on it except System 7.5-related stuff. It makes for much cleaner screen shots and lets me avoid explaining every last difference between your Mac and mine. For the record, my Mac really looks like Figure 4-21.

I'll just point out a few highlights. First, I have two monitors: A 17-inch main monitor and a 12-inch where I keep open windows and palettes. The clock and telephone in the menu bar let me look at my appointments or phone book file without launching my calendar (Now Up-To-Date) or contact database (Now

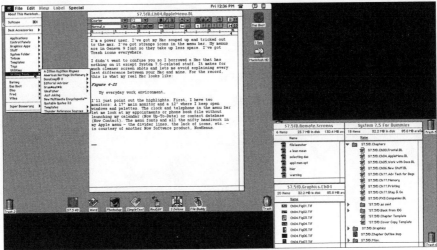

Figure 4-21:
My Mac.

Contact) programs. The small font and all other nifty handiwork in my Apple menu — the divider lines, the lack of icons, and so on — are courtesy of another fine Now Software product, NowMenus.

I have two hard disks — Das Boot and I Spy — totaling almost 2 gigabytes of storage; the Macintosh HD icon is the Mac I'm using for the screen shots, which I access through System 7.5's File Sharing. I have aliases of the Trash in convenient locations screen-wide.

There. I feel better having gotten that off my chest.

Chapter 5

Save Yourself Heartache: Master the Save and Open Dialog Boxes

- -

In This Chapter

▶ Nested folders and paths

▶ Save your document before it's too late

▶ Save versus Save *As?*

▶ The Open dialog box

- -

Mark my words, this is the most important chapter in this book. If you don't understand the Open and Save dialog boxes, the doohickies that appear when you choose File⇨Open or File⇨Save in most programs, you'll never quite master your Macintosh. Yet mastering these essential techniques is perhaps the biggest problem many users have. I get more phone calls that begin, "Well, I saved the file, and now I don't know where it went."

This chapter is the cure. Just pay attention and it'll become crystal clear. And keep saying to yourself, *"The Save and Open dialog boxes are just another view of the Finder."* I'll explain in a moment.

 The Open and Save dialog boxes are virtually unchanged from earlier versions of the operating system, which means that they're just as confusing now as they were before. Too bad. While Apple was souping up System 7.5, it could have made the Open and Save dialogs a little easier to use.

Never mind. They're not that bad. And after you figure out how they work, you'll never forget it. It will soon become second nature to you, and you'll cruise through Open and Save dialog boxes just like the pros, barely thinking about them as your fingers type and click at high speeds.

Nested Folders and Paths (It's Not as Bad as It Sounds)

Before we get started, I need to remind you that you work with Open and Save dialog boxes within applications. I assume that you know how to launch your favorite application and that you know how to create a new document. If you can't do these things, I recommend that you read Poguecello's *Macs For Dummies*. This book has a section on getting the beginning user started with popular Mac programs.

For the rest of this chapter, I'm going to use SimpleText as the sample application. SimpleText comes with System 7.5, so you should have it, too. In fact, you've probably already used SimpleText to read any Read Me files that came with System 7.5.

So if you want to follow along, keystroke by keystroke, launch SimpleText and use File⇨New to create a new document. Type a few words in your document like: "Let us go then, you and I, when the evening is spread out against the sky like a Macintosh sitting on a table." Or something like that (forgive me, T.S. Eliot).

Switch from SimpleText to the Finder (you remember how). You may find the next part easier if you hide SimpleText (you know how to do that, too!) while you work in the Finder. If you've forgotten how to do either, pull down the Application menu, the one at the far right; everything you need is right there.

1. Open your hard disk's icon and create a new folder at root level (that is, in your hard disk's window). Name this folder Folder 1 to reflect the fact that it's one level deep on your hard disk.

2. Open Folder 1 and create a new folder in its window. Name this folder Folder 2 to reflect the fact that it's two levels deep on your hard disk.

3. Open Folder 2 and create a new folder in its window. Name this folder Folder 3 to reflect the fact that it's three levels deep on your hard disk.

You should now have a set of nested folders that looks something like Figure 5-1.

Let me make this perfectly clear: Stuff *inside* Folder 3 is four levels deep. Folder 3 itself is three levels deep. Folder 2 itself is two levels deep, but stuff inside Folder 2, such as Folder 3, is three levels deep. And so on. Got it?

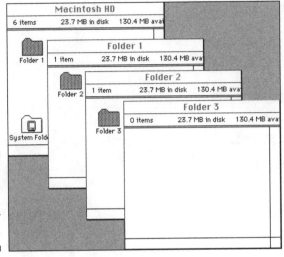

Figure 5-1:
Nested
folders,
going four
levels deep.

What's important here is that you are able to visualize the *path* to Folder 3. To get to Folder 3, you open Macintosh HD, open Folder 1, open Folder 2, and then open Folder 3. Remember this concept. You'll need it in a moment when you look at the Save dialog box.

An easy way to see the path to any open folder is to Command-click on its name in the title bar of its window (hold down the Command key before you press the mouse button). This action displays a drop-down path menu for that folder starting at the Desktop level, as shown in Figure 5-2.

This path menu is live, which means that you can choose another folder from it by sliding the cursor to the folder's name and releasing the mouse button.

Try out this feature with Folder 3. Command-click its title bar, move the cursor down until Folder 1 is highlighted, and then release the mouse button. Folder 1 will pop to the front and become the active window. Try to remember this shortcut, as Command-clicking on title bars can save you lots of time and effort.

OK, our preparatory work in the Finder is through. Use any of the techniques you know to make SimpleText the active application. And don't forget what that path to Folder 3 looked like.

Figure 5-2:
The drop-
down path
menu for
Folder 3
appears
when you
Command-
press on the
window's
name in its
title bar.

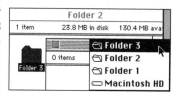

Save Your Document Before It's Too Late

OK, back in SimpleText, it's time to save your masterpiece. Choose File⇨Save (Command-S). This command brings up the Save dialog box (shown in Figure 5-3). Don't panic. These dialog boxes are easy as long as you remember that they're just another view of the folder structure in the Finder.

When the Save dialog box appears, the first thing I want you to do is click the Desktop button to view the icons on your desktop.

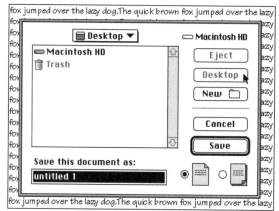

Figure 5-3:
The Save
dialog
box for
SimpleText.

Let's talk about the Save dialog box for a moment. It contains that other view of your hard disk I talked about earlier. You're looking at the icons on your Desktop right now. You know that they're the icons on your Desktop because the active item is the Desktop. Its name appears on the drop-down menu at the top and center.

In programs other than SimpleText, the Save dialog box may look slightly differently because it contains additional options. Don't worry. The Save dialog box always *works* the same no matter what options are offered. Once you can navigate with the SimpleText Save dialog box, you'll be able to navigate with any program's Save dialog box. So don't worry if the one you're used to seeing doesn't look exactly like Figure 5-3; just follow along and learn.

Click Macintosh HD (that is, your hard disk, whatever its name is) in the scrolling list (known as the *file list box*) and then click the Open button or press the Return or Enter key on your keyboard. (In all dialog boxes, the Return or Enter key activates the default button, which is the one with the heavy border around it.)

Open Folder 1 the same way. Open Folder 2 the same way. Open Folder 3 the same way. Your Save dialog box should look like Figure 5-4.

Figure 5-4:
If you Save now, the document will be named Untitled 1 and be saved into Folder 3.

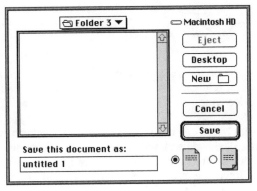

In other words, you navigate through folders in the Save dialog box the same way you navigate through folders in the Finder: by opening them to see their contents.

In the Save dialog box, the name at the top in the drop-down menu is the name of the active item (a folder, disk, or the Desktop). Think of the active item in a Save dialog box as the active window in the Finder. That's where your file will be saved if you click the Save button. That's an important concept. The file will always be saved in the active folder (or disk or the Desktop) — the folder (or disk or the Desktop) whose name appears at the top of the dialog box in the drop-down menu.

To make comprehension easier, think back to when I asked you to remember the path to Folder 3 in the Finder. Now look at the current path to Folder 3 in the Save dialog box by clicking on the drop-down menu. Like the drop-down path menu in the Finder (Command-click the window's name in the title bar), the drop-down menu in the Save dialog box is also live, so if you slide the cursor down to another folder (or Macintosh HD or the Desktop), that item will become the active item (see Figure 5-5).

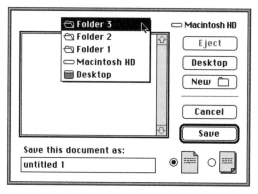

Figure 5-5:
The drop-down menu shows the path to the current folder.

The Save (and Open) dialog boxes treat disk icons and the Desktop the same as folders. Though they're not really folders, you can save items to the Desktop or root level (your hard disk's window).

You always move through hierarchy in the same way. The Desktop is the top level. When you're at the Desktop level, you can see all mounted disks and any folders on the Desktop. If you open a disk icon, you see its folder structure. You always navigate up and down the tree. Your most deeply nested folders are at the very bottom; the Desktop is at the very top.

If you have more than one disk mounted, make sure that the disk name, which appears in the top right next to a little disk icon (hard disks have a hard disk icon; floppies display a floppy disk icon), is correct. If it's not, navigate back up to the Desktop level and choose the correct disk.

Get into the habit of noticing the disk name in the Open and Save dialog box if you often have multiple disks mounted. Nothing is more frustrating than saving a file to the wrong disk and not being able to find it later.

Your file is saved to the active item in drop-down menu when you click the Save button. In other words, when the Desktop is the active item (as it is in Figure 5-3), your document will be saved on the Desktop if you click the Save button. When Macintosh HD is the active item, your document will be saved in the Macintosh HD window if you click the Save button. When Folder 3 is the active item, your document will be saved in Folder 3 if you click the Save button.

1. In the Save dialog box, navigate to Folder 3, that is, make Folder 3 the active item.

2. When Folder 3 appears as the active item, select the words "untitled 1" and type in a more descriptive name. (I called mine "masterpiece.")

3. Click the Save button (or press the Enter or Return key).

That's it. If you switch to the Finder and open up Folder 3 (if it's not already open), you'll see that the file is saved right there in Folder 3.

Congrats. That's all there is to it. You now know how to navigate in a Save dialog box.

Remember the path I asked you to remember, the one you saw when you Command-clicked the title bar of Folder 3's window? Just remember that the path in the Save dialog's drop-down menu (shown in Figure 5-5) is the same.

If that information makes sense to you, you're golden. If you're still a little shaky, go back and try the exercise again and keep trying to understand the relationship between the three folders that you create (one inside the other inside the other) and the drop-down path menus you see when you Command-click Folder 3's title bar or click its name in the drop-down menu in the Save dialog box. Keep reviewing the illustrations. It should just click, and you'll slap yourself in the head and say, "Now I get it."

Don't read on until you get it. This idea of paths and navigating is crucial to your success as a Macintosh user.

There's a little more, but if you get it so far, you're home free.

The rest of what you should know about Save dialog boxes

One thing you need to know is that the file list box and the file name field are mutually exclusive. Only one can be active at a time. You're either navigating the folder hierarchy or you're naming a file. When a Save dialog box first appears, the file name field is active, ready for you to type a name (as shown on the right in Figure 5-6).

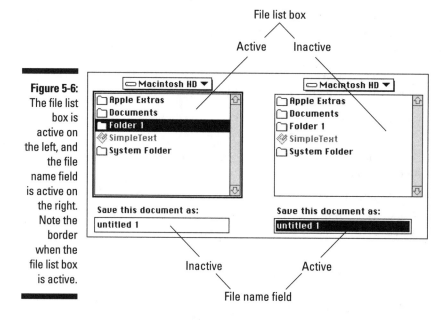

File list box

Active   Inactive

Macintosh HD ▼   Macintosh HD ▼

☐ Apple Extras   ☐ Apple Extras
☐ Documents   ☐ Documents
■ Folder 1   ☐ Folder 1
◈ SimpleText   ◈ SimpleText
☐ System Folder   ☐ System Folder

Save this document as: Save this document as:

untitled 1   untitled 1

Inactive   Active

File name field

When you want to navigate, click anywhere in the file list box. In Figure 5-6, this box is beneath the active item (Macintosh HD), which contains several folders. When you click anywhere in the box, it becomes active and displays a double-lined border around it. If you type something while the file list box is active, the list will scroll and select the folder that most closely matches the letter(s) you typed. Go ahead and give it a try. It's easier to experience than explain.

For what it's worth, you can also type the first letter or two in any Finder window. The icon closest alphabetically to the letter or letters you typed will be selected.

When the file list is active, the letters that you type do not appear in the file name field. If you want to type a file name, you have to activate the file name field again in order to type in it. Here's how:

Regardless of which is active at the time, when you press the Tab key on your keyboard, the other will become active. So if the file name field is active, it will become inactive when you press Tab, and the file list box will become active. Press Tab again and they'll reverse — the file name field will become active again.

If you don't feel like pressing the Tab key, you can achieve the same effect by clicking on either the file list box or the file name field to activate them.

Try it yourself and notice how visual cues let you know which is active. When the file list is active, it displays a double border; when the file name field is active, the file list has no border and the file name field is editable.

The buttons

There are five buttons in SimpleText's Save dialog box: Eject, Desktop, New Folder, Cancel, and Open/Save. The first four are straightforward and almost explain themselves, but the fifth requires a bit of concentration. I'll describe them all (except for the radio buttons, which are application specific).

Ejector Seat

The Eject button is only active when an ejectable disk is selected in the file list box. It's mostly used to save a file to a different floppy than the one currently in the drive. Use the Eject button to eject that floppy so that you can insert another. When you insert the new disk, it becomes the active item automatically. You can tell because its name will appear in two places (see Figure 5-7).

 ✔ At the top-right of the Save (or Open) dialog box above the buttons

 ✔ In the drop-down menu above the file list box

Figure 5-7:
The floppy disk becomes the active item automatically.

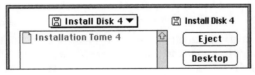

Do it on the Desktop

The Desktop button takes you rocketing up the hierarchy of folders to the very top level, as high as you can go. When you click the Desktop button, the Desktop becomes the active folder (I know that the Desktop isn't really a folder, but play along) in the Save dialog box. From here you can navigate your way down into any subfolder.

If you get lost in a Save (or Open) dialog box, the best thing to do is click the Desktop button and start from the top (the Desktop), which should make it easy to find your way to the folder you desire. Just remember to navigate down through folders in the same order you would in the Finder.

Something new: a New Folder button

This button is a nice touch. If you click the New Folder button, a new folder is created inside the active folder in the Save dialog box. You can then save your document into it. Not every program has this button; in fact, most don't. So don't get too used to it.

What usually happens is that you don't think about needing a new folder until the Save dialog box is on-screen. And in most Save dialog boxes, there's not a thing you can do about it.

What I do in these cases is to Save my file on the Desktop. Later, when I'm back in the Finder, I create a new folder in the proper place on my hard disk and then move the file from the Desktop to its folder.

That's an 86: Cancel

The Cancel button dismisses the Save dialog box without saving anything anywhere. In other words, the Cancel button returns things to the way they were before you brought up the Save dialog box.

The keyboard shortcut for Cancel is Command-period (the Esc key sometimes works too). I said it before and I'll say it again: Command-period is a good command to memorize. It cancels almost all dialog boxes, and it also cancels lots of other things. If something is going on (for example, your spreadsheet is calculating or your database is sorting or your graphics program is rotating) and it's taking too long, try Command-period. It works (usually).

The Open/Save button: the exception to the rule

If you've been paying extra careful attention to the illustrations, you've no doubt noticed that the button near the bottom sometimes says Save and other times says Open. What gives?

In particular, how do you save something when there's no Save button (see Figure 5-8)?

Figure 5-8:
How do you
Save when
this is what
you see?

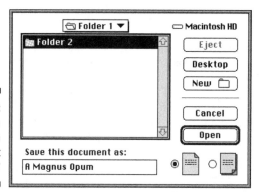

Say I want to save the file A Magnus Opum in Folder 1. I navigate my way to Folder 1. I see it at the top in the drop-down menu. I'm ready to save it but there's no Save button, as is the case in Figure 5-8.

That's because Folder 2 is selected in the file list box and if a folder is selected in the file list box, the button says Open, not Save. To deselect Folder 2, click anywhere in the file list box except on Folder 2 or press the Tab key. When Folder 2 is no longer selected in the file list box, the Open button becomes the Save button, and you can now save (see Figure 5-9).

I know. It doesn't really make sense, but that's how it works. Try it a couple of times. It's not as straightforward as other parts of the Mac interface, but once you get it, you get it for life.

Figure 5-9: The Open button changes to the Save button, which allows me to save A Magnus Opum in Folder 1.

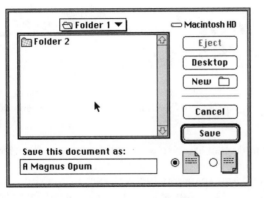

I could have just as easily pressed the Tab key instead of clicking. The net result would be exactly the same — the Open button would change to the Save button.

If this little section confuses you, look again at Figures 5-8 and 5-9. Folder 1 is where I want to save the file. But there's no Save button in Figure 5-8 because a folder, Folder 2, is currently selected. When I click anywhere in the file list box (anywhere except on Folder 2) or press the Tab key on my keyboard, Folder 2 is deselected, the Open button changes into the Save button, and I can save the file named A Magnus Opum in Folder 1.

If you still aren't sure what all this stuff means, try it. It's not particularly intuitive, but it's relatively easy to get the hang of.

1. Select Folder 2 in the file list box of the Save dialog box (Folder 1 is the active folder).

2. Click in the file list box anywhere but on Folder 2. Notice the Open or Save button before and after you click.

3. Press the Tab key. Notice the Open or Save button before and after you Tab.

When the button says Save and you click the button or press Return, the file will be saved in Folder 1. When the button says Open (because Folder 2 is selected) and you click the button or press Return, you move down one level and Folder 2 will become the active folder.

Got it?

It Looks Like Save, It Acts Like Save, So Why Is It Called Save As?

The Save As command, which you'll find in the File menu of almost every program ever made, lets you Save a file that's already been Saved and give it a different name.

Why might you want to do that? Let's say you have two sisters, Jodie and Zelda. You write Jodie a long, chatty letter. You save it as Letter to Jodie. Now you decide you want to send it to Zelda too, but you want to change a few things. So you change the part about your date last night (Zelda isn't as liberated as Jodie) and replace all references to Steve (Jodie's husband) with Zeke (Zelda's husband). Aren't computers grand?

I'll tell you: If you save now, the file named Letter to Jodie will reflect the changes you just made. The stuff in the letter that was meant for Jodie will be blown away and replaced by the stuff you said to Zelda. If you save now, the file name Letter to Jodie will be inaccurate.

That's what Save As is for. If you save as now (it's a different command from Save — look on the File menu and see), you get a Save dialog box where you can type in a *different* file name. You can also navigate to another folder, if you like, and save the newly named version of the file there.

Now you have two files on your hard disk — Letter to Jodie and Letter to Zelda. Both contain the stuff they should.

That's what Save As is for.

Save Early, Save Often = No Heartache

This is as good a time as any to talk about developing good saving habits. Needless to say, it's a very good idea to save your work every few minutes.

After you've saved a file for the first time (and named it something distinctive), you should (re)save it every few minutes while you work on it. You won't see the Save dialog box again; Saving after you've named and saved a file once is transparent.

In most programs, either choose File⇨Save or use the keyboard shortcut Command-S. Think of Save as updating the file on your disk to include everything you've done since your last save.

Here's how it works: Say you've already saved the document Letter to Mom in your Documents folder. Later, you think of some new stuff that you want to add, so you open the Letter to Mom document and begin typing. Ultimately, you add two new paragraphs. If you close the document without saving, your two new paragraphs will disappear into the ether, gone forever. (Don't worry. If you try to close an unsaved document, almost all programs offer you one last chance to save before they let you quit or close the document.) If your Mac crashes or gets unplugged before you save, you'll definitely lose the two paragraphs.

In other words, when you save, changes made since the last time you saved are *written to disk*. Writing the changes to disk makes the changes permanent. Letter to Mom is still in the Documents folder (unless, of course, you've moved it),

but after you save again, it contains the two new paragraphs. (As you'll see in a moment, if you wanted to save it under a different name, such as New Letter to Mom, you would use the Save As command.)

Like backing up your files, saving often is good insurance. Get in the habit of typing Command-S when you pause to take a breath. Or answer the phone. Or grab a glass of lemonade. Or scratch your . . . whatever. Just remember, if the power is interrupted or your Mac has a crash or freeze, you'll lose any work you've done since the last time you saved. If you've never saved the file, you lose everything.

Here's my advice:

- Always save before you switch to another program.

- Always save before you print a document.

- Always save before you stand up.

If you don't heed this advice and your Mac crashes while switching programs, printing, or sitting idle (which, not coincidentally, are the three most likely times for it to crash), you'll lose everything you've done since your last save.

So save early and save often. Command-S is the keyboard shortcut for Save in almost every program I know. Memorize it. See it in your dreams. Train your finger muscles to do it unconsciously. Use it (the keyboard shortcut) or lose it (your unsaved work).

You've made these changes to Letter to Jodie, but you haven't saved again since you decided to make the changes. So now the document on your screen is actually a Letter to Zelda, but its file name is still Letter to Jodie. Think of what would happen if you save now.

It might not be obvious at first, but you can also use Save As to provide a backup when you make massive changes to a document. I use it to hang on to earlier versions of stuff I write. It's kind of like a giant Undo command.

For example, I finished writing this chapter late last night. This morning I had a whopper of an idea about how to make the step-by-step instructions clearer. This is where the giant Undo comes into play — I wanted to retain the option of going back to the way the chapter was if my great idea didn't work out.

So I opened the file (it's called S7.5fD.Ch05.Open & Save if you must know) and used Save As to save a new version for me to experiment with (I called this one Ch.5 Revised).

I then worked on "Ch.5 Revised" for a couple of hours, saving every few minutes like a conscientious Mac user should. In the end, I hated it. So I dragged "Ch.5 Revised" to the Trash and thanked my lucky stars that I had the presence of mind to use Save As before I began revising.

I'm now putting the finishing touches on S7.5fD.Ch05.Open & Save, picking up where I left off last night. Had I not done a Save As before I started this morning, things would have been much harder.

Open (Sesame)

You already know how to use the Open dialog box; you just don't know you know yet.

Using the Open dialog box

Guess what. If you can navigate using a Save dialog box, you can navigate using an Open dialog box. They work exactly the same with a couple of very minor differences.

First, there's no file name field. Of course not. This dialog box is the one you see when you want to open a file! There's no need for the file name field 'cause you're not Saving a file.

There's also no new folder button. You don't need it when you're opening a file. (It sure comes in handy when you're saving a file though, doesn't it? Sure wish every program had one.)

Anyway, that's it. Those are the differences. Navigate the same way you would in a Save dialog box. Don't forget your mantra: "The Open and Save dialog boxes are just another view of the Finder."

The difference between closing a document and quitting a program

I don't know if it belongs here, but like the Open and Save dialog boxes, the difference between closing and quitting is something that often confuses Mac users at first. This info belongs somewhere, so I suppose this place will have to do.

There is a big difference between closing every document window and quitting a program. In an open application, when you close every document, you may see clear through to the Finder, or at least see the desktop pattern (depending on whether the Show Desktop when in background check box in the General Controls control panel is checked), but the program is still running, using valuable RAM. If you make the Finder active and move some files around, pretty soon you forget that you left a program running in the background. There's no physical evidence, such as a document window on-screen, to remind you that it's running. A while later, when you try to open a graphics document, your Mac complains that there's not enough memory to open Photoshop. This message puzzles you, as you used Photoshop just yesterday on this very Mac.

If this kind of thing happens to you, pull down the Application menu (farthest right) and see if you left any programs running with no windows open — or running and hidden.

A program left running with no windows open (or a hidden program) uses just as much RAM as a program in actual use. So get in the habit of quitting programs when you're done with them. Don't close all its windows and leave the program running. Quit when you're done.

You can, of course, ignore this sidebar if you have a zillion megabytes of RAM. It won't matter if you leave a few measly programs running all the time.

I have 32 megs of RAM, so I usually have 6 or 7 programs open, switching between them as needed. Users with 4, 5, or 8 megabytes of RAM — probably the vast majority of you — need to be much more conscientious about using your RAM wisely. You'll run out; I rarely do.

If keeping eight programs — word processor, calendar, address/phone book, graphics program, on-line service program, AppleCD Audio Player, and a couple of others — open at the same time sounds good to you, all you have to do is buy a bunch more RAM.

(Yes, there are alternatives to spending a pile of dough on RAM chips, such as System 7.5's built-in Virtual Memory [not so good] and Connectix RAM Doubler [better], but you'll have to read Chapter 10 to find out about them.)

Figure 5-10 shows two different ways of viewing the same file. The Open dialog box, at top, has navigated to the file Masterpiece in Folder 3. I clicked on the drop-down menu in the Open dialog box to show you the path to the file Masterpiece.

Below the Open dialog box is the Finder view of the path to the file Masterpiece.

If you aren't 100-percent comfortable with the relationship between the two views, please go back and try the hands-on exercises earlier in the chapter again. Please. Keep reviewing the pictures and instructions until you understand this concept. If you don't, your Mac will continue to confound and confuse you. Do yourself a favor — don't read any further until Open and Save dialog boxes feel like the most natural thing in the world to you.

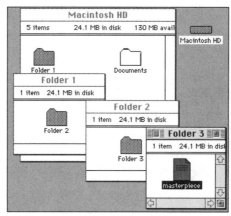

Figure 5-10:
The Open
dialog box,
like the
Save dialog
box, is a
different
view of the
Finder.

A really big show — Show Preview

OK, there's something else about the Open dialog box that's different. As you can see back in Figure 5-10, the Open dialog box for SimpleText has a check box called Preview. What does this little box do? It lets you create little previews for PICT files, which are the type of files created by many popular graphics programs. Click the check box and then click the Create button when a PICT file is highlighted in the file list. After a moment, a little picture will appear (see Figure 5-11). From now on, every time that file is highlighted in an Open dialog box, its preview picture will automatically appear (as long as the Show Preview check box remains checked).

As you might guess, previews are a nice feature to have. Many graphics programs include previews in their Open dialog boxes. At least one, Adobe Photoshop, creates a custom icon for its documents that reflects their contents when it saves them (see Figure 5-12).

Unfortunately, you have to be in the Icon view, which you know I dislike, to see these icons. Still, they're pretty cute.

Figure 5-11:
The Preview
area in this
Open dialog
box shows a
small
picture of
what the
highlighted
file looks
like.

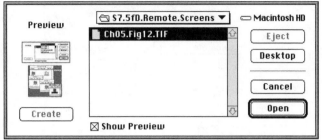

Figure 5-12:
Photoshop
file icon
(shown
double size).

Weird folder names

Every so often you'll see some weird folder names — such as □□□Move &
Rename or Network Trash Folder — in the Open dialog box (see Figure 5-13),
but you don't see these folders when you look at the corresponding windows in
the Finder. Don't worry. It's perfectly natural.

In Figure 5-13 you can see that there are two folders shown in the Open dialog
box that don't appear in the Macintosh HD window in the Finder. The
Macintosh HD window says it contains five items; all five are showing in its
window.

Here's what's going on:

Move & Rename and Network Trash Folder are invisible folders. You aren't
supposed to see them. The System uses them to keep track of stuff that you
don't need (or want) to know about. They're invisible when you look in the
Macintosh HD window but show up in some application's (like SimpleText's)
Open dialog boxes. This anomaly is known as a bug. You shouldn't be able to
see those files. Just ignore them and they won't bother you. If you're lucky, you
won't even see them on your Mac (many people don't).

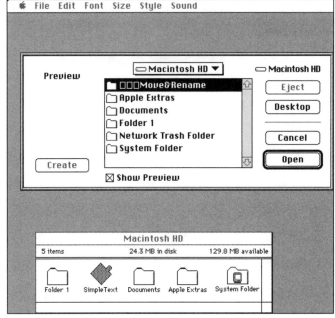

 File   Edit   Font   Size   Style   Sound

Preview   Macintosh HD ▼   Macintosh HD

                    ☐☐☐Move&Rename   Eject
                    Apple Extras
                    Documents   Desktop
                    Folder 1
                    Network Trash Folder   Cancel
                    System Folder
        Create   Open
                    ☒ Show Preview

                        Macintosh HD
        5 items   24.3 MB in disk   129.8 MB available

        Folder 1   SimpleText   Documents   Apple Extras   System Folder

Figure 5-13:
Don't worry
about weird
folders in
the Open
dialog box
that you
don't see in
the Finder.

OK. How many of you have done the math and come up short? There are six folders in the Open dialog box. Two of them are invisible in the Finder. But there are five items in the Macintosh HD window. Add two invisible folders and there should be seven in the Open dialog box, not six. Why don't things add up?

Bzzzzt. Time's up. The items don't add up because you can see the SimpleText application's icon in the Finder but not in the Open dialog box (because SimpleText can't open itself).

Selectively displaying certain items in Open dialog boxes is a feature of most applications. When you use a program's Open dialog box, only files that the program knows how to open appear in the file list. In other words, the program filters out files that it can't open, so you don't see them cluttering up the Open dialog box. Pretty neat, eh?

On the other hand, not seeing every item in an Open dialog box can be a little disconcerting when you're trying to envision the correlation between the Finder and the Open dialog box. Stuff you see in the Finder doesn't always appear in the Open dialog box. That's why I showed you the Save dialog box first. It always includes everything. In a Save dialog box, items that you can't select appear grayed out, but they do appear. Open dialog boxes usually show only files that you can select and open with the current application.

Part II
Making It Purr
(The Lazy Person's
How-To Guide)

The 5th Wave   By Rich Tennant

DARE TO BELIEVE YOUR EYES

HIPPOPOTAMUS MAN

Natures Strangest Joke!

MR. TWEETY
RAISED BY WILD
Parakeets!

DIRECT FROM THE
OUTBACK OF
AUSTRALIA!

GUY WHO BOUGHT
A WINDOWS PC
BECAUSE HE THOUGHT
**IT WORKED
LIKE A MAC!**

SIDE
SHOW
$100

In this part...

1'll start out with a rip-roaring tour of System 7.5's more than 50 improvements and enhancements. Relax, sit back, and enjoy the (conceptual over)view.

Then I'll get back to the how-to. Chapter 7 deals with how to organize your Mac. You'll learn, among other things, how to do routine file-management and navigating tasks the easy way.

Next is the how-to-print chapter, Chapter 8. It includes info on how to decipher Print options and plenty of other how's and why's that will help you become a modern day Guttenberg.

In Chapter 9 you'll learn how to share. Files, that is. It's easy, it's convenient, it's free, and it beats the heck out of sneakernet.

Finally, there's a wonderful chapter (numbered, conveniently enough, 10) on how to manage memory (and other seemingly complicated arcana), an easy-to-understand, almost jargon-free primer on how the whole memory thing works.

Chapter 6

The New Features: 50 Ways to Love Your System

*T*ake a deep breath. Relax a little. This is a different kind of chapter — a kinder, gentler kind of chapter. There will be no step-by-step instruction; in fact, the Hands On icon only appears once in this chapter.

   1. Take your hands off the keyboard and relax.

Actually, it appears one more time. There's one Hands On in the middle of the chapter, but it's something so cool that I don't think you'll mind.

The rest of the chapter deals with ideas, not instructions. Telling, not doing. So relax. It'll be a pleasant respite for you after five chapters of me telling you "do this" and "do that."

According to Apple propaganda, System 7.5 has "more than 50 new enhancements that offer significant immediate out-of-box value." This chapter is an overview of all of 50, give or take a few.

I'll explain almost everything in this chapter somewhere else in the book, more often than not in sickening detail. This chapter is about the big picture, not the details. It's about how these technologies can enable you, not how their control panels work. This is a chapter about the gestalt of System 7.5, not how to use it. (How to use System 7.5 is what the rest of this book is about, in case you hadn't noticed.)

Apple goes on to boast that System 7.5's "enabling technologies are rapidly being adopted by third-party developers to take users into the computing future." This assertion is not so clear. I hope they're right.

You'll find out what I mean and what enabling technologies are in a moment. For now, indulge me as I plow my way through the rest of the introduction.

System 7.5's enhancements fall into seven major categories: Active Assistance, Automation, Productivity and Customization, Compatibility, Advanced Graphics and Printing, Collaborative Technologies, and Mobile Computing. We'll look at each in turn.

But first:

An Overview with a Point of View

System 7.5 provides greater efficiency and productivity than any version before it. Here's what's new and exciting at a glance:

- Step-by-step guidance for learning new tasks
- A higher degree of user-configurability than ever before
- Scripting and automation tools
- Collaboration tools for working with others
- Better, easier printing
- Compatibility with DOS and Windows data files
- Support for TCP/IP (that is, Internet) network connections
- PowerBook enhancements and utilities

Although the enhancements above fall into the aforementioned seven major categories, you can break them down another way as well: programs vs. enabling technologies.

Programs vs. enabling technologies (read at your own risk)

This information is a little hard to explain, so bear with me. Some of the new features of System 7.5 are called "enabling technologies." Enabling technologies are invisible; they run in the background. They don't do anything themselves; rather, they enable other programs to do things.

Most programs don't require an enabling technology, but as time goes on and more people have these enabling technologies installed on their Macintoshes, you'll see exciting new programs that require QuickDraw GX or PowerTalk or your-favorite-enabling-technology's-name-here in order to function.

Now is as good a time as any to talk about System 7.5 extensible architecture and the concept of *extensions* because most enabling technologies from Apple are supplied as Extensions. An Extension (sometimes called System Extension or init) is a special kind of file that (almost always) lives in your Mac's Extensions folder. (A few enabling technologies, most notably the original version of QuickDraw, are built right into the System file or the Macintosh ROM.)

Extensions load automatically from your hard disk into RAM during startup. If you ever used a PC, extensions are like TSRs.

To confuse the issue, many control panel files contain extension code and load into RAM at startup (other control panels act like regular programs and don't load anything into RAM until you open them).

To make this situation even more confusing, not every file in your Extensions folder loads into RAM at startup either; some files, such as printer drivers, don't load into RAM at all. These files just wait in the Extensions folder until your Mac needs them.

Finally, extensions are optional. You can remove ones you don't need.

Extensions and control panels and how to manage them are topics covered in sickening detail not once, but twice: in Chapter 13, which covers all your control panels and gives recommendations for how to configure them, as well as Chapter 15, which tells you the RAM usage, disk space requirements, and net worth to you of every single System 7.5 component. This chapter also explains how to safely get rid of the components that you don't need.

QuickTime is probably the best known example of an enabling technology. QuickTime doesn't do anything at all — it just sits there. But if you're using a QuickTime-dependent application, it will only play movies if QuickTime is loaded. If QuickTime isn't loaded, Premiere (or Movie Player or MYST or whatever) won't play movies. It's that simple.

System 7.5's major enabling technologies (I'll discuss them all in this chapter and elsewhere) are QuickDraw GX, PowerTalk, AppleScript, AppleShare, and QuickTime.

If the concepts are still a little fuzzy for you, here's another way to think of them: enabling technologies are like electricity. By themselves they are invisible and not much use. But connect an appliance like a television or a lamp to a wall socket, and the appliance becomes *enabled*. Programs are like appliances. Some require electricity (that is, an enabling technology) and others don't.

System 7.5's enabling technologies are in their infancy. When electricity was first invented, there weren't many electrical appliances available. As more people got electricity in their homes, the number of electronic appliances grew. Enabling technologies are like that. As more people run these technologies on their Macintoshes, third-party developers will create more programs that take advantage of them.

(continued)

(continued)

(Where does the term "third-party" as in "third-party developer" come from? According to a lawyer friend, Apple is the party of the first part, the developer is the party of the second part, and the consumer is the party of the third part. So third-party developers create products for the party of the third part, which is us.)

Anyway, to summarize: If the enabling technology isn't running, then programs that are *enabling-technology-dependent,* such as Adobe Premiere (requires QuickTime) or QuickMail for AOCE (requires PowerTalk), won't work.

With that stuff safely behind us, let's take a closer look at what's new in System 7.5.

Getting Some Help

There's no right place to start with this discussion of new features, so I'll just jump right in with the ones I personally find most appealing, System 7.5's active assistance, automation, and customization features.

Macintosh Guide: the best of help

You got a brief look at active assistance when you played with Macintosh Guide, System 7.5's new interactive help system, in Chapter 3. There's not much more to say. It's very good. From now on, when you find yourself stymied, choose Macintosh Guide (Command-?) from the Help menu and dig in. More than likely, Macintosh Guide can show you the way.

Macintosh Guide breaks new ground with *coachmarks* — visual cues such as circles, arrows, and highlighted menu items — that guide you through procedures (see Figure 6-1). This wonderful interactivity is unique to the Macintosh. PC owners should be so lucky.

Macintosh Guide is smart, too. It's context-sensitive, which means that it can check to see if you've completed a step and automatically move on to the next instruction if you have.

Macintosh Guide is both an enabling technology and a program. As a program, it's available from the Help menu. As an enabling technology, it's running in the background, so third-party developers can add active assistance to their programs.

Figure 6-1:
Coachmarks include circles around menu names and highlighted menu items.

Macintosh Guide: the last word

Apple refers to Macintosh Guide as an electronic assistant that guides you through specific procedures one step at a time. They haven't over-promised. Macintosh Guide in the Finder is the best help system I've ever seen on a personal computer.

Macintosh Guide as an enabling technology is even better, providing an architecture for third-party programs to offer active assistance, complete with context sensitivity and coachmarks.

Unlike Balloon Help, which was always (and still is) a bit awkward and never really caught on, Macintosh Guide is hot stuff and should be in widespread use by third parties real soon now. I hate manuals, so I can't wait.

I hate manuals. You probably do too. Still, I recommend that you read them carefully. I do. Mac software seems easy, but you'll find that many programs have hidden features that you'll never discover if you don't read the manual.

Maybe someday, when Macintosh Guide is in every program you buy, you won't need a manual. Until then, I strongly recommend that you read the manual for every piece of software you ever buy — cover to cover, no matter how boring.

My wife hates it, but I often read software manuals in bed before going to sleep. Every so often I learn something so nifty, so interesting, that I leap out of bed and run into my office to try it immediately. So read the manual. You might learn something too.

Do It Automatically

System 7.5 includes AppleScript scripting technology and, for the first time, a fully scriptable Finder. These two features enable you to automate many routine and/or complex tasks. Some people call these automated routines "macros," but because the enabling technology is AppleScript, I'm going to refer to them by their proper name, scripts.

Anyway, AppleScript is relatively easy to use, as you'll discover in Chapter 14. Writing scripts can save you significant time and energy. It's not that hard. Read Chapter 14 carefully and you'll have a good start.

Power users have long bemoaned the fact that automation required third-party programs like QuicKeys (CE Software's excellent Mac automation program). Not any more. Although QuicKeys still offers many features not found in AppleScript, Mac users can finally create simple macros without buying additional software, and that is very good news indeed.

Write that zillion-dollar script with AppleScript and the new scriptable Finder

Whether you create your own scripts, use AppleScript's convenient "Watch Me" mode, or rely on scripts created by others (System 7.5 includes more than a dozen), AppleScript is an enabling technology that allows you to easily automate any series of actions. A script can do any of the following:

- Reformat a document
- Make backups from one disk or folder to another
- Schedule file copies
- Create intelligent drop folders
- Perform multipart tasks involving menus, folders, files, and/or dialog boxes (see Figure 6-2)
- And lots more

AppleScript has been around for a while. You could buy AppleScript as a stand-alone product or receive it as part of the late (and ill-fated) System 7 Pro. But it never really caught on. Though it was interesting and somewhat useful in earlier incarnations, it still cost extra, it wasn't as good as QuicKeys, and earlier Finders weren't scriptable. Most users felt that if they were going to spend money, they'd be better served by buying a copy of QuicKeys, which is fairly easy to use and contains many features not yet found in AppleScript.

Figure 6-2:
A simple script to set your Mac's speaker volume to zero, created with System 7.5's Script Editor application.

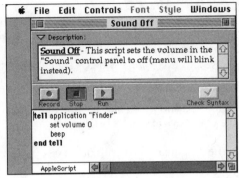

AppleScript for free, on the other hand, will get lots of people to try it. And while some will opt for the increased functionality of QuicKeys (which works very well in conjunction with AppleScript; you don't have to choose one or the other). AppleScript alone will be enough for many.

System 7 Pro?

What was System 7 Pro? An ill-fated attempt by Apple to sell enabling technologies like AppleScript, QuickTime, and PowerTalk for a few extra bucks as a high-performance upgrade to System 7. System 7 upgrades sold for $35; System 7 Pro sold for $149. Does more than a hundred bucks for AppleScript and PowerTalk (you probably had QuickTime already) sound like a good deal to you?

Apparently it didn't to most people. System 7 Pro was a resounding flop. And it slowed down development of neat enabling technology-dependent applications because of the chicken and egg syndrome: Users were hesitant to pay extra for enabling technologies that didn't have much third-party support; developers were hesitant to create programs that took advantage of the enabling technologies because the installed base (computerese for number of owners) was too small.

System 7.5 may change things. Now that all these cool technologies are free (with System purchase, of course), developers should start developing products that take advantage of them. System 7.5 should give them confidence that there will be an installed base of Macintoshes running QuickDraw GX, AppleScript, PowerTalk, QuickTime, Drag and Drop, and all the other new enabling technologies. So there's good news and bad news. The good news is that the chicken and egg cycle is broken, and we should soon see exciting new products and upgrades to existing products that take advantage of one or more of these exciting new technologies. The bad news is that there are very few of these products available today.

AppleScript: the last word

I'm on the record as saying that QuicKeys may be the best piece of Macintosh software ever made. AppleScript provides many of QuicKeys' features for free. And I'm tickled pink that all System 7.5 owners will at least get the chance to try scripting and automating their work.

I give AppleScript a big thumbs up. And if you like scripting and macros as much as I do, be sure to give QuicKeys at least a brief look.

So does AppleScript free in the box mean the death of QuicKeys? I think not.

Years ago, when System 6.0 first came out, Apple included a macro-making utility called MacroMaker. For free. Many, including some at CE Software, braced for QuicKeys' impending demise.

But here's what actually happened: QuicKeys' sales skyrocketed. Why? MacroMaker gave users a taste of the amazing and wonderful things macros could do. But it wasn't very good, and not nearly as good as QuicKeys. Not even close. Even before Apple discontinued MacroMaker (they never quite got it right), people were switching to QuicKeys in droves.

What's the moral of this story? Will AppleScript finally mean the death of QuicKeys? After all, I said how good AppleScript is, and it is free.

I suspect that QuicKeys' sales will skyrocket again. It still does dozens of things you can't do with AppleScript, and it's easier to use than AppleScript for many tasks. And QuicKeys can send and receive AppleEvents, so you can use QuicKeys and AppleScript together. In fact, the combination of the two provides the best possible environment for Macintosh automation.

In other words, if you like AppleScript, consider QuicKeys a high-performance AppleScript upgrade. And if you like the idea of AppleScript but are still a little intimidated about writing scripts (it is a little like programming, after all), consider QuicKeys an easy and powerful alternative to AppleScript.

And no, I am not a CE Software shareholder. I just think QuicKeys is one of the best things ever invented, and I couldn't use my Mac without it.

Ye Shall Be Productive and Customize

Productivity and customization are probably the areas where System 7.5 makes the biggest, most visible strides with many new features both great and small. While many of the new productivity and customization features have been available from third-party developers for years, it's nice to see Apple throwing in useful goodies, like submenus in the Apple menu, for free.

I may have forgotten one or two productivity features in my excitement, but this section contains the highlights.

What a drag it is getting dropped

Macintosh Drag and Drop is a new enabling technology that simplifies the copy and paste metaphor by allowing you to select and drag items — text or graphics — directly from one application to another. The bugaboo here is that the program must support Macintosh Drag and Drop, and at this time, very few do.

Here's how it works, at least in theory. I'll demonstrate using the Scrapbook and the Note Pad, two System 7.5 desk accessories that *do* support Macintosh Drag and Drop.

1. Open the Scrapbook and Note Pad desk accessories.

2. Type some text into Note Pad and select it.

3. Click and hold down the mouse button in the middle of the selected area and drag to the center of the Scrapbook window (see Figure 6-3). The Scrapbook should display a thin, gray border around it to indicate that it is ready to receive the item, as shown in Figure 6-4.

4. Release the mouse button.

The text moves automatically from the Note Pad to the Scrapbook. Neat!

Figure 6-3:
Drag and
Drop in
action.
When I
release the
mouse
button, the
selected
text will be
copied from
the Note
Pad to the
Scrapbook.

Figure 6-4:
The visual
cue that the
Scrapbook
is ready to
receive a
dropped
item is a
thin, gray
border (top).
The
Scrapbook's
normal
border is
shown
below for
comparison.

Macintosh Drag and Drop introduces a new file type, called a *Clippings file*. To create a Clippings file, you select an item (graphic or text) in any application that supports Macintosh Drag and Drop and drag it onto the gray Desktop, onto a folder icon, or into an open window. Release the mouse button and the item automatically becomes a Clippings file that you can drag onto other files later (see Figure 6-5).

Figure 6-5:
Drag and
drop on the
gray
Desktop (or
onto any
folder icon
or open
window) to
create a
Clippings file
for later use.

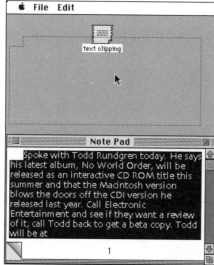

After creating Clippings files, you can view their contents by opening them, as shown in Figure 6-6. A Clipping window appears, showing you the contents of the clipping.

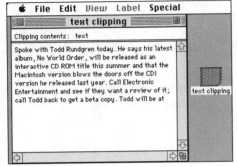

Figure 6-6:
View the contents of Clippings files by opening them.

Apple Menu options

New Apple menu options, managed by the new Apple Menu Options control panel, provide faster and easier access to items that reside in folders under the Apple menu. In addition to the wonderful submenus, a set of "recent items" folders automatically tracks documents, applications, and servers used recently (see Chapter 4 for more details).

Finder hiding

This feature allows the Finder to be inactive when another application is active; if you click outside the application's document window, the application will still remain selected, thus preventing you from getting lost by switching to the Finder or another application accidentally. Great for beginners; not-so-great if you like to switch between programs by clicking.

You can turn Finder Hiding on and off in the General Controls control panel.

Default Document folder

Your Mac automatically saves files to a folder named Documents on Desktop rather than wherever the Save dialog box happened to be pointing, making it easier for beginners to keep track of documents. Once you understand the

Open and Save dialog boxes (let me hear you chant your mantra: "They're just another view of the Finder."), you'll create a folder structure that makes sense to you, and you won't need the Documents folder.

When you tire of it, turn it off in the General Controls panel.

System and Application folder locking

This feature prevents accidental deletion of important files. After you get the hang of using your Mac, you won't want it. When either folder is locked, you can't Trash anything inside it, even by holding down the Option key (which is how you Trash any other locked file).

Turn this feature off in the General Controls panel unless you have kids who use your Mac and think it's neat to indiscriminately drag files to the Trash just to watch it bulge.

WindowShade

WindowShade lets you roll up windows like a window shade (see Chapter 2 for all the details). It's not the same as closing windows; it's better. WindowShade was great as a freeware program (I've used it for years), and it's great as part of System 7.5.

Use the WindowShade control panel to configure this feature or turn it off.

Stickies

Stickies are on-screen Post-it-style notes, described in detail in Chapter 4.

Use the Stickies desk accessory to manage them.

Extensions Manager

Finally, Apple has included a control panel that allows you to turn extensions and control panels on and off selectively. Not that everyone who has more than a handful of third-party extensions or control panels hasn't bought or downloaded a commercial or shareware extension manager already, but it's nice that Apple finally sees the need and is throwing in a pretty decent one.

I still prefer Casady & Greene's commercial extension manager, Conflict Catcher, but I'm an extension maniac. At last count, I was loading more than 50 commercial, freeware, and shareware extensions and control panels, not including the ones from Apple. Conflict Catcher has loads of additional features not found in Extensions Manager. The one that does it for me is Conflict Catcher's ability to isolate conflicting extensions and control panels automatically. See Chapter 18 if you want to learn more about extension conflicts.

And more...

There are even more productivity enhancements worth mentioning that I don't have room to say much about. These include

- ✔ Overall speed boost throughout System 7.5
- ✔ Support for very large (up to 4 gigabytes) hard drives
- ✔ A Universal Enabler instead of 20 *different* enablers — one for every Mac, it seems
- ✔ The Launcher program that's been bundled with Performas for years
- ✔ A menu bar clock (based on the popular freeware clock, SuperClock)
- ✔ Better visual cues in the Finder (gray borders around windows when they're about to receive an item)
- ✔ Automatic power off (on Energy Star compliant Macs only)

Productivity enhancements: the last word

Mac Drag 'n Drop is way cool. I love it. Now if only my favorite applications would support it. (C'mon, Microsoft, Aldus, Adobe, Common Knowledge — go for it. Add Drag and Drop support in your next revision!)

And all the other features are welcome additions to the system as well. For many users, these features will become their favorite things, and with good reason. Many of them have been available as commercial products or shareware for years. People love them. So way to go, Apple. Free is good. My only question is this: Why did you wait so long?

And if you love the new stuff, be sure to read Chapter 17 where you'll see stuff that's even better and more powerful.

You, Me, MacTCP, PC, and DOS Compatibility

This set of features provides an unheard of degree of compatibility with MS-DOS, Windows, and the Internet. For Mac users, it's a breath of fresh air. All of these solutions have been available for years at additional cost. Apple made a wise decision to include them so that everyone and anyone who needs them will have them at their fingertips.

Macintosh PC Exchange/ Macintosh Easy Open

Macintosh PC Exchange and Macintosh Easy Open are a set of utilities that lets you open, edit, and save MS-DOS, Windows, and OS/2 data files (that is, documents) with compatible Macintosh applications.

Macintosh PC Exchange allows the user to insert a DOS-formatted disk into an Apple SuperDrive and view the disk's contents from the Finder — just as if the floppy came from another Macintosh system (see Chapter 2 for an explanation).

When you double-click on a DOS or Windows file to open it, Macintosh Easy Open automatically searches for applications and file translators that are capable of opening it and lists the applications for the user. When you select an application, Macintosh Easy Open manages the translation and opening of the file and then remembers that relationship evermore.

You configure Macintosh Easy Open with the Macintosh Easy Open control panel and Macintosh PC Exchange with the PC Exchange control panel.

Macintosh PC Exchange/Macintosh Easy Open: the last word

Yawn. I hate DOS and Windows, so I don't really care that much. Still, it's a vast improvement over the dreary old Apple File Exchange, the previous Apple no-cost solution for dealing with DOS files.

But much as I hate DOS, I do occasionally have to deal with a DOS-formatted disk and its files. And even I have to admit, the new way is much better. This new functionality — the ability to mount DOS disks on the Desktop and open DOS documents transparently — used to be a separate product Apple sold for around $100, so I suppose it gets a thumbs up just for being included at no extra charge.

It doesn't make DOS any more likable, but hey, it's free.

MacTCP

With System 7.5, Apple includes support for TCP/IP (Transmission Control Protocol/Internet Protocol), the communications protocol used in UNIX networking, college and university networks, as well as in most research communities; it is also the standard protocol for the so-called information superhighway, the Internet communications network.

TCP/IP networking protocols allow different kinds of computers to communicate or connect with each other over a network. MacTCP lets Macintosh users access information on Cray supercomputers, UNIX and Sun workstations, VAX systems, and a variety of hosts. MacTCP also makes it much easier to connect to the Internet.

You configure MacTCP with the MacTCP control panel.

The MacTCP control panel isn't installed automatically when you perform an Easy Install of System 7.5. You must perform a separate custom installation to install MacTCP. (See Chapter 16.)

MacTCP: the last word

What can I say? Another enabling technology at no extra charge. I paid for my copy, but Apple is once again doing the right thing the right way (I wonder if Guy Kawasaki was a consultant to System 7.5?) and throwing it in at no additional cost. If you need it, you'll be thankful; if you don't, no big deal. MacTCP is another win-win addition to your System Folder.

On the Road Again: Mobile Computing Improves

System 7.5 makes PowerBook computing easier in several ways. Although the new features have a great deal of overlap with utilities that many users have already sprung for, such as C.P.U. or PB Tools, it's refreshing to see Apple building in at least this base level of convenience for all PowerBook owners.

Incidentally, if you bought a PowerBook recently, even before System 7.5 came out, it may have included some or all of these PowerBook utilities.

PowerBook utilities and enhancements

System 7.5 includes utilities that manage your portable, extend battery life, and synchronize files between laptop and desktop computers.

Battery management features include automatic backlight dimming and a permanent RAM disk feature that saves information between restarts and shutdowns.

The PowerBook control panel consolidates power-management features (see Figure 6-7).

Apple also threw in a new Control Strip (shown in Figure 6-8), which you can move anywhere on the screen.

Figure 6-7:
The
PowerBook
control
panel
manages
PowerBook
power
consumption.

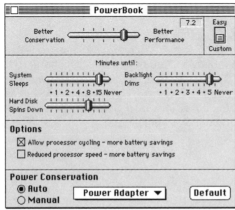

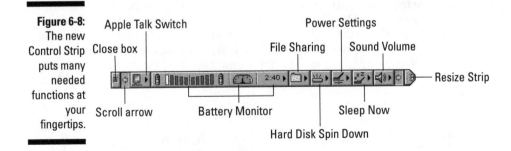

Figure 6-8: The new Control Strip puts many needed functions at your fingertips.

Apple Talk Switch · Close box · Scroll arrow · Battery Monitor · File Sharing · Power Settings · Sound Volume · Sleep Now · Hard Disk Spin Down · Resize Strip

The whole Strip or portions of it can be hidden and rearranged. Here's what each module does:

- ✔ *AppleTalk Switch* turns AppleTalk on or off without a trip to the Chooser. If you never use your PowerBook on a network, for goodness sakes turn AppleTalk off. It sucks up RAM and battery when it's on, even if you're not using it.

- ✔ *Battery Monitor* shows battery charge levels, rate of battery consumption, and a digital readout of battery time remaining. It also tells whether the batteries are charged, charging, or draining. This feature is much nicer than the rickety old Battery desk accessory.

- ✔ *File Sharing* turns File Sharing on or off and changes the sharing setup.

- ✔ *Hard Disk Spin Down* spins down the hard disk with a click. Get in the habit if you're not using your PowerBook for a few minutes and you don't want to put it to sleep. HDSD saves batteries.

- ✔ *Power Settings* pits better conservation against better performance. Pick one. It can also open the PowerBook control panel.

- ✔ *Sleep Now* puts your PowerBook to Sleep with a single click.

- ✔ *Sound Volume* does what its name implies — lets you adjust the speaker volume without opening the Sound control panel.

- ✔ *Video Mirroring* lets you switch video mirroring on or off without a trip to the control panel. (This icon only appears when a PowerBook is attached to an external monitor. Mine isn't, so you don't see this feature in Figure 6-8.)

The last major new PowerBook feature is File Synchronization. PowerBook File Assistant automatically synchronizes files between PowerBook computers and other Macintosh systems by keeping any two files, folders, or disks synchronized whether the machines are wired together over a network or using diskettes. This utility provides drag-and-drop setup and lets users select automated or manual synchronization of data. Synchronization can be one-way or bidirectional.

And then there are what Apple terms the convenience features. And they are indeed convenient. One feature queues up documents to print as soon as you connect your PowerBook to a printer. Another makes the cursor easier to see. A sleep key and button in the Control Strip make it easier than ever to put your PowerBook into sleep mode to preserve your batteries. Finally, when a PowerBook wakes up from sleep, it automatically remounts hard disks and servers.

PowerBook utilities and enhancements: the last word

Very nice. With all of these new features, you won't find yourself running out to buy stuff for your PowerBook. Most of the new features were extra-cost add-ons before, and most PowerBook owners in the past bought one or more utilities to make their PowerBook more powerful. Now Apple's thrown in a decent set of utilities for free. Sure, C.P.U. has more features, but Control Strip is free. A big thumbs up.

Brave New World: Advanced Graphics and Printing

Everything so far has been hunky and dory. All the features I've covered up to this point have merit and can actually be used today. I now come to Apple's new architecture (read: enabling technology) for advanced graphics and printing: QuickDraw GX. You can only use some of its features today; the rest will have to wait for QuickDraw GX-savvy programs from third-party developers.

QuickDraw GX

Here's Apple's pitch: QuickDraw GX is setting the stage for the next generation in graphics. QuickDraw GX greatly extends and expands the graphics capabilities of the Macintosh, creating a new standard for desktop graphics computing and reaffirming the place of Macintosh as the premier publishing platform in the personal computer industry. It offers significant improvements to all customers, from generalist users to publishing professionals.

QuickDraw GX offers greater efficiency and power to Macintosh users by providing

- Simplified printing and print management via a new, customizable print architecture and user interface

- The capability to create *portable* documents from any application that allows other users to print and view the document without having the original application or fonts

- Consistent color between scanners, displays, and printers via ColorSync color-management technology

- Powerful type and text capabilities that, in conjunction with updated or new applications, enable the display and printing of any typeface, in any of the world's myriad script systems

- Tools for developers that will result in new applications that offer greater sophistication in graphics, type, and printing

Apple has set some noble goals, but it remains to be seen if they're achieved. As I mentioned earlier, enabling technologies depend on third-party developers creating programs to take advantage of them. And while QuickDraw GX offers many tantalizing possibilities to developers, such as superior type handling, more powerful graphics handling, and resolution-independent output to any device, I haven't heard of many developers jumping on the bandwagon. Most developers say they plan to add QuickDraw GX support when and if the market demands them. In other words, it will be a while before you can buy many programs that take advantage of QuickDraw GX's advanced features.

QuickDraw GX does provide some functionality out-of-the-box, in other words, without the addition of third-party products. These include

- Simplified and more powerful printing

- Desktop printer icons

- Better management of print jobs

- The ability to view and print documents without the original applications or fonts (kind of like Adobe Acrobat, No Hands Software's Common Ground, or Farallon's Replica)

QuickDraw GX: the last word

The benefits GX provides look good on paper. But Apple's been touting this technology publicly for almost three years, and System 7.5 is its first public appearance. This fact worries me. I'm always wary of the first release of anything, especially System software, and even more especially System software delayed several times while Apple got the bugs out. Most of the other enabling technologies in System 7.5 (PowerTalk, QuickTime, and AppleScript) have been available for a while (though they've never been included with System software, they were available separately or as part of the late, ill-fated System 7 Pro), so they're field proven by now. QuickDraw GX, on the other hand, is brand spanking new.

It may be worth using GX for the out-of-the-box features (remember, most programs have not yet been rewritten to take advantage of QuickDraw GX, and there's no telling how long it will take), but it uses an awful lot of memory (about a megabyte) for those features alone. See Chapter 15 for a comprehensive discussion of its benefits and detriments. This chapter will also detail your options for getting rid of QuickDraw GX if you so desire.

Doin' It Together: Collaborative Technologies

The two new collaborative technologies, PowerTalk and Telephone Manager, are not really new at all. Both PowerTalk and the Telephone Manager have been available to developers for a couple of years. PowerTalk has been sold (in System 7 Pro) and Telephone Manager has been bundled with a few third-party programs. So we should start seeing products that take advantage of them real soon now.

For now, I'll shoot for a mere conceptual overview.

PowerTalk

PowerTalk is a system-software level foundation for collaborative applications and services, based on the Apple Open Collaboration Environment (AOCE).

PowerTalk provides a set of collaborative services that allows users to send electronic mail, share files, and digitally sign and forward documents from within an application. Apple began shipping PowerTalk with System 7 Pro in October, 1993.

The PowerTalk technology includes a number of separate capabilities:

- ✔ *AppleMail* is peer-to-peer mail that allows you to exchange electronic mail with other PowerTalk users without requiring a mail server. It ain't QuickMail, but hey, the price is right — System 7.5 includes everything you need.

- ✔ *PowerTalk support for mail-capable applications* lets you route documents directly from supported applications, avoiding the need to use a specialized mail application that requires documents be sent as an enclosure.

- ✔ *PowerTalk Universal Mailbox* provides a single mailbox for all of your mail. In theory, this mailbox could handle AppleMail, QuickMail, CompuServe, Internet, fax, pager, and voice mail. Someday this will be a great feature when the on-line services I use — and I use quite a few — all have *gateways,* the software PowerTalk needs to connect to them. They don't yet.

- ✔ *PowerTalk authentication and privacy* ensures that communications are kept secure and private.

- ✔ *PowerTalk Digital Signatures* let you attach reliable approval signatures to documents.

- ✔ *PowerTalk Directories* are central repositories of information, and they are critical for communicating and collaborating with others. This information can be shared between applications.

- ✔ *PowerTalk messaging between applications* provides the plumbing that allows PowerTalk-savvy applications to communicate with each other over the network to create collaboration solutions.

- ✔ *PowerTalk Key Chain security* lets you unlock password-protected resources, including network servers, with a single password entry. I like this feature, as I'm usually the only one in my office. I hated typing my password 20 times a day to mount disks and get electronic mail.

Telephone Manager

With Telephone Manager, Apple paves the way for integrated computer and telephone functions. System 7.5 includes built-in support for the Macintosh Telephony Architecture, including the Telephone Manager.

In the near future, a new breed of integrated telephone/Macintosh programs should appear on the scene. Expect to see programs such as contact managers that can initiate telephone calls, databases that can present information automatically based on incoming calls, calendar programs that can automatically dial scheduled conference calls, accounting applications that can automate accounts receivable follow-up phone calls, and electronic-forms applications that allow individuals to call the originator of a form before approving it.

Another potential use for the new Telephony functions is screen-based telephony applications that provide the user interface for a virtual telephone on the user's Macintosh desktop. At worst, they serve as an alternative to the keypad on a telephone, letting you place calls, answer calls, transfer and hold calls, and so on with a simple Macintosh interface on-screen. Programs like this could log call times for professionals charging hourly rates. Receptionists who juggle many calls simultaneously may also find such programs useful. Given how frequently most people use their telephones, these applications can quickly become essential to day-to-day productivity.

Finally, programmed telephony applications might allow you to script a Macintosh to handle incoming calls and interact with callers to create telephone-based information retrieval systems, voice mail, fax broadcasts, and personal agents.

Telephony applications can be combined with PowerTalk's catalogs technology for the storage of telephone numbers and other personal information. This feature provides a real-time application of PowerTalk's integration of store-and-forward collaboration to the Macintosh user experience.

Collaborative Technologies: the last word

If you think this section (and the previous one on QuickDraw GX) sounds a little like a press release from Apple, you're right. Because there are very few programs around that take advantage of either PowerTalk or Macintosh Telephony Architecture, much of what I say is speculation based on what Apple tells us PowerTalk and Macintosh Telephony Architecture are capable of. Now it's up to third-party developers to create some compelling applications.

Collaborative computing is more than a buzzword. Every year I transact more and more of my business via modem. So I'm looking forward to having one mailbox and being able to digitally sign forms. But it seems to me that my wishes won't come true until two events take place:

1. Third-party developers invent products good enough to spend money on.

2. System 7.5 is widely adopted.

The truth is, I foresee both happening soon, so I'll give the collaborative technologies a thumbs up, mostly on the basis of what they promise, and not what they can deliver today.

PowerTalk's modest office email is usable, especially at the price. That alone is probably worth a thumbs up, particularly if you don't already have some kind of email system. Though it's a little wimpy without the store-and-forward capabilities of the optional PowerShare Collaboration Server (an additional $999), it's still better than no email at all. It's functional, but nowhere near as good as a full-featured email system like QuickMail.

The Last Word

OK, I lied. This isn't the last word yet. I thought I was done, but I realized I left out one of my favorite parts of System 7.5, QuickTime.

QuickTime

QuickTime is the enabling technology that lets movies play on your Mac screen. No QuickTime, no movies. It's that simple. If you have one of the AV model Macs, you can import video and create your own QuickTime movies without any additional hardware (a VCR or camcorder is required, of course). Other Macs can import and export QuickTime with an inexpensive video digitizing board (starting at well under $400). QuickTime movies are usually smaller than full-screen and usually play back at less than the 30 frames per second used in television and videotape productions.

You can display QuickTime movies on your screen. With the proper hardware (read: not cheap), you can create full-screen QuickTime movies at 30 frames per second and even record them to videotape.

You can have your Mac automatically play a QuickTime movie at startup, even if you don't have a QuickTime movie-playing program on your hard disk. Just name the QuickTime movie Startup Movie (the space is important) and drag it into your System Folder.

In the past, QuickTime was readily available, and usually free, but it wasn't included with your System disks. You could buy a QuickTime Starter Kit from Apple for under $50 or find it bundled with games that required it. (The game developers license QuickTime from Apple for a reasonable annual fee and are allowed to include it with their products.) Free with your System software is even better.

QuickTime: the last word

What's not to like? QuickTime is totally cool, giving your Macintosh the capability to view and edit video. Yes, it requires a lot of horsepower — RAM and disk space — to really get into it. But even users with older, slower Macs can play back movies at a reasonable speed and resolution if they have at least 4 or 5MB of RAM (though more is better).

The Last Word, Really

This section really is the last word on the whole shebang. And you have to admit, after reading this chapter, System 7.5 sure sounds good on paper.

It is good in real life, too. It's a solid upgrade with lots of new functionality and convenience. Although many of its improvements have been in widespread use for years — hierarchical Apple menus, WindowShade, menu bar clock, recent items folders, and more — it's good to see Apple throwing them in for free. As a power-user guru, I'm always turning people on to my favorite commercial and shareware utilities; many of System 7.5's improvements mean that they'll get something similar absolutely free when they upgrade.

And I think that free is a very good thing.

As far as the enabling technologies go, I'm reserving judgment. I'm not using PowerTalk or QuickDraw GX on a regular basis until I discover a compelling reason, which I expect to do in the not-so-distant future. So for now, I give them a tentative thumbs up.

I guess you could sum up this chapter by saying that Apple has done its part. It's provided plenty of solid usability enhancements and included the plumbing for several promising new enabling technologies.

Now it's up to third-party developers (or Apple) to provide applications that make us want to use those technologies. I hope we don't wait too long.

Chapter 7
File Management Made Simple

• •

In This Chapter

▶ Using Launcher (or not)

▶ Getting yourself organized (or something like it)

▶ Using aliases

▶ Looking at other people's Macs

• •

*I*n Chapters 1–5, you learned the basics about windows and icons and menus. In this chapter, you'll apply what you've learned as you begin a never-ending quest to discover the fastest, easiest, most trouble-free way to manage the files on your Mac.

I can help. I'm not a doctor, but I play one in books and magazines. I've been wrangling with the Macintosh interface for almost ten years now, and I've learned a lot about what works and what doesn't — at least what works for me. This chapter will spare you at least part of the ten-year learning curve.

Remember: we're talking about a Macintosh here. And we're talking about developing your own personal style. There is no right way to organize your files, no right way to use aliases, no right way to use the Apple menu, and no right way to use Drag and Drop. The only thing for sure is that these features are useless if you don't use them.

Please take the time to understand these wonderful features. They make your Mac so much easier to use. I'll show you how I do it and then give you a glimpse of how a few of my friends do it. After absorbing that info, you'll have all the ammunition you need to create your own personal Macintosh experience, a Mac environment designed by you, for you.

Launcher (or Not)

Launcher is a new (unless you have a Performa — Apple's included a similar Launcher for a while) control panel that creates a window in the Finder with single-clickable icons that launch (open) frequently used files.

The advantage of Launcher is that the icons in the Launcher window can represent items in many different folders on your hard disk (see Figure 7-1).

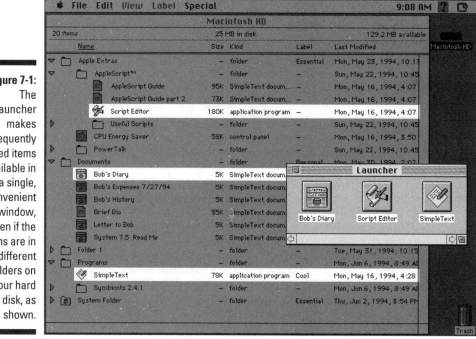

Figure 7-1:
The Launcher makes frequently used items available in a single, convenient window, even if the items are in different folders on your hard disk, as shown.

So Launcher, at least in theory, saves you time by saving you from rooting through folders every time you need one of these items.

Launcher is easy to configure. If you want an icon to appear in the Launcher window, create an alias of the icon and place that alias in the Launcher Items folder, which you'll find in your System Folder (see Figure 7-2).

If you want something to appear in the Launcher, put an alias of it in the Launcher Items folder. That's it. The whole enchilada.

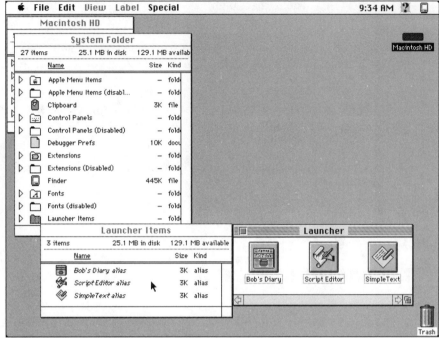

Figure 7-2:
If an item's
alias is
in the
Launcher
Items folder,
the item
appears
in the
Launcher
window.

I think I've been objective up to this point. Now I'll tell you why I think Launcher stinks:

✔ It doesn't float in front of other Finder windows, so it's easy to lose behind other windows.

✔ It has only a Large Icon view, so it wastes valuable screen real estate.

✔ It can't be chosen from the Application menu.

✔ It's no different from a regular window in View by Icon mode except that ...

✔ ... It uses single clicks to open icons, a clear violation of Macintosh Human Interface Guidelines, the bible of Macintosh interface design.

So why did Apple start including Launcher, first with Performas and now with System 7.5? And why, after ten years of rabid insistence that double-click means *open,* did Apple change its mind?

My take on it is that Apple is afraid that new users are too stupid to grasp the concept of double-clicking to open a file. And too stupid to realize that you can do everything Launcher does and more by customizing your Apple menu (as you'll see later in this chapter).

I don't think you're that dumb. I say get rid of the lame-o Launcher. (See Chapter 15 for complete instructions on shuffling Launcher off this mortal coil.)

With what you learn in this chapter, you'll instead be able to create your own customized environment, which I promise will let you find and launch items faster and more flexibly than Launcher.

On the other hand, if for some unfathomable reason you *like* Launcher, by all means enjoy it. It doesn't use that much disk space or RAM, so there's no great advantage to trashing it.

No advantage beside never seeing Launcher again (which I consider a big advantage).

Getting Yourself Organized (or Something Like It)

I won't pretend to be able to do this task for you. Organizing your files is as personal as your taste in music. You develop your own style with the Mac. So in this section, I'll give you some food for thought, some ideas about how I do it, and some suggestions that should make organization easier for you, regardless of how you choose to do it yourself.

And it's root, root, root for the root level

Root level is the window you see when you open your hard disk's icon. It's the first level down in the hierarchy of folders. How you organize root level is a matter of taste, but let me try to give some guidance.

Kiss: keep it simple, stupid

I find that less is more when it comes to organizing files and folders. I try to use the simplest structure that serves my needs. For example, if I have more than a handful of icons at root level, I begin to look for ways to reorganize. I shoot for no more than 10 items at root level; fewer is better.

At the very least...

Root level must contain the System Folder. It won't work properly if you put it somewhere else (like in another folder or on the Desktop). Beyond that, what you place on the root level is up to you.

I think most people should start with two other folders, Applications and Documents, at the very least, but even these don't *have* to go at root level. The Desktop is an equally good place for them, as you'll see in a later section.

Documentary evidence: the Documents folder

Remember, you don't have to have a Documents folder, but if you do, here are some tips for organizing it:

  ✔ Don't create subfolders (within the Documents folder) until you need them.

Creating a bunch of empty folders because you think that you might need them someday is more work than creating them when you need them. You end up opening an empty folder when you're looking for something else — a complete waste of time.

I recommend saving everything in the Documents folder for a week or two (or a month or two, depending on how many new documents you save each day). Once a decent-sized group of documents has accumulated in the Documents folder, take a look at them and create logical subfolders to put them into.

  ✔ Let your work style decide file structure.

You should create the subfolders based on a system that makes sense to you. Here are some ideas for subfolders:

  ✔ By type of document: Word Processing documents, Spreadsheet documents, Graphics documents
  ✔ By date: Documents May-June, Documents Spring '94
  ✔ By content: Memos, Outgoing Letters, Expense Reports
  ✔ By project: Project X, Project Y, Project Z

When things start to get messy, and you start noticing some folders bulging (that is, filled up with tons of files), subdivide them again and use a combination of the methods I just mentioned.

For example: If you start by subdividing your Documents folder into four subfolders, Memos, Expense Reports, Letters, and Other Documents (as shown in Figure 7-3), a few months later, when those folders begin to get full, you might subdivide them in one or more of the ways, as shown in Figure 7-4.

The Other Documents folder hasn't required subdividing yet as it only contains five items. If I accumulated a few more poems there, I might consider a Poems subfolder inside the Other Documents folder.

Figure 7-3:
A Documents folder containing four subfolders.

Documents		
4 items	25.5 MB in disk	128.7

		Name
▷	📁	Expense Reports
▷	📁	Letters
▷	📁	Memos
▷	📁	Other Documents

Figure 7-4:
The same Documents folder several months later, with new subfolders for three of the original four subfolders.

Documents			
18 items	25.5 MB in disk		128.7 MB available

Name	Size	Kind	Lat
▽ 📁 Expense Reports	—	folder	
▷ 📁 Expenses Aug/Sep '94	—	folder	
▷ 📁 Expenses Jun/Jul '94	—	folder	
▷ 📁 Expenses Oct/Nov '94	—	folder	
▽ 📁 Letters	—	folder	
▷ 📁 Collection Letters	—	folder	
▷ 📁 Fan Letters	—	folder	
▷ 📁 General Business Letters	—	folder	
▽ 📁 Memos	—	folder	
▷ 📁 Memos to CEO/CFO	—	folder	
▷ 📁 Memos to Marketing Dept.	—	folder	
▷ 📁 Memos to my staff	—	folder	
▽ 📁 Other Documents	—	folder	
📄 Brief Bio	35K	SimpleText docum...	
📄 Lecture Notes	5K	SimpleText docum...	
📄 Poem	5K	SimpleText docum...	
📄 Poem for Lisa	5K	SimpleText docum...	
📄 System 7.5 Read Me	5K	SimpleText docum...	

The point is that your folder structure should be organic, growing as you need it to grow. Let it happen. Don't let any one folder get so full that it's a hassle to deal with. Create new subfolders when things start to get crowded.

How full is too full? That's impossible to say. If I find more than 15 or 20 files in a single folder, I begin thinking about ways to subdivide it. On the other hand, some of my subfolders that contain things I don't often need, such as my "Correspondence 1992" folder, contain over a hundred files. Because I don't use the folder that much (but want to keep it on my hard disk just in case), its overcrowded condition doesn't bother me. Your mileage may vary.

After almost ten years of growth, my Documents folder contains only about a dozen subfolders, most of which contain their own subfolders (see Figure 7-5). Being a nonconformist, I call my documents folder "Stuff."

Stuff		
25 items	35.7 MB in disk	82.3 MB available

Name	Size	Kind	Last Modified
▷ 📁 Correspondence	–	folder	5/20/94, 10:41 PM
▷ 📁 Databases	–	folder	6/6/94, 11:27 AM
▷ 📁 Done.Writing	–	folder	5/16/94, 1:19 PM
▷ 📁 Dr. Mac Training Seminar	–	folder	1/12/94, 10:35 AM
▷ 📁 FamilyPC Done	–	folder	5/21/94, 2:29 PM
▽ 📁 Finances	–	folder	1/19/94, 10:32 PM
▷ 📁 1989	–	folder	12/31/91, 5:12 PM
▷ 📁 1990	–	folder	4/1/91, 5:28 PM
▷ 📁 1991	–	folder	12/31/91, 5:13 PM
▷ 📁 1992	–	folder	9/20/93, 1:39 PM
▷ 📁 1993	–	folder	1/12/93, 12:29 PM
▷ 📁 1994	–	folder	1/19/94, 10:32 PM
▷ 📁 General Information	–	folder	6/4/94, 3:26 PM
▽ 📁 HelpFolder	–	folder	6/6/94, 1:26 PM
▷ 📁 HelpFolders – 1990	–	folder	9/13/93, 9:06 AM
▷ 📁 HelpFolders – 1991	–	folder	9/13/93, 9:06 AM
▷ 📁 HelpFolders – 1992	–	folder	9/13/93, 9:06 AM
▷ 📁 HelpFolders – 1993	–	folder	9/13/93, 9:06 AM
▷ 📁 HelpFolders – 1994	–	folder	5/31/94, 9:21 PM
▷ 📁 Lisa's Folder	–	folder	4/17/94, 5:50 PM
📄 Mystery Novel	10K	Microsoft Word do...	3/24/94, 10:18 AM
▷ 📁 Online Archives	–	folder	2/1/94, 5:25 PM
▷ 📁 Public Relations	–	folder	5/20/94, 10:54 PM
▷ 📁 Public Speaking	–	folder	1/13/94, 10:53 AM
▷ 📁 ZMC/MacUser Forum	–	folder	5/22/94, 3:30 PM

Figure 7-5:
My
Documents
folder
and its
subfolders.

Other folders at root level

You can follow this same philosophy for other folders at root level, subdividing them as needed. If you use a particular folder a great deal, move it from the Documents folder to root level or to the Desktop (more about that in a few pages) to make it easier to use.

The only thing I might caution you against is storing your stuff in the System Folder that doesn't belong there. There's no harm in it, but the System Folder is already the repository for many files used by both the System software and applications. For most people, the System Folder is the most crowded folder on their disk, so sticking items that don't belong in it will only cause further clutter. Word processing documents and spreadsheets (and indeed almost all documents) don't belong in the System Folder. You know how the file system works. Create a folder somewhere else for your documents.

Other than that, the only rule is that there are no rules. Whatever works for you is the best way.

Apply here: the Applications folder

I recommend an Applications folder for all your programs. The best place for this folder is either at root level or on the Desktop. Your Applications folder can also be subdivided when the need arises. As Figure 7-6 shows, mine has subfolders for business programs, graphics programs, writing tools, utilities, toys, and on-line (modem) stuff.

Figure 7-6: My applications folder contains six subfolders.

It'll probably be a while until you need so many subfolders — unless you're like me and try a lot of new software. Either way, organize your applications the same way you organized your documents — in a way that makes sense to you. Follow this advice and I promise that you'll always be able to find what you're looking for.

The Greatest Thing Since Sliced Bread: Aliases

When System 7 first arrived several years ago, many of its features were heralded as breakthroughs. But of these features, none has proved to be more useful than the alias.

An alias, if you've forgotten, is a quick-opener for another file. With aliases, a file can be in two (or more) places at once. When you create an alias of a disk, file, or folder, opening its alias is the same as opening the item. And an alias takes up only the tiniest bit of disk space.

Why is this feature so great? First, it lets you put items in more than one place, which, on many occasions, is exactly what you want to do. For example, it's convenient to keep an alias of your word processor on your Desktop and another in your Apple menu. You may even want a third alias of it in your Documents folder for quick access. Aliases let you open your word processor quickly and easily without navigating into the depths of your Applications folder each time you need it.

Here's another example: If you write a memo to Fred Smith about the Smythe Marketing Campaign to be executed in the 4th quarter, which folder does the document go in? Smith? Smythe? Marketing? Memos? 4th Quarter?

With aliases, it doesn't matter. You can put the actual file in any of the folders and then create aliases of it and place them in all the other folders. So whichever folder you open, you'll be able to find the memo.

Finally, many programs need to remain in the same folder as their supporting files and folders. Some programs won't function properly unless they are in the same folder as their dictionaries, thesauri, data files (for games), templates, and so on. Ergo, you can't put these programs on the Desktop or in the Apple Menu Items folder without impairing their functionality.

Icons on the Desktop

How about a little hands-on training? You'll create an alias for your favorite application and put it on Desktop, a very good place for it.

1. Find your favorite application — ClarisWorks, Microsoft Word, Spectre Supreme — and select its icon, not the folder that it's in. Be sure and select the program's icon.

2. Choose File⇨Make Alias, or press Command-M, as shown in Figure 7-7.

   An alias of the application appears right next to the original. The alias's file name will be the same as the original's, except that it is in italics and has the word *alias* appended at the end.

3. Drag the alias onto the Desktop and move it to a convenient place.

Figure 7-7:
Make an
alias of your
very favorite
program.

I like to keep my Desktop icons across the bottom of the screen. Directly under the hard disk icon is another prime location (see Figure 7-8).

There. You've just made it easier to use your favorite program. Next time you need your favorite program, just open its alias right there on your Desktop instead of opening several folders and cluttering up your screen.

Frequently used folders or documents are good candidates for aliases-on-the-Desktop. In fact, any icon you use more than a couple of times a day is a good candidate for an alias on the Desktop.

Remember, aliases don't take up much disk space (a measly 3 or 4K each), so there's no penalty for making an alias and later deciding that you don't like it. Big deal. Drag it to the Trash.

The temporary alias theory

I use a lot of *temporary* aliases on my Desktop. When I first create a file, I save it in its proper folder, inside my Documents folder somewhere. If it's a document that I plan to work on for more than a day or two, such as a magazine article, I make an alias of the document and put it on the Desktop. When the article is done and I've submitted it to my editor, I trash the alias. The original file is already stashed away in its proper folder.

With bigger projects, like books, which have multiple subfolders of their own, I keep an alias of the parent folder on the Desktop for easy access. When I submit the last chapter, the alias goes into the Trash.

Incidentally, the same technique can be used without the aliases. Just save all your new documents on the Desktop (click the Desktop button in the Save dialog box or use the shortcut Command-D). Later, when you're done with them, you can file them away in their proper folders.

My point is that the Desktop is an excellent place for the things that you need most often. Whether you use aliases of documents or save the actual files on the Desktop until you figure out where you want to store them, the Desktop is a fine place for the things you use most. Keep frequently used programs on the Desktop forever, and use the Desktop as a temporary parking place for current projects.

Whatever you do, I encourage you to do it on the Desktop.

What a drag it is not to drop

Macintosh Drag and Drop, as described in Chapter 6, deals with dragging text and graphics from one place to another. But there's another angle to Drag and Drop, one that has to do with documents and icons.

Drag and Drop can be used to open a file using a program other than the one that would ordinarily launch when you open the document. This concept is easier to show than to tell, so follow along on your own computer:

1. Make a screen shot picture of your Desktop by holding down the Command and Shift keys and pressing the 3 key. Command-Shift-3 takes a picture of your Desktop.

2. You hear a cute snapshot sound, and a document called Picture 1 automatically appears in your hard disk's root level window. Open it.

3. Assuming that there's a copy of SimpleText on your hard disk, SimpleText will launch and display Picture 1.

    But you don't want to use SimpleText. SimpleText can open and display a picture file but can't make changes to it. You want to open the picture with a program that can edit it. What do you do? Use Drag and Drop.

4. Quit SimpleText.

5. Drag the icon for Picture 1 onto the alias of your favorite program that you created earlier. Figure 7-9 shows how made changes to Picture 1.

If the alias of your favorite program didn't highlight when you dragged Picture 1 on top of it, or if dragging Picture 1 onto the alias launched the program but didn't open Picture 1, then your favorite program isn't capable of opening picture files.

Your solution if your favorite program couldn't open Picture 1: Get a different favorite program. Just kidding. The solution is to try dragging Picture 1 onto other program icons (or aliases of program icons) until you find one that opens it. When you do, you might want to put an alias of that application on the Desktop, too.

What happens if you don't have a copy of SimpleText on your hard disk when you try to open Picture 1? Macintosh Easy Open kicks in and offers you a choice of other programs that can open it (see Figure 7-10).

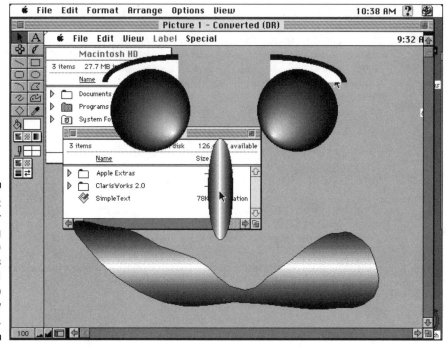

Figure 7-9:
After
dragging
Picture 1 to
a graphics
program, I
was able to
make a few
changes.

Figure 7-10:
Macintosh
Easy Open
lets you
choose from
compatible
applications
if you try to
open a
document
and don't
have the
program
that created
it on your
hard disk.

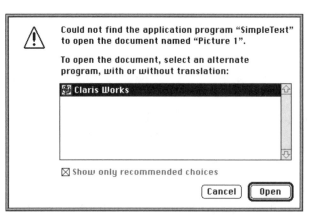

When I trashed SimpleText and tried to open Picture 1, Figure 7-10 is what I saw. In a more technical book, I'd go on to explain about file Type and Creator codes and how they have to do with what program gets launched when you open a document. But this is *Macintosh System 7.5 For Dummies,* so I won't.

Suffice it to say that System 7.5 is smart enough to figure out which applications can open what documents and offer you a choice. Earlier versions weren't that smart.

Smart Apple menu tricks

Remember when I called the Launcher lame? Here's something way better. I talked a bit about the Apple menu in Chapter 4; now I'll show you how to make it work for you.

First, make sure that you've turned the wonderful submenus on in the Apple Menu Options control panel. If you don't see little black triangles to the right of all folders in the Apple menu, they're not turned on.

Now do something useful. Let's make a file launcher that enables you to open every file on your hard disk from a single Apple menu item!

The hard-disk-alias-in-the-Apple-menu-trick

1. Select your hard disk icon and make an alias of it by selecting your hard drive and choosing File⇨Make alias or by using the shortcut Command-M.

2. Put the alias of your hard disk in the Apple Menu Items folder (which is in your System Folder).

3. Pull down the Apple menu and admire your handiwork (see Figure 7-11).

If having your hard drive on the Apple menu is too overwhelming for you, consider putting an alias of your Documents folder or your Applications folder in the Apple menu. It's easy, it's fast, and it's convenient. Get in the habit of putting frequently used items (it's not just for desk accessories and folders anymore) in the Apple menu. You'll be glad you did.

A quick trick for adding an alias to the Apple menu

1. Select the icon of the item that you want to appear in the Apple menu.

2. Choose Apple menu⇨Automated Tasks⇨Add Alias to Apple Menu.

This script will automatically create an alias of the selected item and put it in the Apple Menu Items folder, as shown in Figure 7-12.

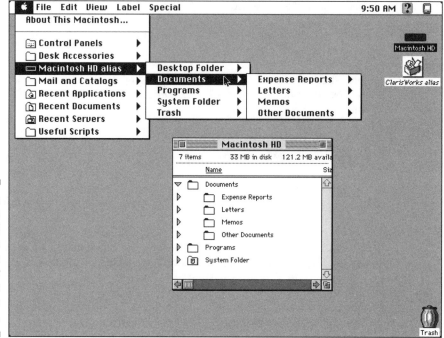

Figure 7-11:
Put an alias
of your hard
disk in the
Apple menu
to gain easy
access to
every file on
your disk.

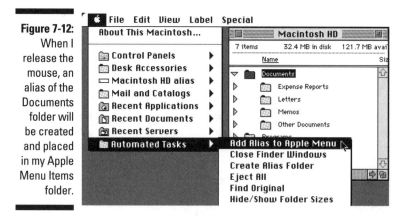

Figure 7-12:
When I
release the
mouse, an
alias of the
Documents
folder will
be created
and placed
in my Apple
Menu Items
folder.

The old alias-of-the-Apple-Menu-Items-folder-on-the-Desktop trick

Are you growing fonder of your Apple menu? You should be. It's a great resource and it's easy to customize. If you find yourself customizing yours a lot,
here's a tip to make it easier to use.

Make an alias of the Apple Menu Items folder and put it on your Desktop for
easy access.

If you make frequent changes to your Apple menu, this tip saves you at least one step. And here's another tip: You can also put an alias of the Apple Menu Items folder in the Apple menu so that you can select it even if a window is covering the alias on your Desktop (see Figure 7-13).

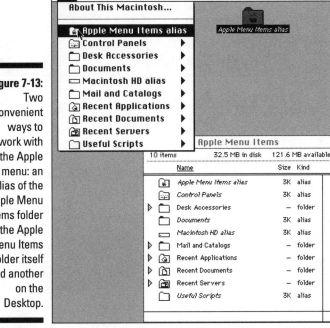

Figure 7-13:
Two convenient ways to work with the Apple menu: an alias of the Apple Menu Items folder in the Apple Menu Items folder itself and another on the Desktop.

When you put an alias of the Apple Menu Items folder in your Apple menu, it won't have subfolders, which makes sense when you think about it. If it had subfolders, they would create an endless loop.

By the way, you'll learn some more very cool Apple menu tricks in Chapter 12.

Macstyles of the Not So Rich and Famous

Earlier in the chapter I promised you a peek at some of my friends' Desktops. Personally, I find electronic voyeurism fascinating. I hope you will too. You can learn a lot about people (and a lot of cool tricks to use on your own Mac) by looking over their shoulders at their Macs.

So here are some glimpses into the Macs of a few of my friends.

Robin Williams: Renaissance Woman

Robin Williams (no, not Mork or the voice of Genie) is the author of *The Little Mac Book, The Mac Is Not a Typewriter,* and *The Non-Designer's Design Book.*

I'd have never expected her Desktop to be so … well, so austere, but take a look at Figure 7-14.

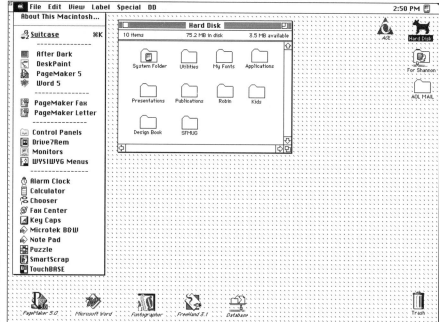

Figure 7-14:
Robin
Williams's
austere
Desktop and
Apple menu.

Steven Bobker: The Godfather of MacUser

Steven Bobker is a legend in Mac circles as the crusty but benevolent Editor-in-Chief of *MacUser* magazine during its first golden age. He's forgotten more about the Mac than most of us will ever know. Figure 7-15 shows how he keeps house.

Lofty Becker: Triple Threat

Loftus E. Becker Jr., known to all as Lofty, is a triple Mac threat. He's a consummate power user who uses his Mac for three (count 'em) diverse jobs, often all three at the same time. First, he's a law professor. Then he's a sysop for

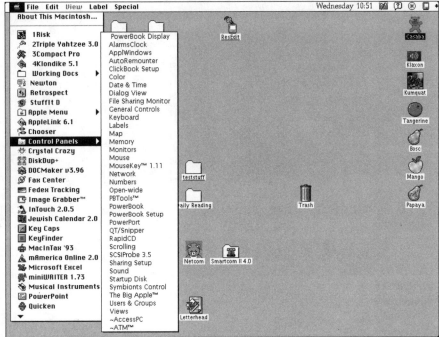

Figure 7-15:
Steven
Bobker
relies
almost
exclusively
on his Apple
menu for file
launching
and folder
navigation.

CompuServe's popular MAUG forums. In his spare time, he's an ace product reviewer for *MacWEEK* magazine. A busy guy like that has to make the most of his time. Let's look at Lofty's Desktop (in Figure 7-16).

Glenn Brown: Federal Agent and Extension King

Glenn Brown works in international customs for Revenue Canada. He's also the king of customizing Macs. In fact, Glenn and I once wrote a book called, coincidentally enough, *Customizing Your Mac for Productivity and Fun.* Glenn holds the world record for running a Mac with the most extensions and control panels at the same time, over 150 at once! Figure 7-17 shows Glenn's highly customized Desktop.

Rich Wolfson: The Unkempt Professor

Rich Wolfson is a professor of technology at Montclair State College as well as the supervisor of their Mac lab. He's also the author of *The PowerBook Companion* and a frequent contributor to *MacUser* magazine. Figure 7-18 shows his Desktop.

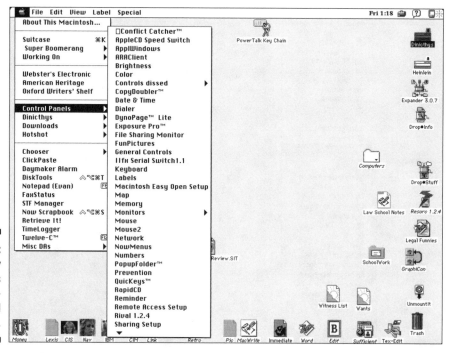

Figure 7-16:
Lofty
Becker's
well-
organized
Desktop.

Figure 7-17:
Glenn's
Desktop
is as
customized
as they
come.

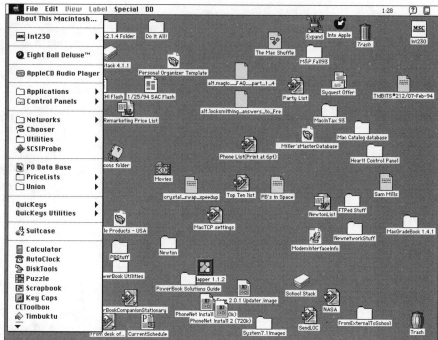

Figure 7-18:
Rich doesn't
keep a
very tidy
Desktop.

Robyn Ray: Bad Influence

By now I'm sure you're asking yourself, OK, so that's what the Desktops of a bunch of hot-shot writer-types look like. But what about normal folks? What about beginners? What do their Desktops look like?

To answer that question, we'll turn to my childhood friend Robyn Ray, who is now a casting director for feature films like *Threesome*, *Frank & Jesse*, and *Bad Influence*, and a close personal friend of the Jackson 5. She got her first Macintosh a few weeks ago. Figure 7-19 shows what her Desktop looks like today.

Guy Kawasaki: A Marketing Pro

I asked Guy Kawasaki, author of *The Macintosh Way* and back-page opinion columnist for *Macworld* magazine, to submit his Desktop for this little section of my book. Never shy about self-promotion, he sent me a giant screen shot of his Desktop with his next book, *How to Drive the Competition Crazy: Disrupting the marketplace for fun and profit,* prominently displayed in the middle. He figured I'd run the picture full size and his book would get a nice little dose of free publicity. He even sent me a note that said, "Just for this chutzpah, you should put the whole thing in."

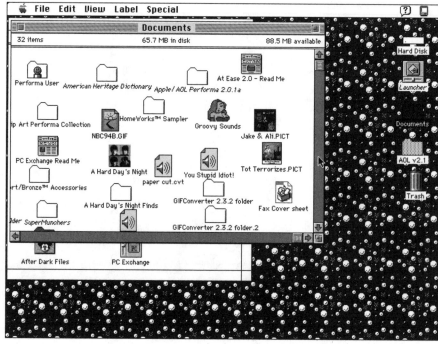

Figure 7-19:
New Mac
user
Robyn's
Desktop.

Nice try, Guy. His Desktop was boring anyway. The only remotely interesting part is the Apple menu (see Figure 7-20).

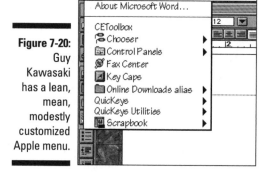

Figure 7-20:
Guy
Kawasaki
has a lean,
mean,
modestly
customized
Apple menu.

Chapter 8

Publish or Perish: The Fail-Safe Guide to Printing

· ·

· ·

*P*rinting is like being. It just is. Or at least it should be. It should be as simple as typing Command-P and then pressing the Return key. And usually that's how it is. Except when it isn't, and printing turns into a raging nightmare.

You won't be having any nightmares. If you get your printer and printing software configured properly, printing is simple as can be. And that's pretty darn simple. QuickDraw GX adds a few wrinkles, but it's nothing you can't manage.

So this is a chapter about avoiding nightmares. We'll go through the entire process, as if you just unpacked a new printer and plugged it in. If you upgraded from an earlier version of System 7 and are able to print with System 7.5 already, you can probably skip some of the steps. The objective here is to familiarize yourself with the printing process from start to finish.

 One thing I suggest is that you read the documentation that came with your specific printer. There are hundreds of different printer makes and models available for the Mac, so I may contradict something that your printer manual says. If you run into this discrepancy, try it the way the manual says first. If that doesn't work, try mine.

Another thing you need to know is that every application can use its own custom print and Page Setup dialog box. Though many will look like the ones in this chapter, others won't. For example, the Print and Page Setup dialog boxes for Microsoft Word include choices not covered in this chapter, such as Even or Odd Pages Only, Print Hidden Text, and Print Selection Only. If you see commands in your Print or Page Setup dialog boxes that aren't explained in this chapter, they're specific to that application and should be explained in its documentation.

OK. Let's get started then. Begin by connecting the printer to the Printer port on the back of your Mac (with both the Mac and the printer turned off, of course — but you knew that, didn't you?). If you don't have a cable (and many Apple printers don't come with cables), contact your printer manufacturer and ask where it is. Plug the printer into an outlet. Turn it on. If the printer came with software, install it on your hard disk, following the instructions that came with the printer. That's it.

Ready, set, print!

Ready: Choosing a Printer in (What Else?) the Chooser DA

The path to printing perfection begins with the humble Chooser DA. In earlier versions of System 7, it was a necessary evil, but with System 7.5's nifty new Desktop Printers, you'll use it once to set up your printer, and under ordinary circumstances, you'll rarely use it again.

Many of the steps involving the Chooser require that the printer be turned on and warmed up, so if yours isn't, it should be. Do that now so that you'll be able to choose a printer:

1. Choose Apple menu⇨Chooser.

The Chooser desk accessory opens. If you have previously chosen a printer, its icon is selected when the Chooser opens; if you've never printed before, the Chooser appears with no printer icon selected.

The Chooser is also used to choose network connections. You may see icons for AppleShare or your fax modem there. Don't mess with them yet. I'll talk about File Sharing in the next chapter.

If no icon is selected in your Chooser, click on the printer icon that matches your printer. If you have an Apple printer and you used System 7.5's Easy Install option, there should be an icon that matches your printer.

If you have an Apple printer and there is no icon that matches your printer, try clicking the one that sounds most like your printer.

If you have a non-Apple printer, see its manual for instructions on installing printer drivers for your printer. Or try using one of the Apple printer drivers.

Some of the icons in the Chooser represent *printer drivers*. Printer drivers translate between your Mac applications and your printer, ensuring that what you see is what you print. Technically, a printer driver is a special piece of software called a Chooser Extension. When you drag a printer driver onto your System Folder, System 7.5 will automatically place it in the Extensions folder for you. As long as a printer driver is in the Extensions folder, you should see an icon for it in the Chooser DA.

If you have a printer made by someone other than Apple, you might want to contact them about getting a new QuickDraw GX-savvy driver. Many printer manufacturers are offering new drivers with enhanced functionality. If you have a modem, you may find new drivers for your printer on on-line services such as eWorld, America Online, or CompuServe. Check with your printer manufacturer for details.

You can install Apple printer drivers by using System 7.5's Custom Install option. You remove them by dragging them from the Extensions folder to the Trash. It's perfectly safe to remove printer drivers for printers that you never intend to use. Removing unneeded printer drivers can free up more than a megabyte of hard disk space.

If you have a printer made by someone other than Apple and you have an older printer driver, one of the souped-up new Apple GX drivers (they have "GX" after their names) *may* work with your particular printer. The only way to find out is to try it. If a page prints and it looks OK, the driver probably works.

OK. Now let's get down to business. At the top of the Chooser on the right side is a pop-down menu. It may offer four choices for connecting your printer: AppleTalk, Serial, SCSI, and Servers. I can't tell you which kind of connection your printer uses (look in its manual), but here are some general guidelines:

- ✔ Most PostScript laser printers use AppleTalk.
- ✔ Most ImageWriters and StyleWriters use Serial.
- ✔ Most SCSI printers have the letters SC in their model number or name and use a cable with a huge connector like the ones on external hard disks, CD-ROM drives, and scanners.

> ✔ If you have a print server, chances are good that you have a system administrator who can show you how it works. Ask him or her.

If all has gone right, the right side of the Chooser is displaying either your printer's name (see Figure 8-1) or a pair of icons (see Figure 8-2).

If you have an AppleTalk printer

If you have an AppleTalk printer, click on your printer's name to select it, even if only one name appears, as shown in Figure 8-1.

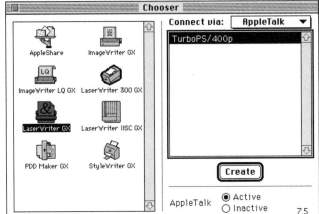

Figure 8-1:
The Chooser
DA for an
AppleTalk
printer.

If you have a serial printer

If you have a serial printer, you'll see two icons on the right side of the Chooser instead of a printer name. Choose whichever port the printer cable is connected to on the back of your Mac (Figure 8-2).

If you have a SCSI or server-based printer

If you have a SCSI or server-based printer, you're on your own. What you see on the right side of the Chooser depends on the SCSI printer's manufacturer or your server's setup. I couldn't beg or borrow one, so I don't know what you'll see. With luck, you'll figure it out.

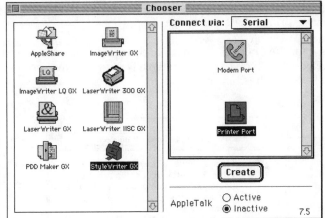

Figure 8-2:
The Chooser
DA for a
serial
printer.

My printer is a NewGen TurboPS/400p, a compact, inexpensive 400 dot-per-inch PostScript AppleTalk laser printer. I've had the NewGen for a couple of years and it's performed like a champ. At some point I plan to upgrade to a 600 or 800 d.p.i. printer, but it's not mission critical as long as the NewGen keeps chugging along.

In the past, I've avoided Apple printers as being too expensive, but lately they've become more competitive in both price and features. Who knows, my next printer could actually be an Apple.

Before you close the Chooser...

You're going to go through the rest of this exercise using my printer, an AppleTalk printer, as the example. If you have a different kind of printer — a serial, SCSI, or server — and you can print to your printer at this point (close the Chooser, open a document, and choose File⇨Print — if the document comes out of the printer, you can print to your printer), everything in the rest of the chapter should work the same for you.

The AppleTalk Active/Inactive radio buttons

OK. Here's something I can help you with. Should AppleTalk be active or inactive? My answer: Inactive unless you need it.

How do you know if you need AppleTalk? Well, for starters, if you're on a network and use File Sharing, you need it. If your printer is an AppleTalk-only printer (many are), you need it. If you're in neither of these situations, you probably don't need AppleTalk. There's no reason to keep it turned on if you don't need it.

If in doubt, just give it a try. You'll know if your printer works with AppleTalk inactive if your printer spits out a page.

OK. That's it for the Chooser. Go ahead and close it. You will see a warning that looks like Figure 8-3 if you haven't created a Desktop Printer for the printer that you just selected in the Chooser.

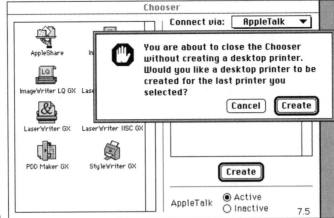

Figure 8-3: The first time you choose a printer after installing QuickDraw GX, the Chooser coaxes you to create a Desktop Printer.

If you see this dialog box warning, go ahead and click the Create button for now. I'll talk more about these mysterious Desktop Printers later in the chapter, and if for some strange reason you hate it, you can Trash it later.

Set: Setting Up Your Page with Page Setup

The hard part is done. Now you should be able to print a document quickly and easily. Right? Not so fast, bucko. Though you may not need it right this second, you need to know about the Page Setup dialog box.

Almost every program that can print a document has a Page Setup command on its File menu. Some programs call it Page Setup and others call it Print Setup. (Print Setup is the quaint, old-fashioned term, more popular in the System 6 era than today.) Either way, this dialog box allows you to choose paper type, page orientation, scaling percent, page flipping, and page inverting.

Depending on what program you use, the Page Setup dialog box may look like Figure 8-4 or Figure 8-5. Figure 8-4 is the Page Setup dialog box for ClarisWorks 2.1, which uses the older-style of Page Setup and Print dialog box. Figure 8-5 is the Page Setup dialog box for Apple's SimpleText, which uses the newer-style, GX dialog boxes. Newer programs will have the GX style; older programs will have one like Figure 8-4.

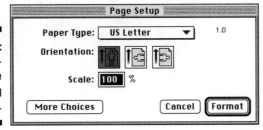

Figure 8-4:
An old-style
Page Setup
dialog box.

Figure 8-5:
A new GX-
style Page
Setup dialog
box.

For the rest of the chapter, I'll refer to the two kinds of Page Setup dialog boxes as old-style and GX-style.

You'll find the GX-style dialog boxes in programs that have been updated or upgraded to take advantage of at least some of QuickDraw GX's features (see Chapter 16). You should start seeing fewer and fewer of the old style and more and more of the new style as time passes. The newer style is more streamlined and easier to use, and it has a modular architecture, so you can take advantage of third-party printing extensions if you like. If all you seem to see are old-style Page Setup dialog boxes, don't worry — they both do about the same thing, although only the GX-style allow add-on printing extensions.

For what it's worth, I know of only one printing extension so far, Peirce Print Tools (it modifies the Print dialog box, not the Page Setup dialog box). I have yet to see a product that adds an icon to the GX-style Page Setup dialog box, but it's likely that someone will invent one soon.

Paper type

In either type of Page Setup dialog box, the objective here is the same — choose the type of paper currently in the paper tray of your printer, or choose the type of paper that you're about to feed manually.

In the old-style dialog box, you make this choice by using a combination of radio buttons for the more common choices or a pop-up menu (see Figure 8-6).

Figure 8-6:
In the old-style Page Setup dialog box, you choose your paper using either radio buttons or the pop-up menu.

In GX-style Page Setup dialog boxes, there is only a pop-up menu with no radio buttons (see Figure 8-7).

Figure 8-7:
Choosing paper in the GX-style Page Setup dialog box.

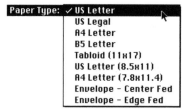

Choose the type of paper you plan to use for your next print job.

Page Setup dialog box settings remain in effect until you change them. So if you are printing an envelope this time, don't forget to change your Page Setup back to US Letter before trying to print to letter-size paper.

Page orientation

Page Orientation lets you tell the printer whether the page you're about to print is a portrait (letter, longways) or landscape (spreadsheet, sideways) oriented page (see Figure 8-8).

The old-style dialog gives you a portrait or clockwise-rotated landscape, as shown in Figure 8-9.

The GX-style Page Setup dialog lets you rotate landscape pages clockwise or counterclockwise (see Figure 8-10).

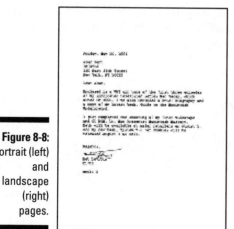
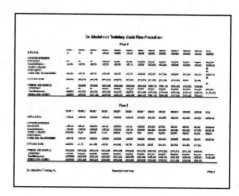

Figure 8-8:
Portrait (left) and landscape (right) pages.

Figure 8-9:
The old-style Page Setup dialog box only offers one landscape choice.

Orientation:

Figure 8-10:
The GX-style Page Setup dialog box gives you two landscape choices.

Orientation:

I suppose that the additional landscape choice is a good feature if you've got paper in the tray that has letterhead on one side or the other.

Wait a gosh darn second. How many people have landscape-oriented letterhead? Now how many have portrait-oriented letterhead? A lot more. So wouldn't a button that let you print upside down on letter-sized paper be a better idea?

When I get to the section about page flipping, you'll see how truly ludicrous this feature is. (OK, here's a hint: The two page flipping check boxes in the Page Setup Options dialog box can rotate your page a quarter or half-turn in either direction without using these Page Orientation icons at all!)

Reduce or Enlarge/Scale

This control, called Reduce or Enlarge in old-style Page Setup dialog boxes and Scale in GX-style dialogs (see Figure 8-11), lets you print pages bigger or smaller than their size on the screen.

Reduce or Enlarge: 🔼🔽 **100** %

Scale: **100** %

Just type a new value into the text entry box, replacing the number 100. In old-style Page Setup dialog boxes, you can also use the arrow buttons on the screen to change the value.

The range of scaling is 25–400%. If you try to enter a higher or lower number, your Mac will beep at you and change it automatically to the closest acceptable number. Nice touch.

Options: Page flipping and page inverting

But wait, there's more. The Page Setup dialog box offers two (three if you're using the old-style) additional options.

To get at them in the old-style dialog box, click the Options button and the More Options dialog box will appear, as shown in Figure 8-12.

In a GX-style dialog box, first click the More Choices button. Then, after the dialog box expands, click the LaserWriter Options icon in the icon list on the left side of the screen (see Figure 8-13).

Figure 8-12:
The old-
style Page
Setup
Options
dialog box.

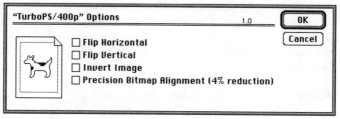

Figure 8-13:
The GX-
style Page
Setup
Options
dialog box.

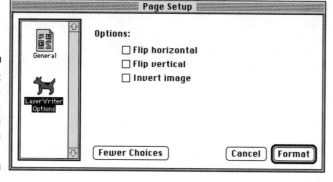

Page flipping

Flipping the page vertically or horizontally merely requires that you check the appropriate check box with either style of Page Setup dialog box.

Here's a case where the old style is definitely better than the new. In the old-style dialog, the dogcow on the miniature page reflects your choices (see Figure 8-14).

Figure 8-14:
The old-
style
Options
dialog gives
visual
feedback —
the dogcow
flips, inverts,
or shrinks.

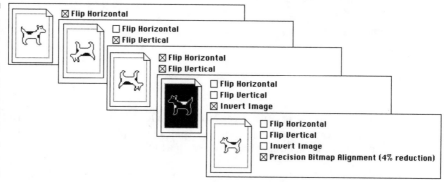

The GX-style dialog provides no visual feedback. The dogcow icon on the left (refer to Figure 8-13) doesn't flip or invert or anything.

So? I really don't get it. Why would Apple make the Page Setup Options dialog box harder to use?

Bring back the dogcow. Let Apple know how you feel:

Bring Back the Dogcow
c/o Apple Computer, Inc.
1 Infinite Loop, Mailstop 303-2E
Cupertino, CA 95014-6299

Personally, I can't believe that they crippled Clarus the dogcow. In fact, excuse me for a moment, I've got a letter to write.

OK. I'm back and I feel better.

Page inverting

Checking this option inverts your page, making light areas dark and dark areas light, like a photograph negative (see Figure 8-15).

Figure 8-15:
The page seen in Figure 8-8 with the Invert Image option in effect. The black prints as white and the white prints as black.

Note that this option will generally use a lot of toner or ink. And printing a large number of inverted pages could cause a laser printer to overheat or an inkjet printer to clog. So use this feature sparingly.

I suppose that the Invert Image option is useful for creating artsy effects or making negative images of documents that will be printed to film. I've never used it in the nine years I've used a Mac.

The tail of the dogcow

The dogcow has appeared in the Page Setup dialog box since time immemorial. He is a kind of unofficial Macintosh mascot. His name, they say, is Clarus. His bark, they say, is *Moof.*

As you can see in Figure 8-14, Clarus is more than just a mascot. He's an elegant way to give you visual feedback on your choices. Look at Figure 8-14. It works.

Precision bitmap alignment

This option helps bitmapped pictures print more clearly with less jaggedness. It is only available in the old-style Page Setup Options dialog boxes.

Checking this option reduces the size of your page to 96 percent, which will cause bitmapped pictures, which usually have a resolution of 72 d.p.i. (dots per inch), to print more cleanly. For a 300 d.p.i. printer, 96 percent is equal to 288 d.p.i.. Because 288 is evenly divisible by 72 (288 ÷ 72 = 4), there is less jaggedness than at 300 d.p.i., which can't be divided evenly by 72 (300 ÷ 72 = 4.1666666666667).

Why this option isn't included in the GX-style Page Setup Options dialog box is anyone's guess. Mine is that most graphics are not 72 d.p.i. bitmaps anymore; they're color PICT and TIFF files instead, files that don't always benefit from being reduced to 96 percent of their original size.

If you have a picture that prints with jagged edges and obvious stair-stepping, and your program has an old-style Page Setup dialog box, check this option and try printing the document again.

Print: Printing to Most Printers

Now we come to the final step before that joyous moment when your printed page pops out of the printer. It's the Print dialog box, and it's the last thing standing between you and your output.

While most of you will see Print dialog boxes that look like the ones in this chapter, others won't. The features in the Print dialog box are strictly a function of the program with which you're printing. Many programs choose to use the standard issue Apple dialog boxes as shown in this chapter, but others don't. If a feature isn't explained in this chapter, chances are it's a feature specific to the application that you're using and should be explained in that program's documentation.

The Print dialog box

Your printer is chosen in the Chooser. Your page is set up in Page Setup. If, up to this point, you haven't been working with a document that you want to print, find one now and open it because it's time to...

    1. Choose File⇨Print (Command-P).

One of the best things about the Mac is that Apple has published a set of guidelines that all Mac programs should use. Consistency between programs is one of the Mac's finest features. Notice how 99 percent of all programs have Open, Close, Save, Save As, Page Setup, Print, and Quit commands in their File menus and Undo, Cut, Copy, and Paste commands in their Edit menus. That's the kind of thing the Human Interface Guidelines recommend.

Apple's Human Interface Guidelines say the Print command should always appear in the File menu, which is good. The Human Interface Guidelines also say that the keyboard shortcut Command-P should be reserved for Plain Text (the way Command-B is often used for Bold or Command-I for Italic). This is bad.

Fortunately, software developers listened to Apple about the first item and ignored Apple about the second, so Command-P is almost always the shortcut for the Print command in the File menu.

Every so often you come across a program that doesn't follow these conventions, but I'd say at least 90 percent of commercial Mac programs put the Print command in the File menu and use Command-P for its keyboard shortcut.

The point is that there is a slight chance that Step 1 won't work for you. If the Print command is on a different menu, if there is no Print command, or the keyboard shortcut is anything but Command-P, you'll have to wing it.

Then write the software company a brief note mentioning that they *could* make things easier on everyone by putting the Print command in the proper place and using the generally agreed-upon keyboard shortcut.

Anyway, the Print dialog box appears. The old-style one looks like Figure 8-16; the GX-style one looks like Figure 8-17.

Figure 8-16:
The old-style Print dialog box.

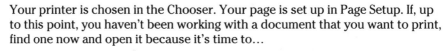

Figure 8-17:
The GX-
style Print
dialog box.

```
┌─────────────────────────────────────────────┐
│                   Print                       │
│  Print to:  [ TurboPS/400p  ▼]    1.0f2c12   │
│  Pages:  ● All                                │
│          ○ From: [        ]  To: [        ]   │
│  Copies: [1        ]                          │
│  ( More Choices )          ( Cancel ) (( Print )) │
└─────────────────────────────────────────────┘
```

Among the choices you make in both the old-style and GX-style Print dialog boxes are

- ✔ How many copies to print
- ✔ Which page numbers to print
- ✔ Automatic or manual feed paper
- ✔ Destination: printer or PostScript file

Only the old-style dialog offers a cover page option (which almost nobody uses). The GX-style dialog box adds several extra features:

- ✔ Print quality (only available for certain printers)
- ✔ Print time for delayed printing
- ✔ Alerts for starting and ending of a print job
- ✔ Paper matching

A wimpier version of delayed printing appears in the Print Monitor application in earlier versions of System 7.

Try pressing the Tab key and watching what happens. The active field will jump to each of the text fields in the dialog box in rotation. Shift-Tab makes the active field jump backward. In GX-style Print dialogs, the Tab key also selects the icon list on the left side of the window. When the list is selected, you can use the arrow (cursor) keys on your keyboard to select an icon. Try it; you'll like it.

Number of copies

The Print dialog box defaults to one copy in most applications, so you'll probably see a 1 in this field when the dialog box appears. Assuming that's the case, don't do anything if you only want to print one copy. If you want to print more than one copy of your document, select the 1 that appears in the Copies field and type in a new number (see Figure 8-18).

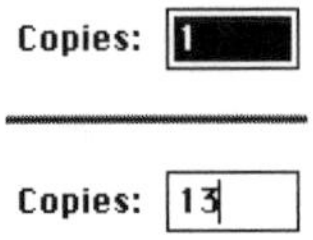

Figure 8-18:
To print 13
copies,
replace the
1 with 13

Copies: `1`

Copies: `13`

Pages to print

This option is easy. If you want to print your entire document, click the "All" radio button. If you only want to print a specific page or range of pages, type them in the "From" and "To" text entry boxes.

For example, say you have a ten-page document. You print the whole thing and then notice a typo on page 2. You fix the typo and then print only page 2 by typing a 2 in both the From and To fields, as shown in Figure 8-19.

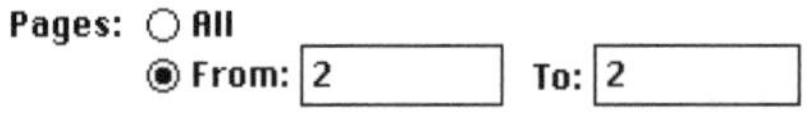

Figure 8-19:
Printing only
the second
page of a
document.

Pages: ○ All
　　　　● From: `2`　　To: `2`

You can type any valid range of pages into the To and From fields.

Cover page

This option is only available in old-style Print dialog boxes. Clicking the First Page or Last Page radio button (see Figure 8-20) adds a page at the beginning or end of your print job. The cover page contains your name, the program and document names, date and time, and printer name. In other words, a page that looks like this:

User: Bob LeVitus
Application: ClarisWorks
Document: Brief Bio (WP)
Date: Tuesday, August 14, 1994
Time: 3:54:02 AM
Printer: TurboPS/400p

Figure 8-20:
Cover page
options.

Cover Page: ⦿ No ○ First Page ○ Last Page

I may have used this feature once in the past ten years. I suppose if you're on a network sharing a printer, there might be a reason to waste trees by printing useless pages with hardly anything on them. But unless you must have a cover page, leave the No button selected and save a tree.

Paper source/feed

In the old-style dialog box, this option is called Paper Source, and your choices are Paper Cassette or Manual Feed. In GX-style dialog boxes, this option is called Paper Feed, and your choices are Automatic or Manual (see Figure 8-21).

What? You don't see it in your GX-style dialog? Oops. Click the More Choices button. In the GX-style Print dialog, you have to click the More Choices button to see the Paper Feed control option.

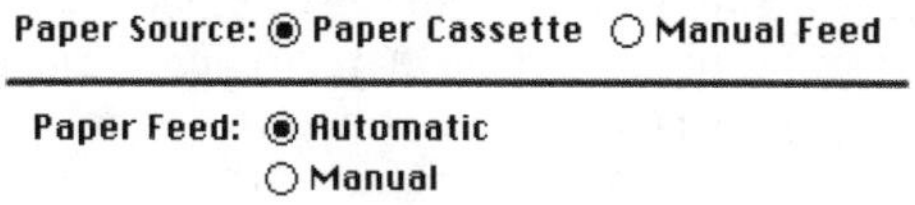

Figure 8-21:
Old-style
paper
source
selector
(top) and
GX-style
(bottom).

Paper Source: ⦿ Paper Cassette ○ Manual Feed

Paper Feed: ⦿ Automatic
             ○ Manual

Their names may be different, but they both work the same. If you plan to use the paper in your printer's paper tray, choose Paper Cassette (old-style) or Automatic (GX-style). If you plan to feed a single sheet, choose Manual Feed or Manual.

It's that simple.

Destination: printer or PostScript file

This control lets you choose to print to your printer or create a PostScript file on disk instead. When you click the radio button to create a PostScript file instead of printing to a printer, the Print button becomes a Save button. When you click the Save button, a standard Save dialog box appears, as shown in Figure 8-22.

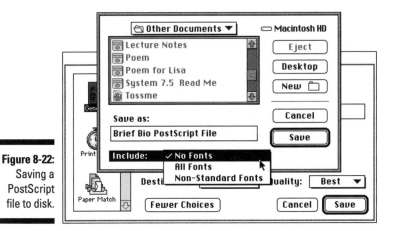

Figure 8-22:
Saving a
PostScript
file to disk.

Use the Save dialog box to navigate to the folder that you want to save the PostScript file in and then click the Save button to save the PostScript file to disk.

The pop-up menu allows you to include no fonts, all fonts, or only nonstandard fonts. Nonstandard fonts are fonts other than the ones the System 7.5 Installer installs. Choose whichever setting is appropriate for the recipient.

The safest bet is to include all fonts, just in case. The downside to this solution is that the PostScript file will be much larger than the original. For example, the Brief Bio file in Figure 8-22 uses 5K of disk space in its original form, saved as a SimpleText document. When saved as a PostScript file with all fonts included, it grows more than tenfold, requiring a whopping 80K of disk space.

Several things can inflate the size of the PostScript file. Including all fonts adds a lot of K. High-resolution images add a lot of K. And long documents use a lot of K. It's common for color artwork or page layout documents printed to disk as PostScript files to be larger than a high-density floppy disk. So if you plan to save a PostScript file to your hard disk and then copy it to a floppy disk, you may have to use a backup or compression utility to segment the file so that it will fit on several floppy disks.

Print quality (only available for certain printers)

The print quality option is only available in the GX-style Print dialog box after clicking the More Choices button.

Clicking the Fewer Choices collapses the dialog box back to its previous size.

Heck. There was only one choice on my menu, and if you have a laser printer, chances are there's only one choice on yours: Best or Best.

The PostScript saga

PostScript is the page description language invented by Adobe Systems and used almost universally in high-end imaging and typesetting devices, printers, imagesetters, color printers, and so on. Your Mac sends the PostScript commands to the printer and the printer prints that page at the highest resolution it can. The page will look the same—fonts, line breaks, and pictures appear in exactly the same place regardless of the resolution of the printer. You can proof on a 300 d.p.i. laser printer and then print the final, camera-ready copy on a 2540 d.p.i. imagesetter.

The entire process is transparent to you and is handled behind the scenes by the application that creates the document, the printer driver for your PostScript printing device, and the CPU inside your PostScript printing device (which is actually a small, single-purpose computer that interprets PostScript commands).

There are several reasons why you might want to create a PostScript file rather than print to the printer:

- The person you're giving the file to has a PostScript printer but not the application that you used to create the document. This is the most common reason.

- The person you're giving the file to has a PostScript printer but not the fonts that you used to create the document. This is the other most common reason.

- You're sending the file to a service bureau, and they asked for a PostScript file instead of a PageMaker/Quark/Illustrator/FreeHand/whatever file. This is the other other most common reason. Any combination of the three is also a good reason.

In order to print a PostScript file on a PostScript printer, the recipient must have two things: a PostScript printer and a utility capable of sending a PostScript file to the printer.

Though a PostScript file can be opened up in any word processor or text editor (it's nothing more than a long text file), it must be sent to the printer as PostScript commands, which requires a special application.

LaserWriter Utility is such an application and it comes free with System 7.5. It's not installed when you choose the Easy Install option, so it probably isn't on your hard disk yet. You can install it by choosing Custom Install in the QuickDraw GX Installer program and then installing only the QuickDraw GX Utilities.

PostScript files on disk can't be viewed on-screen, or at least they can't be viewed on-screen and look like what will print. After you save a file as PostScript, it can only be printed on a PostScript printer. If you try to open a PostScript file with a word processor, it looks like gobbledygook.

If you were to print this file from your word processor, you'd get a very long document covered in PostScript code, much like the figure to the right. If, on the other hand, you send this file to a PostScript printer using a PostScript downloading utility, you'll get a document that looks exactly like the one that was on your screen when you created the PostScript file.

```
ifelse
grestore
} Bdef
/AvoidLimit {
/@1 exch store
/@2 exch store
currentflat dup /@3 exch store
{
gsave
@2 load stopped not
{
@1 0 gt {
PointsAvailable @1 ge
{exit} if
} {exit} ifelse
} if
grestore
/@3 @3 2 mul dup setflat store
@3 1000 gt {exit} if
} loop
@3 1000 lt {
grestore
@3 setflat
@2 load exec
} {
pop
@2 ExecLimChk
} ifelse
```

I don't know why this option's there. Most laser printers don't allow draft printing. So if a laser printer is selected in the Chooser, you really don't have any choice when it comes to print quality.

Impact and inkjet printers do allow draft printing. If an impact or inkjet printer is selected in the Chooser, the Print quality option is available.

But even when the current printer is a laser printer, the pop-up menu appears in the GX-style dialog. It doesn't do anything, it just appears.

If your program uses the old-style Print dialog box, you only see a print quality option if the printer that you selected in the Chooser offers a choice of print quality (flip forward to Figure 8-27). Like the dogcow debacle, this is a case where the old seems better than the new.

Print time

This function is available in the GX-style Print dialog, and again, only if you've clicked the More Choices button.

If your program uses the old-style Print dialog, you still have some control over when it prints. See the section later in the chapter on Desktop Printers for the details.

To set a printing time for your document:

1. Click the Print Time icon in the icon list on the left side of the window.

   The print time options appear (see Figure 8-23).

2. Click the radio button next to your desired print time priority. Here's what the priorities mean:

   - The Normal option prints the document now. If other documents are in the print queue, it takes its place behind documents printed before it.

   - The Urgent option prints the document now but places it ahead of any documents in the print queue.

   - The Print at option lets you choose a specific time. When you click on its radio button, you can adjust the time and date (see Figure 8-24).

   - The Hold document option lets you prepare a document for printing but not print it at this time. (There's more about this feature in the section about Desktop Printers later in the chapter.)

Alerts for starting and ending

The two Show Alert check boxes, available after clicking More Choices and the Print time icon in the GX-style Print dialog box, tell your Mac to alert you via another dialog box (see Figure 8-25) when your print job starts and finishes.

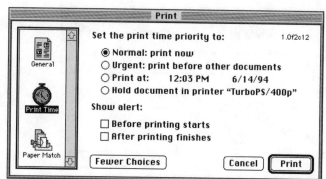

Figure 8-23:
The Print
Time
options.

Figure 8-24:
Use the
Print At
button to set
the date and
time.

⦿ Print at: **12**:19 PM ⬍   6/14/94

Figure 8-25:
The alerts
for the start
(top) and
finish
(bottom) of a
print job.

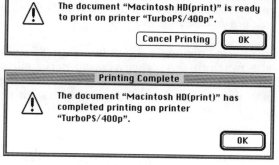

Paper Match

The Paper Match options, available after clicking More Choices and the Paper Match icon in the GX-style Print dialog box, give you additional control over how your document is formatted.

- ✔ The Print matching option matches the pages in your document to the pages in your printer.

- ✔ The Ignore matching option overrides the normal matching of pages and lets you choose a different paper source if one is available (see Figure 8-26).

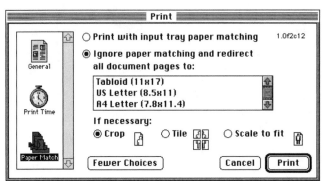

Figure 8-26:
Paper
Matching
options.

The If necessary buttons let you crop, tile, or scale the pages to fit the chosen paper source. They are only available if you choose the Ignore paper matching option.

Background printing

Background printing has been around for a while. It's the thing that allows you to continue using your Macintosh while it's printing. Wonderful stuff.

It didn't used to be that way. In the bad old days, in the pre-System 6 era when there was no background printing, you sat and waited until the printing was done before you could use your Mac again.

Under System 7.5, background printing is always turned on. You may notice your Mac feeling a little twitchy or jerky when a document is printing in the background. That's normal. Ignore it. After a while, you hardly notice it at all. And it's much better than the alternative — being unable to work until your print job is done.

Things you may see if you have a StyleWriter

StyleWriter and StyleWriter II users, as well as users of other inkjet printers, will see slightly different versions of the Print dialog box in programs that use old-style Print dialog boxes (see Figure 8-27).

As Figure 8-27 shows, all the controls have been previously discussed; they're just laid out a little differently here.

Figure 8-27:
The
StyleWriter
old-style
Print dialog
box.

StyleWriter GX		1.0	

Copies: **1**   Pages: ⦿ All ○ From: [   ] To: [   ]

Print Quality: ○ Best   ⦿ Normal   ○ Draft

Paper Source: ⦿ Sheet Feeder   ○ Manual

[**Print**]
[Cancel]
[Help]
[Options]

Oops. There is one other option: When you click the Options button (old-style Print dialog) or click the Options icon in the icon list (GX-style Print dialog), you'll find an option to Clean Ink Cartridge Before Printing. It's a good idea to choose this option every so often. See your printer manual for details on how often is often enough.

The Latest Thing: Desktop Printers

Desktop Printers are unique and a huge improvement over earlier printing schemes. When combined with GX-style Print and Page Setup dialog boxes, which more and more programs should have as time goes by, the new architecture for printing makes the entire experience easier.

What is a Desktop Printer anyway?

A Desktop Printer is an icon on your Desktop that represents a printer that is connected to your computer. To print a document, drag its icon onto a Desktop Printer (see Figure 8-28).

In Figure 8-28, when I release the mouse, Lecture Notes will print immediately.

Figure 8-28:
Printing
Lecture
Notes by
dragging it
onto the
Desktop
Printer.

Technically, SimpleText, the application that created the Lecture Notes document, will launch, the file will print, and then SimpleText will quit automatically.

There is no Print dialog box when you use a Desktop Printer; the Page Setup and Print dialog box settings last used with the document are used automatically.

What if SimpleText isn't available? If you have a translator that can open SimpleText documents, you'll see a dialog box where you can choose another application. If you don't have a compatible application or translator, you'll see an error message telling you that the document cannot be opened.

If you foresee that you may not have a compatible application for printing a document, read the section on PDD documents, which can be used as a workaround for any situation where you're not sure that the right application will be available for your document.

You create new Desktop Printers with the Chooser desk accessory. If you haven't already created one for your printer, try it right now. Here's how (assuming QuickDraw GX is installed and turned on):

1. Open the Chooser desk accessory.

2. Select your printer's icon on the left side.

3. Select a method of connecting from the pop-up menu and/or the icons on the right side.

4. Click the AppleTalk Active or Inactive button, depending on whether your printer requires AppleTalk.

5. If everything is configured correctly for your printer, click the Create button.

A printer icon will appear on your Desktop. In Figure 8-29, I've just created a Desktop Printer for my AppleTalk laser printer.

If you want to change the name of your printer to something more meaningful, use the aforementioned LaserWriter Utility program.

Using Desktop Printers

Before I talk about using Desktop Printers, I need to tell you why you should use Desktop Printers. Three words: It saves steps. Rather than open a document, choose File⇨Print, and diddle with the Print dialog box, you can drag that document onto a Desktop Printer and then go out for a Jolt cola or whatever. In a word, it's easy. No Print dialog box. No muss, no fuss. Just drag and drop, and in a few moments, paper starts popping out of your printer.

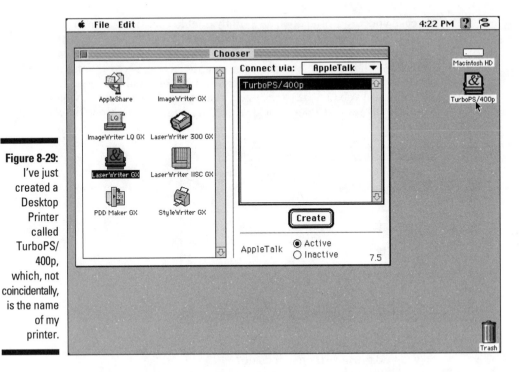

Figure 8-29:
I've just created a Desktop Printer called TurboPS/ 400p, which, not coincidentally, is the name of my printer.

So basically, you use Desktop Printers by dragging documents onto them. As long as the application that created the document is available, they'll be printed with no further ado.

But there's more to using Desktop Printers than just drag and drop. When you select a Desktop Printer (by single-clicking it), a new Printing menu appears in the menu bar, as shown in Figure 8-30.

To view the print queue, open the Desktop Printer (see Figure 8-31).

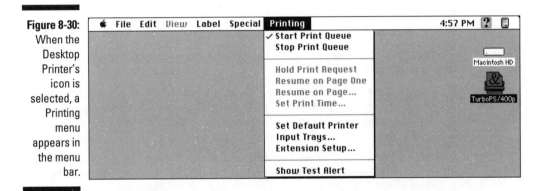

Figure 8-30:
When the Desktop Printer's icon is selected, a Printing menu appears in the menu bar.

(In case you forgot, you open an item by double-clicking its icon or by selecting its icon and choosing File⇨Open [Command-O]).

In Figure 8-31, there are four documents in the queue. Lecture Notes is currently printing. Poem is selected. Clicking the Hold button would suspend the printing of Poem until you choose to resume. Clicking the Remove button would permanently remove Poem from the printing queue, and it would never print.

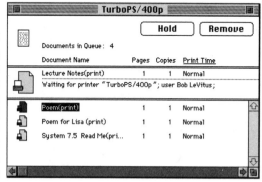

Figure 8-31:
Open the
Desktop
Printer icon
to see and
manipulate
the print
queue.

So what do the menu commands do?

- ✔ **Start and Stop Print Queue** are like the Play and Pause buttons on your VCR. To pause the printing process and be able to resume where you left off later, choose Stop Print Queue. To resume, choose Start Print Queue.

- ✔ **Hold Print Request** stops the selected print files from printing. This command is only enabled if a file — the currently printing file or a file from the queue — is selected in the Desktop Printer's window.

- ✔ **Resume on Page One** resumes printing of a file placed on hold, beginning with the first page, even if some pages had been printed before the file was placed on hold.

- ✔ **Resume on Page** resumes printing of a file placed on hold, beginning with the page number that you specify in a dialog box, even if some pages had been printed before the file was placed on hold.

- ✔ **Set Print Time** lets you defer the printing of a file in the queue until a specific time.

- ✔ **Set Default Printer:** This item should be checked if you want this Desktop Printer to be automatically selected when you print a document from within an application. If you only have one Desktop Printer, it's automatically selected as the Default printer.

- ✔ **Input Trays** displays a dialog box where you can specify the type of paper currently loaded in the paper tray or trays of the selected printer (see Figure 8-32). This command works in conjunction with the Paper Match option in GX-style Print dialog boxes.

✔ **Extension Setup** displays a dialog box so that you can choose printing extension files to use with this particular Desktop Printer (see Figure 8-33).

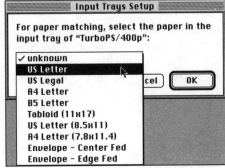

Figure 8-32: Choose the type of paper in the paper tray here and never worry about it again.

Figure 8-33: I've turned on Print Tools for use with this Desktop Printer.

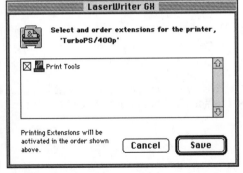

If I had more than one printing extension (I don't, at least I don't yet), I could change the order in which they are activated by dragging them in the list.

Because there's only one printing extension that I know of so far, Print Tools from Peirce Software, I'm not sure why you want to activate printing extensions in a specific order. Maybe we have printing extension conflicts to look forward to.

One last thing about these here Desktop Printers: If your program uses GX-style dialog boxes, you can choose your Desktop Printers from the pop-up menu in the Print dialog box! That's right, the Print To pop-up menu in GX-style Print dialog boxes gives you a choice of any printer that appears on your Desktop. No more trips to the Chooser! Hooray! This feature makes it almost painless to have a dedicated label printer, something I've considered but rejected in the past as too much trouble with all those trips to the Chooser.

Of course, you'll have to wait until your favorite programs are updated to include GX-style Print dialog boxes to take advantage of this feature.

Font Mania

To a computer user, a font is a typeface. Although professional typographers will scream, we'll go with that definition for now.

Each font looks different. There are tens of thousands of different fonts available for the Macintosh. You can buy single fonts and font collections anywhere you can buy software. There are also plenty of shareware and public domain fonts available from on-line services and user groups. Some people have thousands of them.

How to install fonts

This is a very short section. To install any font except a Type 1 font, drag it onto your System Folder. When you drag a font onto your System Folder, your Mac will ask if you want to place it in the Fonts folder. Click OK.

When you click OK, the deed is done and the font is installed. To remove a font, drag it out of the Fonts folder (which is in the System Folder). After a font is installed, it appears in the font menu of all your applications.

You can store fonts anywhere on your hard disk, but a font will only be available in an application if it's in the Fonts folder when you launch that application.

Type formats

There are four different kinds of fonts that you need to know about:

- *Bitmap* fonts, unlike other font formats, come in different sizes. You need a separate bitmap file for each size of the font that you want to diplay or print.

- *TrueType* fonts come with System 7.5. They are the Apple standard issue and are in wide use on Macs as well as on Windows machines. These fonts are scalabe, which means that there is only a single outline for the font, and your Mac makes it bigger or smaller when you choose a bigger or smaller font size in a program.

- *Type 1* fonts, sometimes referred to as PostScript Type 1 fonts, are the standard for desktop publishing on the Mac. There are tens of thousands of Type 1 fonts available (and not nearly as many TrueType fonts exist).

  Type 1 fonts usually come in two pieces, a bitmap font suitcase and a second piece, called a printer font. Some Type 1 fonts come with 2, 3, or 4 printer fonts. They usually have related names.

✔ *TrueType GX* is the latest font format. The advantages of TrueType GX are primarily features for the professional typographer such as alternate and swash character sets, true drawn small caps, old-style figures, extensive kerning and tracking capabilities, style variations, and more. There are also some features for non-pros, such as automatic character substitution, automatic hanging punctuation, even rebus functions that automatically substitute pictures and symbols for words.

Font advice in brief

You don't need to know a thing about font types. Really. When you get a font, just drag it (or all of its parts) onto your System Folder. If you're interested in all the ins and outs of the various kinds of fonts, see Sir Poguelot's *Macs For Dummies*.

Print to Disk PDD format

System 7.5 is the first version of the operating system to include a way to view and print documents without the original applications or fonts. QuickDraw GX includes a new type of document file format, known as a portable digital document (Apple calls it "print and view"; I call it "print to disk"). PDD documents can be opened, viewed, and printed on any other Macintosh with QuickDraw GX installed.

Even if the other Macintosh doesn't have the same application or typefaces that were used to create the document, the file is a perfect representation of the document, complete with all the graphics and typographic information of the original document. It looks like the original document on-screen and will look like the original document when you print it. No new software is required: Portable documents can be created using any of today's applications.

You can create a Desktop Printer to create PDD documents if you like.

1. Open the Chooser desk accessory (Apple menu⇨Chooser).

2. Click on the PDD Maker GX icon on the left.

3. Click the Create button.

A PDD Maker GX icon appears on your Desktop. To create a PDD document, drag any document onto the PDD Maker icon. A PDD version of the file will appear on the Desktop.

You can select a default folder for all future PDD documents by selecting the PDD Maker GX icon and then choosing Printing⇨PDD Maker Setup.

When you open a PDD document, you may see the translation dialog box asking if you want open the file in SimpleText. You do.

SimpleText is the only PDD viewer I know of, so it's a good idea to keep a copy on your hard disk even if you don't use it for anything else. I don't know of another program (yet) that can open QuickDraw GX PDD documents.

PDD documents, when viewed in SimpleText, look exactly the same as they would if you printed them out on a printer even if the Mac you're viewing them on doesn't have the fonts in the document or the application that created the document.

PDD documents aren't the first attempt at paperless paper. There have been many other products — Adobe Acrobat, No Hands Software's Common Ground, Farallon's Replica to name a few. None really caught on. On the other hand, they all cost money; PDD documents don't.

So will the PDD format become ubiquitous? Will programs other than SimpleText support it? Will Read Me files start coming in PDD format? Stay tuned. We'll know soon, or, as they say in the computer business, "RealSoonNow."

The 5th Wave   By Rich Tennant

"YES, WE STILL HAVE A FEW PROBLEMS WITH THE PRINTER. BY THE WAY, HERE'S A MEMO FROM MARKETING."

Chapter 9

File Sharing for the Rest of Us

Computer networking has a well-deserved reputation for being complicated and nerve-wracking. The truth is, there's nothing scary or complicated about sharing files, folders, and disks (and printers, for that matter) among computers. As long, of course, as the computers are Macintoshes.

If you have more than one computer, File Sharing is a must. It's fun, it's easy, and it's way better than SneakerNet[*].

[*]SneakerNet: Moving files from computer to computer on a floppy disk; i.e., walking from one computer to the other with floppy disk in hand.

Your Macintosh includes everything you need to share files and printers. Everything, that is, except the printers and the cables. So here's the deal: You supply the printers and cables, and I'll supply the rest.

This chapter is kind of unusual. You won't actually share a file until the next-to-the-last section. The first four sections provide an overview and tell you everything you need to know to share files successfully. Trust me, there's a method to my madness. If you try to share files without doing all of the required prep work, the whole mess becomes confusing and complicated — kind of like networking a pair of PC clones.

So just follow along and don't worry about why you're not sharing yet. You'll share soon.

What It Is

Macintosh File Sharing lets you use files, folders, and disks from other Macs on the network as easily as if they were on your own local hard disk.

Devices connected directly to your computers, such as hard disks or CD-ROM drives, are *local*. Devices you access (share) over the network are *remote*.

File Sharing also lets any computer on the network access (if you desire) *your* files, folders, and disks as easily as if they were on someone else's local hard disk.

Finally, File Sharing lets you *link* programs on your computer to programs on other computers. Why would you want to do that? You'll find out.

For our purposes, a network is two or more Macs connected by LocalTalk-compatible cables.

This chapter assumes you're working on a small network, the kind typically found in a home or small business.

There are also huge corporate networks, spaghetti-like mazes with thousands of computers and printers connected by cable, phone, infrared link, and ISDN, complete with confusing-sounding hardware such as routers and hubs and hublets and transceivers and netmodems. *That* kind of network *is* complicated even if the computers *are* Macs. And, of course, this chapter isn't about that subject.

If you're part of a mega-monstrous corporate network and you have questions about your particular network, talk to the P.I.C. (person in charge, a.k.a. your network administrator).

If you're trying to *build* one of these mega-networks, I regret to inform you that you'll need a book a lot thicker than this one.

Portrait of a LocalTalk network

This chapter describes my office network. It consists of two Macintoshes and a network laser printer. (By the end of the chapter, that's not all we'll be sharing, if you know what I mean.)

This two-person network is merely an example. In real life, a network can and often does have dozens or hundreds of users. Regardless of whether your network has two nodes or two thousand, the principles and techniques in this chapter will be the same.

My little network looks like what's shown in Figure 9-1.

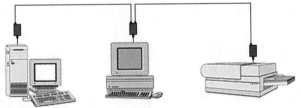

Figure 9-1:
Left to right:
Bob's Mac,
Lisa's Mac,
printer.

The black lines between the devices are cables; the gray box near each device is a connector. You need one connector for each device and enough cable to run between them. We happen to use the Apple LocalTalk Locking Connector Kits (part number M2068) and Apple Locking Cable Kits (M2066). LocalTalk connectors look like Figure 9-2.

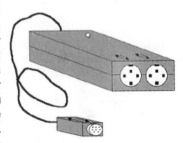

Figure 9-2:
The plug coming out the far side goes into the modem or printer port of your Mac. The two holes (ports) on the near side are where you connect your Apple Locking Cables.

We could have used PhoneNet connectors from Farallon instead of the Apple connectors. The big difference is that PhoneNet connectors use regular telephone cord from Radio Shack (or Target or anywhere) instead of expensive Apple Locking Cables. PhoneNet connectors are also less expensive than Apple LocalTalk connectors. Finally, PhoneNet connectors perform as well as (if not better than) Apple's LocalTalk connector.

So why did I use the Apple cables? Because they were here. They came with my loaner computer. If I were paying my own money, I'd have gone with PhoneNet instead.

When discussions of networks take place, you're likely to hear the words AppleTalk, EtherTalk, TokenTalk, and/or LocalTalk bandied about with great regularity. The first three are *protocols*, a kind of language networks speak. The last, LocalTalk, is a collection of wires and connectors. I'll talk more about this aberration in a moment.

Of the three network protocols, AppleTalk is the slowest but it's also the cheapest — it's free. Your Mac includes all the software and ports that you need to set up an AppleTalk network; all you have to provide are LocalTalk-compatible cables and connectors (such as the Apple or Farallon products mentioned earlier).

EtherTalk and TokenTalk are higher-speed protocols for using EtherNet or Token Ring networks. System 7.5 includes EtherTalk and TokenTalk software if you need it. Most Macs require an additional piece of hardware — an EtherNet or Token Ring adapter or transceiver — to use that type of network. (I say *most* because some recent Mac models include EtherNet ports.) To install EtherTalk or TokenTalk software, use the Custom Install option in the System 7.5 Installer.

LocalTalk is an aberration. It's not a protocol even though it sounds like one. In the old days, Apple referred to both the wires and the protocol as AppleTalk. Then one day a few years ago, Apple decreed that AppleTalk was a protocol and LocalTalk was the wires and connectors.

I suppose disassociating the protocol and the wires makes sense. LocalTalk sounds like a protocol (AppleTalk, EtherTalk, and TokenTalk) even though it's not. Anyway, LocalTalk refers to the physical connections that an AppleTalk network uses.

Got it? AppleTalk, EtherTalk, and TokenTalk are protocols, the languages that the network speaks. LocalTalk is a collection of physical parts — connectors (LocalTalk Connectors), ports (like the Modem or Printer port), and cables (LocalTalk-compatible cables) — that hook the machines together.

Getting turned on

The first thing to do is turn AppleTalk on. No network activity can take place until it is.

1. Open the Chooser (Apple menu⇨Chooser).

2. Click the Active radio button to turn on AppleTalk (see Figure 9-3).

3. Close the Chooser by clicking its close box in the upper-left corner or by choosing File⇨Close (Command-W).

Figure 9-3:
Click the
AppleTalk
Active radio
button in the
Chooser
desk
accessory.

AppleTalk   ◉ Active
             ○ Inactive   7.5

If you're using a LocalTalk network, that's all there is to getting started.

If you're using EtherTalk or TokenTalk, you also have to open the Network control panel and click the icon for the network connection that you want to use. If your network has multiple zones, you'll also have to choose a zone in the Chooser at this time.

Zones are mini-networks connected together. Once a network gets to about 50 users, zones help network managers keep network traffic under control. If you have zones, there's probably somebody around whom you can ask if you need to know more.

Sharing Setup

OK. AppleTalk is on and you're ready for a quick game of Name That Mac before you turn File Sharing on.

Get a network identity

1. Choose Apple menu⇨Control Panels⇨Sharing Setup.

   The Sharing Setup control panel will open (see Figure 9-4).

    ▭▭▭▭▭▭▭▭ Sharing Setup ▭▭▭▭▭▭▭▭

    🖥 **Network Identity**

        Owner Name: Lisa LeVitus
        Owner Password: ••••••
        Macintosh Name: Lisa's Macintosh

Figure 9-4:
The Sharing
Setup
control
panel for
Lisa's Mac.

    📁 **File Sharing**
                    ┌Status─────────────────────────────
        [Stop]   │ File sharing is on. Click Stop to prevent other
                    │ users from accessing shared folders.
                    └───────────────────────────────────

    🏠 **Program Linking**
                    ┌Status─────────────────────────────
        [Stop]   │ Program linking is on. Click Stop to prevent other
                    │ users from linking to your shared programs.
                    └───────────────────────────────────

2. Type in all three pieces of information in the Network Identity section at the top: your name, a password, and a name for your Mac.

> **Owner Name:** This one should be self-explanatory — type your name.
>
> **Owner Password:** Your password can be any combination of up to eight letters and numbers. When you click anywhere outside the Password field, the letters or numbers in your password will turn into bullets, as shown in Figure 9-4.
>
> **Macintosh Name:** Select a Macintosh name that's unique and memorable. *Lisa's Macintosh* is a better choice than *Mac*.

You can press the Tab key to move from field to field in the Sharing Setup control panel.

Turn File Sharing on

File Sharing and Program Linking each have a Stop/Start button. It's a toggle: If it's turned on, the button reads "Stop." If it's not turned on, the button reads "Start."

1. Turn File Sharing and Program Linking on if they're not on already by clicking each section's Start button.

The status of File Sharing and Program Linking appears to the right of their buttons, as seen in Figure 9-4. Both are presently on. How do I know? The buttons read Stop and the status boxes to the right of the buttons say that they're on.

You want your Sharing Setup control panel to look like Figure 9-4, so if File Sharing and Program Linking aren't on, click their Start buttons (click each one once). In other words, if *your* buttons say Start, click them. If they say Stop, don't click them.

Turn Program Linking on

Program Linking lets certain Macintosh programs exchange information with other programs. Programs implement linking in various ways and not all programs can link. See the documentation that came with your program to see if linking is supported and how to use it.

There is no penalty for turning Program Linking on, so I keep it running — even though I can't recall ever using it — in case I need it someday. You turn Program Linking on and off for each Mac in the Sharing Setup control panel; you allow or disallow its use by each user in the Users & Groups control panel (more on that subject in a second).

If Program Linking is not on (in the Sharing Setup control panel), other users on your network cannot program link even if the Allow user to link check box is checked in the user privileges window of the Users and Groups control panel.

Users and Groups and Guests (Oh My)

Macintosh File Sharing is based on the concept of users and groups. Shared items — disks or folders — can be shared with no users, one user, or many users. Access to items on your local hard disk is entirely at your discretion. You may configure your Mac so that nobody but you can share its folders and disks, so that only one other person can share its folders and disks, or so that many people can share its folders and disks.

People who share folders or disks are called *Users*.

Users

Before you can go any further, you need to create User identities for the people on your network. You perform this little task with the Users & Groups control panel. I'm going to demonstrate on Lisa's Mac:

1. Open the Users & Groups control panel (Apple menu⇨Control Panels⇨Users & Groups).

   A Users & Groups window appears, as shown in Figure 9-5. If you haven't previously created users or groups, you will see two user icons in the window.

   Owner: Lets you configure sharing for the owner of your Mac, the person whose name appears in the Owner Name field of the Sharing Setup control panel. This icon should have your name on it.

   <Guest>: Allows you to configure a guest account for your Mac.

   Notice how the File menu changes slightly when the Users & Groups window is the active window (see Figure 9-5). The New Folder command disappears, replaced by two commands: New User (Command-N) and New Group.

2. Choose File⇨New User to create a New User. (The Users & Groups window must be the active window.)

3. Rename the new user something meaningful.

4. Open the icon with your name on it (the name that you typed in the Owner Name field of the Sharing Setup control panel).

5. Open the new user's icon.

   You should see something similar to Figure 9-6.

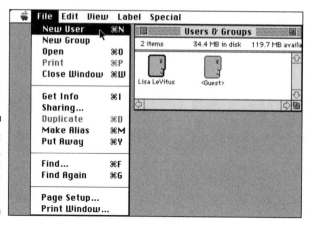

Figure 9-5:
The Users &
Groups
control
panel.

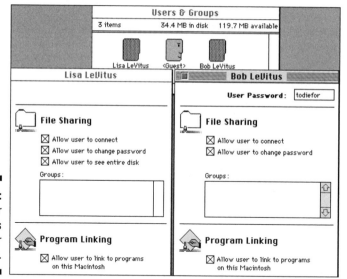

Figure 9-6:
The user
privileges
windows for
Lisa and me.

The check boxes determine what privileges each user has. Since Lisa and I are partners and want full access to each others' computers, we check all the choices.

- ✔ **Allow user to connect:** Lets the user connect to this Mac from a remote Mac (as long as he/she knows the proper password).

- ✔ **Allow user to change password:** Does what you expect. Lets that user choose his/her own password and change it at any time.

- ✔ **Allow user to see entire disk:** This choice is only available for the owner of the Mac. It means you can see every file on your hard disk if you connect from a remote machine.

When you create a new user, you have the option of assigning a password. If network security is unimportant to you (if only people you trust use the network), it's OK to leave the password field blank.

When you close a User window, you'll be asked if you want to save any changes you've made. The answer is usually yes. After you click the Save button, that user is said to be *registered.* In a forthcoming section, you'll learn about the three categories of users on the network; registered users are one of the three.

Groups

Groups are a convenient way to deal with a bunch of users at once. In the preceding example, say I want to create a group so that I can assign privileges to everyone at once: Lisa, our daughter Allison, who occasionally uses our computers, and myself. First, I open the Users & Groups control panel (Apple menu⇨Control Panels⇨Users and Groups). Next, I create a new user icon for Allison. Then I create a new group (File⇨New Group) and name it The LeVitus Family. Finally, I drag the icons for Lisa, Bob, and Allison onto the group icon. The group icon will invert as shown in Figure 9-7.

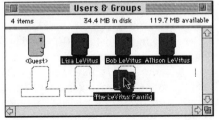

Figure 9-7:
Creating a
group.

If you open a group icon and look inside, you'll see icons representing the individual users. They appear in little picture frames (see Figure 9-8). Opening one of the little picture frame icons is the same as opening its user icon in the Users & Groups window. In other words, the little Bob LeVitus icon in the LeVitus Family group icon is like an alias of the bigger Bob LeVitus icon in the Users & Groups window.

Giving privileges to a group is the same as giving those same privileges to each individual member of the group.

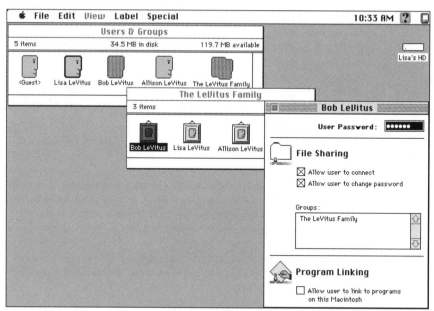

Be our guest

Notice the icon in your Users & Groups window called <Guest>. The <Guest> icon represents any users who haven't been assigned individual access privileges. Use this icon to allow or disallow guests to connect to your shared folders or disks. Even when Guest access is on, no one but you has access to any of your folders or disks until you specifically share them. I'll talk about assigning access privileges to disks and folders in the next section.

Removing Users or Groups

To remove a user or group icon from the Users & Groups window, drag it to the Trash. It's that simple.

Access and Privileges (Who Can Do What)

Now that File Sharing is on and you've created users and/or groups for your networks, you're ready to begin deciding who can use what.

Sharing a folder or disk

To share a folder or disk with another user, take the following initial steps.

1. Select the folder or disk icon and choose File⇨Sharing.

   The access privileges window for the selected item opens (see Figure 9-9).

2. Click the Share this item and its contents check box.

   If you want to be the owner of the folder, leave the Owner pop-up menu alone (more about ownership in a sec).

3. Choose a user or group from the User/Group pop-up menu (see Figure 9-10).

4. For the owner and each user or group, click in the appropriate See Folders, See Files, and Make Changes check boxes to assign access privileges for the folder or disk. Each of these access categories is explained in the following sections.

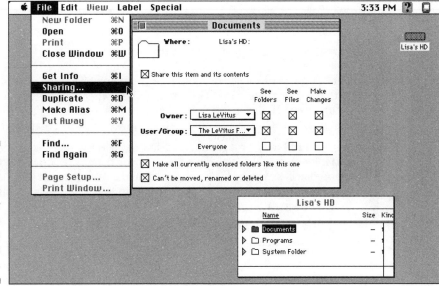

Figure 9-9:
The Access
Privileges
window
for the
Documents
folder on
Lisa's HD.

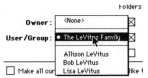

Figure 9-10:
Choose a
user or
group from
the pop-up
menu.

If what you see is different

You may not see exactly what's in Figures 9-9 and 9-10 on your screen. Well, of course you won't. I'd be surprised if *your* network's users were named LeVitus. But there are other differences you might see as well:

- ✔ If you've selected a folder inside another shared folder, the check box at the top will say, "Same as enclosing folder" instead of "Share this item and its contents."

- ✔ If you've selected a folder on another computer, the Owner and User/ Group areas are text entry boxes, not pop-up menus.

- ✔ If you've selected a folder that someone else owns, all the check boxes and their labels are dimmed.

Setting access privileges

The check boxes to the right of the Owner and User/Group pop-up menus control the access. In other words, they control who can use what and how much they can use it.

There are three categories of users on the network:

- ✔ **The Owner:** The owner of a folder or disk can change the access privileges to that folder at any time. The name in the Owner Name field of the Sharing Setup control panel is the default owner of shared folders and disks on that machine. Ownership may be given away (more on that in a moment).

- ✔ **A registered user or a group:** A registered user has access to shared disks and folders over the network as long as the user or group has been granted access by the folder or disk's owner. A registered user is any user who has an icon in the Users & Groups window. A group is nothing more than a bunch of registered users.

- ✔ **Everyone:** This category is an easy way to set access privileges for everyone at once — the Owner, registered users and groups, and guests.

Useful Settings for Access Privileges

Here are some ways you can combine access privileges for a folder or disk:

Allow everyone access

Figure 9-11 shows the settings that allow access for everyone on a network.

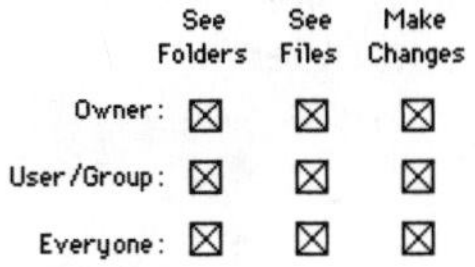

Figure 9-11:
Allow
everyone on
the network
to open, read,
and change
the contents
of this shared
disk or folder.

	See Folders	See Files	Make Changes
Owner:	☒	☒	☒
User/Group:	☒	☒	☒
Everyone:	☒	☒	☒

Allow nobody but yourself access

Figure 9-12 shows the appropriate settings that allow only the owner access.

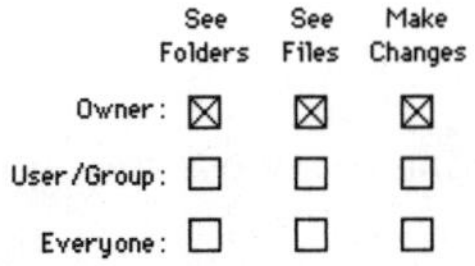

Figure 9-12:
Allow
nobody
except the
owner to
see or use
the contents
of this
shared disk
or folder.

	See Folders	See Files	Make Changes
Owner:	☒	☒	☒
User/Group:	☐	☐	☐
Everyone:	☐	☐	☐

Allow one person or one group access

Figure 9-13 shows the settings that allow only one person or group (in addition to the owner) access.

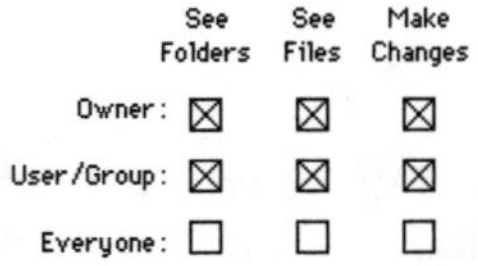

Figure 9-13:
Allow the
owner and a
single user or
single group to
see, use, and
change the
contents of this
shared disk or
folder.

	See Folders	See Files	Make Changes
Owner:	☒	☒	☒
User/Group:	☒	☒	☒
Everyone:	☐	☐	☐

Allow others to deposit files and folders without giving them access (a drop box)

Figure 9-14 shows the settings that allow users drop files or folders without being able to see or use the contents of the disk or folder.

Figure 9-14:
No users can
see or use the
contents of this
shared folder or
disk, but they
can deposit files
or folders of their
own in it.

```
                   See      See     Make
                 Folders   Files  Changes
         Owner:    ☒        ☒       ☒
    User/Group:    ☐        ☐       ☒
      Everyone:    ☐        ☐       ☒
```

After a file or folder is deposited in a drop folder, the dropper cannot retrieve it, as he or she doesn't have access privileges to see the items in the drop folder.

Read-only bulletin boards

Figure 9-15 shows the settings that allow everyone to access the contents of the disk or folder without the ability to make changes.

Figure 9-15:
Everyone can
open and read
the files and
folders in this
shared folder or
disk, but only the
owner can make
changes.

```
                   See      See     Make
                 Folders   Files  Changes
         Owner:    ☒        ☒       ☒
    User/Group:    ☒        ☒       ☐
      Everyone:    ☒        ☒       ☐
```

The two other privileges

There are two more check boxes at the bottom of the Access Privileges window. The "Make all currently enclosed folders like this one" option does exactly what its name implies. This feature is a fast way to assign the same privileges to many subfolders at once.

The second check box, "Can't be moved, renamed, or deleted," protects the folder (this check box doesn't appear in the Access Privileges window for disks) from being moved, renamed, or deleted by users whose privileges would otherwise allow them to move, delete, or rename that folder.

The Actual Act of Sharing

OK. This is the moment you've all been waiting for. You've done everything leading up to the big moment: Sharing is set up; users & groups are registered; and access privileges are assigned.

If you've been following along, you know how to do all of the prep work and more. So make sure that you've shared at least one folder on your hard disk and you have full access privileges to it. Now go to another computer on the network and I'll show you how to access that folder remotely.

Interestingly, File Sharing doesn't have to be turned on on the other machine. A Mac can access shared files over the network even with File Sharing turned off. If File Sharing is turned off, you can't create users & groups or assign access privileges, but you can access a remote shared disk or folder if you have been granted enough access privileges by its owner, even with File Sharing turned off on your Mac.

If File Sharing is turned off, though, others won't be able to access your disk or folders, even if you've shared them previously.

Connecting to a shared disk or folder

In my example, I've been showing Lisa's Mac and hard disk so far. Now I'm going to move over to my own Mac, and I'm going to access the Documents folder on Lisa's Mac, which Lisa owns but has granted me full access to (see Figure 9-16).

Figure 9-16:
The Documents folder on Lisa's HD. I have full privileges, so I will be able to access this folder from my (remote) computer.

			Documents			
	Where:		Lisa's HD :			
☒ Share this item and its contents						
				See Folders	See Files	Make Changes
Owner:	Lisa LeVitus ▼			☒	☒	☒
User/Group:	Bob LeVitus ▼			☒	☒	☒
	Everyone			☐	☐	☐
☒ Make all currently enclosed folders like this one						
☒ Can't be moved, renamed or deleted						

On my computer, I choose Apple menu⇨Chooser and then click on the AppleShare icon.

AppleTalk, of course, is active on my machine. If it's not, I won't be able to use the network. While File Sharing doesn't have to be turned on for me to access a remote disk or folder, AppleTalk does.

I select Lisa's Macintosh in the Chooser's file server list and then click OK (see Figure 9-17).

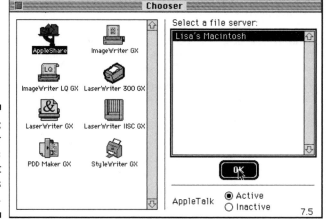

Figure 9-17:
The Chooser on my Mac as I connect to Lisa's Mac.

After I click OK, the Connect dialog box appears. Because I'm the owner of this Mac, my name appears in the Name field. I type in my password and then click OK (see Figure 9-18).

Figure 9-18:
The Macintosh owner's name appears automatically. Type the correct password, click the OK button, and you're connected.

I now encounter another dialog box where I can select one or more items to use on my Mac. Because that single folder, Documents, is the only file on Lisa's Mac that has been shared with me, it's the only one that appears in Figure 9-19.

Figure 9-19:
The last dialog box before Documents appears on my Desktop.

I click OK and the Documents icon appears on my Desktop, as shown in Figure 9-20.

Figure 9-20:
The Documents icon, which represents a shared folder from Lisa's hard disk, appears on my Desktop.

The unique icon for the Documents folder clearly indicates that this is a shared folder accessed over the network. Those are, of course, wires coming out the bottom of the icon. This icon is what you see whenever a remote disk or folder is mounted on your Desktop.

If there are multiple items in the item selection dialog box (refer to Figure 9-19) and you want to select more than one, click on the first item and then hold down the Shift key and click once on each item that you want to add to the selection. After you've selected all the items that you want to use, click the OK button and they'll all be mounted on your Desktop.

Connecting automatically at startup

If I wanted the Documents folder, which is on Lisa's Macintosh, to appear automatically on *my* Mac's Desktop every time I turn it on, I would click the check box to the right of Documents in Figure 9-19.

I only expect to use this folder occasionally, so I won't.

Reopening the remote Documents folder quickly and easily

Now that I've mounted the Documents folder on my Desktop for the first time, I can make it easier to use in the future by creating an alias for it. Next time I want to use the Documents folder, I open the alias and the Connect dialog box appears. I type in my password and the folder appears (is mounted) on the Desktop. No Chooser; no other dialog boxes; no muss and no fuss.

 If you use remote folders often, mount each one on your Desktop, create an alias for each one, and put the aliases in a folder called Remote Folders. Move the Remote Folders folder to your Apple Menu Items folder, and you'll be able to mount these remote folders on your Desktop almost instantly.

Getting on your own computer from a remote computer

Because Lisa is the owner of her computer, if she walks over to my computer, she can mount her entire hard disk on my Desktop. She checked the Allow user to see entire disk check box in her owner window in the Users & Groups control panel. In other words, after she opened the icon representing herself in her Users & Groups control panel, she gave herself the privilege of seeing her entire disk remotely by checking the appropriate check box.

Anyway, if Lisa's at my Mac and wants to use her hard disk, she'd do almost the same things that I did to mount the Documents folder on my Desktop, with one small difference.

Here's how she'd do it: First, she'd walk over to my Mac. Then she'd select Apple menu⇨Chooser. In the Chooser, she'd select her Macintosh from the list of servers. Now, here's where the procedure is a little different. When the password dialog box appears, it has the owner's name in it, as shown back in Figure 9-18. She would delete the "Bob" part and replace it with "Lisa." Then she would click OK. After typing her password, instead of seeing a list of folders, she'd see her hard disk in the next dialog box (see Figure 9-21).

If Lisa had logged on as a guest or used my name and password, she'd have seen the Documents folder instead of her hard disk in the dialog box in Figure 9-21.

Figure 9-21:
Lisa is
sitting at
my Mac.
When she
connects to
her Mac,
her entire
hard disk is
available to
her, not just
folders that
she shares
with guests
and me.

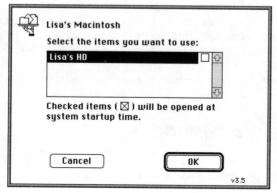

Lisa's Macintosh

Select the items you want to use:

| Lisa's HD | ☐ |

Checked items (☒) will be opened at system startup time.

[Cancel]   [OK]

v3.5

Here's a great tip for Lisa. If she plans to use her hard disk while working at my Mac, there's an even easier way. Before she leaves her computer, she should make an alias of her hard disk and copy it to a floppy disk.

When she gets to my computer, all she has to do is insert that floppy and open the alias of her hard disk. The Connect dialog box will appear, and as long as she types the correct password, her hard disk will mount on my Desktop. Neat.

This technique is often called office-on-a-disk. If you work in a largish office and find yourself trying to connect to your hard disk from someone else's computer, carry one of these office-on-a-disk floppies with you at all times.

Disconnecting from a shared folder or disk

When you finish using the shared disk or folder, close any open files or programs on the shared disk or folder and then disconnect using one of these three methods:

- ✔ Select the shared disk or folder icon and choose File➪Put Away (Command-Y).

- ✔ Drag the shared disk or folder icon to the Trash.

- ✔ If you're done working for the day, choose Special➪Shut Down. Shutting down automatically disconnects you from shared disks or folders.

A Few Other Things You Ought to Know

That's the gist of it. But there are still a few aspects of File Sharing you might want to know about. For example, how do I know who is using the network? How do I change my password? How can I unshare a folder or disk?

The answers to these and other fascinating questions await you. Read on.

Monitoring File Sharing

When File Sharing is on, you can see what's going on out on the network with the File Sharing Monitor control panel (see Figure 9-22).

Figure 9-22:
The File Sharing Monitor control panel tells you what's happening on the net.

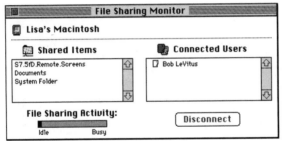

A list of shared folders and disks appears on the left, and a list of connected users appears on the right. To disconnect a user at any time, select his or her name in the list and then click the Disconnect button. A dialog box will appear asking you how many minutes until the selected user is disconnected (see Figure 9-23).

Figure 9-23:
Type in a number and click OK; the user will be disconnected after that many minutes have passed.

Type in a number and click OK. When that amount of time has passed, the user will be disconnected. The shared disk or folder icon will become grayed out on the user's Desktop, indicating that the item is no longer available. The disconnected user will see a dialog box saying that he or she has been disconnected (see Figure 9-24).

Figure 9-24:
If you see this dialog box, you've been disconnected.

"Lisa's Macintosh"

You were disconnected from the file server [10:07 AM on 6/24/94].

OK

In the dialog box shown in Figure 9-23, if you set the number to zero and click OK, the user is disconnected immediately.

The File Sharing Activity monitor at the bottom of the screen tells you how much activity there is on the network. If yours is always up in the busy range, you may need to rethink your network strategy.

AppleShare file servers and PowerTalk collaboration servers can ease network traffic — so can hardware add-ons like hubs and routers. If your network appears busy in the File Sharing Activity indicator most of the time, you should beef up your network with one or more of the aforementioned items.

Changing your password

You can change your password at any time.

1. Open the Sharing Setup control panel (Apple menu⇨Control Panels⇨Sharing Setup) from your own computer.

2. Delete your old password.

3. Type in a new password.

4. Close the Sharing Setup window.

Your new password is now in effect.

Unsharing a folder or disk

To unshare a folder or disk you own, merely select it, choose File⇨Sharing, and uncheck the Share this item and its contents check box. The folder or disk becomes inaccessible over the network as soon as you close the Sharing window.

Chapter 10

How to Manage Memory and Other Seemingly Complicated Arcana

• •

In This Chapter

▶ Running out of RAM

▶ The Memory control panel

▶ The Disk Cache

▶ Virtual memory

▶ 32-bit addressing

▶ Modern Memory Manager

▶ The RAM disk

▶ Memory-related troubleshooting

• •

*T*he Mac lets the user — that's you — get along fine without knowing much about memory. Many users go through their entire lives with a Macintosh without knowing anything more than "it has 5 megs."

On the other hand, a working knowledge of the way your Mac's memory works can be invaluable in getting the most out of your Mac.

In other words, you don't have to know this stuff, but it's likely to come in handy someday. It's not particularly complicated nor particularly technical, so it wouldn't hurt to just jump right in.

Baby, Baby, Where Did Our RAM Go?

RAM is the TLA (three-letter acronym) for Random Access Memory. RAM is the special kind of memory in which your System software and applications live while your Mac uses them. System software (including extensions and control panels) loads into RAM on startup; applications load into RAM when you open them.

Your Mac probably came with 4, 5, or 8 megabytes of RAM. Depending on what you want to do, that amount may or may not be enough.

If you never plan to do anything more than use a single program that doesn't require a massive amount of RAM (that is, not Photoshop or PageMaker, both of which require at least 5MB of RAM) and never plan to use two or more programs at once, a 4 meg Mac may let you squeak by.

If you have 4 megs of RAM or less, read this chapter and Chapter 15 very, very carefully. The less RAM you have, the more important it is to manage it wisely.

If you want to keep a word processor, a calendar, a phone book, and a graphics program all open at the same time, an 8MB Mac may not even have enough RAM for you.

The simple rule is that the more stuff you want to run at once, the more RAM you're gonna need. If you have one or more programs that require a lot of RAM, you'll need enough RAM to run them and your System software simultaneously. You'll also need even more RAM if you want to keep several programs open at the same time.

Go ahead: add more RAM

You can add more RAM to most Mac models easily and relatively inexpensively (about $35–50 per megabyte today, but prices change quickly, so check around before you buy).

If you are so inclined, you can install RAM yourself with a minimum of technical skills. Memory comes mounted on cute, little printed circuit boards called SIMMs (fancy acronym for Single Inline Memory Module) that snap into little printed circuit board-holders inside your Mac. Installing RAM yourself will, of course, void your warranty. (On the other hand, if your Mac is more than 366 days old, it doesn't have a warranty.)

If you are technologically challenged and never want to lift the lid off your Mac (I don't blame you),

you can have RAM installed for you at any Apple dealer. But this service costs significantly more than doing it yourself.

I'm a klutz. I don't repair things around the house. But I've managed to install RAM upgrades in several Macs without incident. It's not terribly difficult, and it doesn't require soldering or other specialized skills. If you can turn a screwdriver, you can probably handle the task.

If you do decide to go the do-it-yourself route, I recommend TechWorks (800-234-5670 or 512-794-8533). Their prices are fair; their support and manuals are superlative; and they offer a lifetime guarantee on every RAM chip they sell.

Essentially, you should remember that three things use RAM:

- ✔ The System and Finder
- ✔ Extensions and control panels
- ✔ Applications

The first, the System and Finder, you have no control over. That dynamic duo is going to chew up about 1,400K of RAM no matter what you do.

You do, however, have control over extensions, control panels, and applications, and you use this control to make the most of the memory you have.

OK. RAM is used *primarily* for three things. There's other stuff — PRAM (parameter RAM), debuggers, rdev and scri files — that could be rattling around in there, using up small amounts of your RAM. But their impact on the amount of RAM that you have to work with is negligible, so they're not important to this discussion. Besides, most people will never need to know what a scri file is.

Sigh. OK, just this once. A *scri file* is a special kind of extension that automatically loads before all other extensions. The old System Update 3.0 that you should have been using with System 7.1 (but don't need with System 7.5) is a scri file.

System software memory theory: where some of the RAM goes...

To observe how RAM is being used on your Mac, look at the About This Macintosh window (Apple menu⇨About This Macintosh).

Figure 10-1 shows a Mac running System 7.5. No extensions or control panels are loaded. The System software uses 1,356K of RAM.

How do you get System 7.5 alone to load, without loading any extensions or control panels? Easy. Hold down the Shift key during startup until you see the "Extensions Off" message on the Welcome to Macintosh screen. Memorize this tip; it's a good thing to know. If you run into memory problems (that is, you see error messages with the word *memory* in them), starting up with Extensions off will allow you to run your Mac so that you can pinpoint problems related to any of your control panels or extensions.

Figure 10-1:
System 7.5 alone, with no extensions or control panels loaded, uses 1,356K of RAM on this Mac.

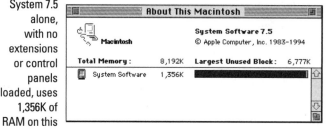

On this 8MB Mac, after the System software eats up its share of RAM, 6,777K of RAM is available for extensions, control panels, and applications.

Your mileage will vary and you'll probably see a slightly different number on your Mac. Don't worry about it. The System software for each Mac model requires slightly different amounts of RAM.

When I restart my Mac the old-fashioned way, without holding the Shift key down, the extensions and control panels load as usual, and the System software expands to take up 5,737K (see Figure 10-2).

Figure 10-2:
System 7.5, with its full comple-ment of extensions and control panels loaded, uses 5,737K of RAM.

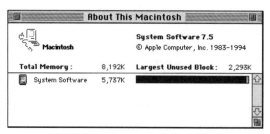

This situation often causes confusion. When you look at the bar for System software in the About This Macintosh window, it displays not only the RAM used by your System and Finder but also the RAM used by your extensions and control panels that load at startup.

There's no way to tell how much of that bar is the System and Finder and how much is the extensions and control panels. The important thing is that the System software bar tells you how much combined RAM the System, Finder, extensions, and control panels use.

If you're good at math, you can figure out that loading the full complement of System 7.5 extensions and control panels costs 4,381K of RAM.

5,737K – 1,356K = 4,381K.

On my 8-meg Mac, I'm left with only 2,455K available for applications.

You can free up more RAM for applications by turning off extensions and control panels in the Extensions Manager control panel. Read Chapter 15 for details on exactly how much RAM each extension and control panel uses and what happens if you turn them off.

Application memory theory: where the rest of the RAM goes

If you haven't read the first part of Chapter 4, which explains the "About This Macintosh" item in the Apple menu and provides you with your first glimpse of memory management, you should do so now. There's a very important technique there — how to adjust Application memory — and I'm not going to waste space repeating it.

Sigh. I guess I have to repeat at least part of it. This *is,* after all, a chapter about memory management.

When you launch an application, the application grabs a chunk of memory (RAM). You can see how big a chunk of RAM it grabs by going back to the Finder after you launch it and choosing Apple menu⇨About this Macintosh (see Figure 10-3).

Figure 10-3:
ClarisWorks
grabs 950K
of RAM.

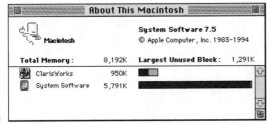

The beginning of Chapter 4 has a lengthy discourse on changing the amount of RAM a program grabs when you launch it and why you may want to do so. If you weren't paying attention, you diddle a program's RAM usage by selecting its icon and choosing File⇨Get Info or using the keyboard shortcut, Command-I (see Figure 10-4).

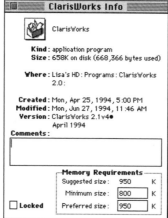

ClarisWorks Info

ClarisWorks

Kind: application program
Size: 658K on disk (668,366 bytes used)

Where: Lisa's HD : Programs : ClarisWorks 2.0 :

Created: Mon, Apr 25, 1994, 5:00 PM
Modified: Mon, Jun 27, 1994, 11:46 AM
Version: ClarisWorks 2.1v4● April 1994
Comments:

Memory Requirements
Suggested size : 950 K
Minimum size : 800 K
Preferred size : 950 K

☐ **Locked**

Figure 10-4: ClarisWorks grabs 950K of RAM, its Preferred size, when opened.

Here's a brief review of what these memory sizes mean:

- ✔ The Suggested size is the size the manufacturer of the program recommends. In most cases, the Preferred size should be set to at least this amount. You can't change the Suggested size.

- ✔ The Minimum size is the smallest amount of memory the program needs to run. It is usually (but not always) slightly smaller than the Suggested size.

- ✔ The Preferred size is the amount of memory the application requests (and will get) as long as there is that much memory available when the application is launched. Your Mac doesn't let you set the Preferred size lower than the Minimum Size.

When you try to open an application, if the available RAM (Largest Unused Block in the About This Macintosh window) is less than the Preferred size but more than the Minimum size, the program launches. But its performance may be degraded, or you may encounter memory-related errors.

In summation

Make sure that you're clear on this theory stuff before you move on to execution. RAM is used by three things: System software, extensions and control panels, and applications.

You can make more RAM available for your programs by holding down the Shift key at startup, which disables all extensions and control panels.

You can fiddle with the amount of RAM that a program uses in its Get Info box.

Everything else you need to know about memory involves the Memory control panel, which you're about to meet.

The Shift key at startup technique is wonderful, but it's absolutely absolute. Either your control panels and extensions are on, or they're off. The Shift key provides no way to turn some off and leave others on. When they're all off, you lose the ability to share files, to use Desktop Printers, and much more.

That's why Apple provides the Extensions Manager control panel. You can use it to selectively disable and enable control panels and extensions. As I keep saying, this dandy tool is discussed in Chapter 15, a chapter designed to help you figure out which extensions and control panels you truly need. You'll find out how much precious RAM and disk space each control panel and extension uses, and you'll also learn how to get rid of the ones that you don't want (both temporarily and permanently).

In other words, Chapter 15 may be the most useful chapter in this book.

Memories Are Made of This: The Memory Control Panel

You configure memory-related functions for your Mac in the Memory control panel, which is in the Control Panels folder. You can open the Memory control panel by choosing Apple menu⇨Control Panels⇨Memory.

Here's a look at the Memory control panel's components, which are for the most part unrelated.

Cashing in with the Disk Cache

The *Disk Cache* (pronounced "cash") is a portion of RAM set aside to hold frequently used instructions. In theory, if you set a reasonably sized cache, say 5 percent of your total RAM, your Mac should feel like it's running faster. In reality, many people can't tell the difference.

The first important thing to know is that the size of the Disk Cache is added on to the RAM used by the System software. Therefore, memory assigned to the Disk Cache is not available for programs to use. In Figure 10-2, the System software is using 5,737K of RAM. The Disk Cache is set to 32K.

If you increase the size of the Disk Cache to 1,024K (see Figure 10-5) and restart the Mac, the System software balloons to 6,807K (see Figure 10-6).

Figure 10-5:
The Disk
Cache is
increased
to 1,024K
in the
Memory
control
panel.
See the
results in
Figure 10-6.

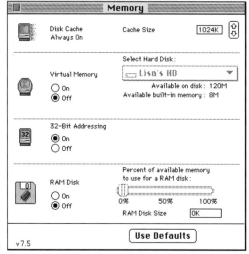

Figure 10-6:
System
software
uses 1,024K
more RAM
than before
(compared
to Figure
10-2).

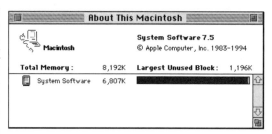

Those of you who caught the math thing a few pages ago have certainly noticed that the numbers here don't add up correctly. 6,807 – 5,737 = 1,070, not 1,024.

The vagaries of RAM usage are well known. The amount of RAM System software uses changes from hour to hour, seemingly at random. I opened About This Macintosh three times today and got three different numbers ranging from a low of 6,807 to a high of 6,852.

In other words, RAM usage is not a precise science. Take all numbers in this chapter with at least a grain of salt.

How to set your Disk Cache

If RAM usage is an imprecise science, telling you how to set your Disk Cache is imprecise science *fiction*. Bearing that in mind, here's some excellent advice on figuring out the best setting for you.

As I said, some people don't notice the speed improvement provided by a larger Disk Cache. So first you must determine whether you can tell the difference in speed by cranking the Disk Cache size way up. Here's how to crank up the Disk Cache size:

1. Choose Apple menu⇨Control Panels⇨Memory to open the Memory control panel.

2. Click the up-arrow key for the Cache Size repeatedly until it won't increase any further (see Figure 10-7).

Figure 10-7:
Click the up-arrow key repeatedly until it won't go any higher and then click the down-arrow key two times.

3. Click the down-arrow key two or three times (so you leave enough RAM available to open an application).

4. Restart your Mac.

   You now have a huge Disk Cache, larger than you would actually use in real life. But I want you to exaggerate its effects for this experiment.

   When your Mac gets back to the Finder, proceed to Step 5.

5. Open the System Folder, noticing how long it takes for the window to appear completely.

6. Close and then reopen the System Folder window, again noticing how long it takes to appear on-screen.

The difference in speed (the second time the System Folder should have opened noticeably faster) is a result of the increased size of the Disk Cache.

You should also notice a speed improvement when you scroll through documents. Launch your favorite application and scroll around a document for a while.

If you don't notice any speed improvement in the Finder or in your favorite application, return to the Memory control panel, set the Cache Size to its lowest setting (32K), and be done with it.

If you notice (and like) the speed improvement, you still have a little more work to do. As you may remember, memory assigned to the Disk Cache is not available for applications. So you want to set the Disk Cache to the lowest possible number that still feels fast to you.

To lower the Disk Cache, repeat the preceding steps, lowering the Disk Cache one click each time. Restart after each change. Then close and reopen the System Folder two times and note the difference in speed the second time. When you begin to notice sluggishness when closing and opening or when scrolling through documents, then you've discovered your threshold. Return to the Memory control panel, increase the Cache Size one click, and be done with it.

The old rule-of-thumb about the Disk Cache is to allow 32K per megabyte of RAM. I've always thought that this suggestion was bunk, as many people can't tell the difference between a 32K Disk Cache and a 1,024K Disk Cache. And why should they waste a megabyte of perfectly good RAM? So I've always encouraged people to try the experiment I've just described and see for themselves.

That said, I have to admit that the Disk Cache in System 7.5 feels a lot zippier than earlier Disk Caches. On a Quadra 605 with 8MB of RAM, I notice a definite speedup with the Disk Cache set to 256K. Under System 7.1 the speedup doesn't feel as great.

For what it's worth, I'm leaving mine set to 256K for now and may even bump it up to 384K. That only leaves me about 2MB of RAM for applications, but I'm willing to trade a couple of hundred K of RAM for the speedup. Your mileage may vary.

It's not real: it's Virtual (Memory)

Virtual Memory allows you to use spare hard disk space in place of RAM. If it sounds too good to be true, it is. For the most part, Virtual Memory is a loser.

The truth is that you should have enough real RAM to use your favorite application or applications (if you like to keep more than one program running) comfortably. You should have enough real RAM to open all the documents and programs you need.

If you can't afford that much RAM, pop for a copy of Connectix RAM Doubler, which does what Virtual Memory does but does it better and faster for about $50 (see the "RAM Doubler" sidebar). If you can't manage to find $50, you're stuck with Virtual Memory.

What's so bad about Virtual Memory? About the only thing it has going for it is that it's free. I suppose it could come in handy in an emergency, when you absolutely, positively have to open another application or document but don't have enough RAM installed.

But I wouldn't use it very often. Why not?

- Virtual Memory is piggishly slow. If you don't have enough real RAM to open a program, you can open the program using Virtual Memory, but the program works more slowly. Sometimes MUCH more slowly.

- Virtual Memory puts a big invisible file on your hard disk. Very big. The size of the invisible file is equal to the amount of Virtual Memory in use PLUS all the installed RAM! So if you have an 8MB Mac and want to make it think it has 16MB (see Figures 10-8 and 10-9) using Virtual Memory, you'll have an invisible 16MB file on your hard disk taking up space (see Figure 10-10).

  Of course, I had to know that the file was named VM Storage to use Find File to show it, but that's neither here nor there. Notice that you don't see VM Storage in the Lisa's HD window in Figure 10-10. That's because it's invisible. Insidious, isn't it?

- Many games don't work if Virtual Memory is on.

Figure 10-8:
Making an
8-meg Mac
think it has
16MB of
RAM with
Virtual
Memory.

Figure 10-9:
After
Restarting,
this Mac
thinks it
has 16
megabytes
(16,384K) of
RAM.

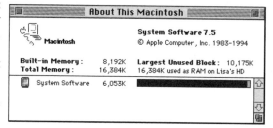

Figure 10-10:
The
unpleasant
side effect
of Figures
10-8 and
10-9: an
invisible file
(shown
using Find
File) called
VM Storage
that takes
up 16
megabytes
of disk
space.

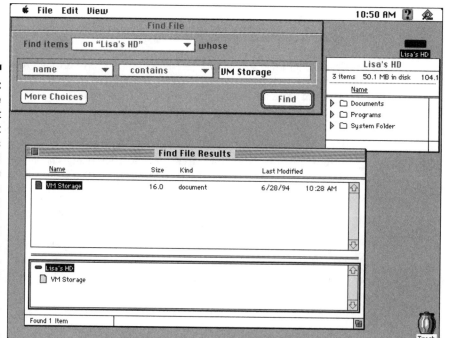

OK. So if after all of my advice you still want to use Virtual Memory, there are three more things you need to know. First, you may have to turn on 32-bit addressing (see the next section). Second, after you make changes in the Memory control panel, you have to restart your Mac for the changes to take effect. Finally, Virtual Memory is more effective when you are using several small programs simultaneously than when you are using one large program.

32-bit addressing does its bit

Most Macs can use large amounts of memory by taking advantage of a feature known as 32-bit addressing. If you have 8 megabytes of RAM or less, you don't need 32-bit addressing. Turn it off.

If you have more than 8 megabytes of RAM, 32-bit addressing must be on or your Mac acts like it only has 8MB of RAM.

Technically, 32-bit addressing allows the use of long (32-bit) binary numbers to control the way data is manipulated.

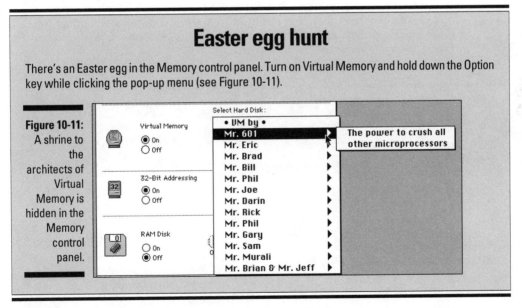

Easter egg hunt

There's an Easter egg in the Memory control panel. Turn on Virtual Memory and hold down the Option key while clicking the pop-up menu (see Figure 10-11).

Figure 10-11:
A shrine to the architects of Virtual Memory is hidden in the Memory control panel.

Select Hard Disk:

Virtual Memory
● On
○ Off

32-Bit Addressing
● On
○ Off

RAM Disk
○ On
● Off

• VM by •
Mr. 601   ▶   The power to crush all
Mr. Eric   other microprocessors
Mr. Brad   ▶
Mr. Bill   ▶
Mr. Phil   ▶
Mr. Joe   ▶
Mr. Darin   ▶
Mr. Rick   ▶
Mr. Phil   ▶
Mr. Gary   ▶
Mr. Sam   ▶
Mr. Murali   ▶
Mr. Brian & Mr. Jeff ▶

So it's really very simple:

- ✔ 8 megs or less = 32-bit addressing off.
- ✔ 9 megs or more = 32-bit addressing on.

Some older software is incompatible with 32-bit addressing. If you have a program that crashes when you launch it or when you perform some specific action (choose a menu item, spell check a document, and so on), try turning 32-bit addressing off. (Don't forget to restart.) If the program doesn't crash again when you perform that same action with 32-bit addressing off, the action is probably incompatible with 32-bit addressing.

For what it's worth, almost all software sold today works beautifully with 32-bit addressing.

Modern Memory Manager (Power Macintosh only)

If you have a Power Macintosh, you have no choice — 32-bit addressing is always on. There is no option to turn it off in the Memory control panel. In its place are a pair of radio buttons for something called Modern Memory Manager, which is shown in Figure 10-12.

RAM Doubler

If you have to have more RAM but can't afford the chips, then consider RAM Doubler, an alternative Virtual Memory program from Connectix Corporation. It installs with a single click and magically transforms your 8MB Mac into a 16MB Mac (or your 5MB Mac into a 10MB Mac, or whatever). Its speed is much better than Apple's Virtual Memory. It doesn't require a permanent, invisible file on your hard disk, and it works with almost everything Virtual Memory works with. It's kind of like Virtual Memory without any of the side effects.

I'd be remiss if I didn't mention that if any single program has its Preferred size set higher than the amount of free RAM installed in your Mac, performance will more than likely be degraded. Even so, in the same situation, the degradation from Apple's Virtual Memory will likely be worse. While RAM Doubler is a miracle, even miracles have limitations.

If you like Virtual Memory, you'll like RAM Doubler even better. Even if you hate Virtual Memory, you may like RAM Doubler. If you need more RAM but can't afford it right now, give RAM Doubler a try. It's the next best thing to real RAM.

Figure 10-12:
The Power
Macintosh's
Modern
Memory
Manager.

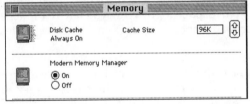

Modern Memory Manager (MMM) should usually be kept on. If you have an older program that crashes when you launch it on your Power Macintosh, you may be able to use it after turning off Modern Memory Manager in your Memory control panel. You must restart for changes in the MMM setting to take effect.

Faster than a speeding bullet: it's a RAM disk

A RAM disk enables you to use part of your installed RAM as a temporary storage device, a virtual disk made of silicon. Using a RAM disk is much, much faster than any other kind of disk and, if you're using a battery-powered Mac, much more energy efficient.

Many Macintoshes include a RAM disk feature. To find out if yours is one of them, open your Memory control panel. If you see the RAM disk controls like those shown Figure 10-13, your Mac has the RAM disk feature.

Figure 10-13:
If your Mac
supports a
RAM disk,
you'll see
these
controls in
your
Memory
control
panel.

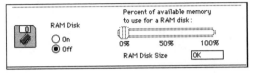

Memory assigned to a RAM disk is not available for opening programs or loading extensions and control panels. So unless you have 8 or more megabytes of RAM, a RAM disk is probably not practical. Even with 8 megabytes, it may not be useful.

RAM disks are wickedly fast while you use them, but they are temporary. When you shut down your Mac (or if the power is interrupted to a non-PowerBook Mac), the contents of a RAM disk are wiped out. In addition, certain kinds of System crashes can erase a RAM disk's contents. The contents of a RAM disk do, however, survive a restart.

Even so, you should never store your only copy of a file on a RAM disk. If you save files on a RAM disk, make sure to copy them to your hard disk every so often — just in case.

Creating a RAM disk

To create a RAM disk, click the On button in the RAM Disk portion of the Memory control panel (refer to Figure 10-13) and drag the slider to choose the percentage of the available memory that you want to use for your RAM disk. Close the control panel and restart your Mac. The new RAM disk appears on your Desktop (see Figure 10-14).

Figure 10-14:
A RAM disk acts like any other disk, except that it's much faster.

Erasing a RAM disk

There are three ways to erase the contents of a RAM disk. One, of course, is to shut down your Mac. You'll see a warning that the contents of the RAM disk will be lost; when you click OK, it's gone.

You can also erase a RAM disk by doing the following:

- Selecting the RAM disk's icon and choosing Special⇨Erase Disk.
- Dragging everything on the RAM disk to the Trash and then choosing Special⇨Empty Trash.

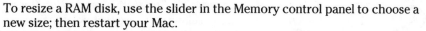

Resizing or removing a RAM disk

To resize a RAM disk, use the slider in the Memory control panel to choose a new size; then restart your Mac.

The contents of a RAM disk are lost when you resize it, so copy anything important to your hard disk before you resize.

To remove a RAM disk, click the Off button in the Memory control panel and then restart your Mac. The RAM disk must be empty or the Off button is disabled.

Good things to try with a RAM disk

Some applications run a lot faster when they're on a RAM disk. Copy your favorite program to a RAM disk and give it a try.

Your Mac runs screamingly fast if your System Folder is on a RAM disk. You need at least 16 megs of RAM to create a RAM disk big enough for your System Folder.

It is possible to use a RAM disk containing just a System and a Finder as your startup disk. It's not very useful, but it is possible. Here's how you do it:

1. Create a RAM disk large enough to hold your System and Finder (about 3MB).

2. Create a new folder on the RAM disk. Name it System Folder.

3. Copy the System file and the Finder file from the System Folder on your hard disk to the newly created System Folder on the RAM disk.

4. Open the Startup Disk control panel and click your RAM disk's icon to designate it as the startup disk.

5. Restart your Mac.

Your Mac boots up from the RAM disk instead of your hard disk.

While this particular execution won't do much for you, if you have enough RAM to create a 5 or 6 megabyte RAM disk, you can add a few extensions and control panels to the System Folder on the RAM disk and have a relatively useful, blindingly fast startup disk.

If you have a lot (12 megs or more) of RAM and want a really good RAM disk, get Maxima from the aforementioned Connectix Corporation (for well under $100). Connectix specializes in selling software that does the same things (only better) as software that Apple gives you for free. Connectix does stuff so much better that if you need a particular feature (Virtual Memory, a RAM disk and so on), you'll probably happily pay for a better one. And, compared to the freebie from Apple, Maxima is definitely a better RAM disk.

First, Maxima is nonvolatile, which means it survives a shutdown. Second, it's fast and easy to use. Finally, it includes RAM Doubler technology that lets you create a RAM disk approximately double the size of the largest one you could create with the Apple RAM disk.

Part III
U 2 Can B A Guru

The 5th Wave   By Rich Tennant

"OH, SCARECROW—I DON'T THINK YOU'LL NEED YOUR POWERBOOK IN THE EMERALD CITY ANYWAY."

In this part...

OK. Now you know how to use your Mac. You've learned how to click, drag, double-click, and all that jazz. You've mastered the Finder and triumphed over Open and Save dialog boxes. In other words, now you're ready to learn tips, tricks, and techniques to make using your Mac easier and more fulfilling. More succinctly, this part is about how things work and how you can make them work better.

After two chapters full of tips and tricks, I'll crawl through the Control Panels folder and discuss each and every control panel and its recommended settings.

Moving right along, I'll next delve into automating your Mac using AppleScript, complete with some easy-to-follow info guaranteed to get you scripting with the best of them.

Finally, in what may be the most useful chapter in the book, I'll look at every single file installed with System 7.5. I'll tell you who needs it, how much RAM it uses, how much disk space it uses, and most important of all, how to get rid of it safely if you don't need it.

Chapter 11

Sure-Fire, Easy-to-Use, No (or Low)-Cost, Timesaving Tips

. . . .

In This Chapter

▶ Flying fingers

▶ In living color — or not

▶ Getting your Views under control

. . . .

Some of what you're about to read has been mentioned somewhere in the first ten chapters already. But this chapter isn't a blatant attempt at upping my page count. No siree. This chapter is here because, by now, you lust for speed.

Now that you understand the basics, if you're normal, you wish your Mac worked faster. (You're not alone — all users wish that their Macs worked faster at some time, even those with Power Mac 8100s.) So in this chapter, I'll cover things that can make your Mac at least seem faster, most of which won't cost you a red cent.

Let Your Fingers Do the Flying

One way to make your Mac faster is to make your fingers faster. Here are a couple of ways:

Use those keyboard shortcuts

I know I've told you this tip already, but the less often you remove your hand from the keyboard to fiddle with the mouse, the less time you'll waste. Learn to use those keyboard shortcuts. Memorize them. Make your fingers memorize them. The more keyboard shortcuts you use, the faster you'll get done with what you are doing. Trust me.

Learn to type better

Learning to type faster may be the very best way I know to make your Mac faster. As a Macintosh consultant and trainer, I get to spend a lot of time with beginners. And almost all of them are lousy typists. When they complain that their computer is too slow, I ask them to perform a task for me. Then I perform that same task for them. I can type about 50 words per minute, and I type without looking at the keyboard. I always accomplish the task in less time; if the task involves a lot of typing, I accomplish it in much less time.

Because you're there and I'm here, I can't provide you with as dramatic an illustration. But trust me, typing fast saves you time at your Mac — a lot. And this speed gain isn't just in word processors and spreadsheets. Once you're a decent touch-typist, you'll fly when you use those nifty keyboard shortcuts that I mention so frequently.

There are several fine typing programs out there, and any one of them will do just fine. Most cost under $30 by mail order and are worth every penny. I happen to like a program called Mavis Beacon Teaches Typing (The Software Toolworks) for a number of reasons. First, it allows you to choose whether there should be one space or two after a period. The correct answer, of course, is one — at least if you're typing on a Mac.

What? You learned to put two spaces after a period in your high school typing class? Well, you learned wrong, at least if you're going to use a computer. The double-space after punctuation is a throwback to the days when typewriters were king and we had no personal computers or printers. Because of the way typewritten text is monospaced (each letter is the exact same width), a double-space after a punctuation mark looked better than a single space.

With the advent of the computer and laser printer, most fonts are no longer monospaced (Courier and Monaco *are* monospaced). Today, on most personal computers, most fonts are spaced *proportionally*. In other words, some characters are wider than others. The width of a space in a proportionally spaced font is just the right size to use a single space after punctuation. If you use a double-space, it looks unattractive.

Mavis Beacon Teaches Typing (or any of the typing programs) will teach you to type significantly faster in just two weeks. If you give it about 30 minutes per day of your undivided attention, you will learn to type quickly without looking down. Mavis Beacon includes timed speed and accuracy drills (see Figure 11-1) as well as a typing game (see Figure 11-2) where you try to type fast enough to keep your computerized opponent's car in the rearview mirror and not ahead of you. The program keeps track of your drills and lets you see graphs and charts of your progress at any time.

The important thing isn't how the typing program works or which program you buy. You simply need to commit the time. Just remember: The easiest way to speed up your Mac is to speed up your fingers.

End of sermon.

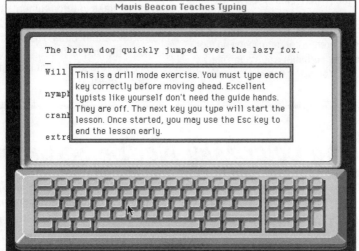

Figure 11-1:
A typing drill in the Mavis Beacon Teaches Typing program.

Figure 11-2:
A game in the Mavis Beacon Teaches Typing program.

The Mac is not a typewriter

The Macintosh is more of a typesetting machine than a typewriter. So when you use a Macintosh, you should follow the rules of good typography, not the rules of good typewriting. If you want your documents to look truly professional, in addition to single spaces after punctuation, you need to understand the difference between inch and foot marks ("and ') and typographer's quotation marks (' and ' or " and "). You also need to know when

and how to use a hyphen (-), an en dash (–), and an em dash (—).

In other words, the Mac is not a typewriter. If you want to make your documents look more elegant and professional, get ahold of Robin Williams' excellent book *The Mac Is Not a Typewriter.* It's wonderful, easy to understand, and covers all the stuff I just mentioned (and much more) in great detail.

Why Living Color May Not Be So Great

Chances are good that your Macintosh has a color monitor (most do). And chances are also good that you keep that monitor set to the maximum number of colors it supports. That may be a mistake.

Monitor settings

Your screen consists of thousands of square dots (over 300,000 for the average Mac monitor) known as *pixels* (an acronym of sorts for PICture ELement). Most 13" or 14" monitors display a picture that is 640 pixels wide by 480 pixels high — over 300,000 pixels on the screen for your Mac to deal with. Larger monitors have more pixels; smaller monitors have fewer.

The number of colors that you choose to display on your monitor has a significant impact on how quickly your screen *updates.* The more choices your Mac has to make about the color of each pixel, the longer it takes for the screen to update completely so that you can continue your work.

When I say *update,* I'm talking about the amount of time it takes for your screen to paint all the pixels their proper color or colors after opening or closing an icon or document. For example, when you open a color picture in a graphics application or open a window in the Finder, the screen updates until every element is drawn on-screen in its proper place and in its proper color.

Some people call screen updating screen *redrawing*. It means the same thing: the time you spend waiting for Finder windows to draw themselves completely or the time it takes for documents to appear completely in their windows on-screen. When your screen is updating, you have no choice but to wait for it.

(You might sometimes hear this scourge referred to as *refreshing*, but that term is incorrect in this context. *Screen refresh rate* is a technical term, measured in hertz [Hz], that has to do with the video hardware. Even so, people use the three words — update, redraw, and refresh — more or less interchangeably.)

How quickly your screen updates depends on a few things, mostly CPU speed, hard disk speed, and video circuitry (built-in or on a video card).

You shouldn't find it surprising that much of what's in the rest of the chapter is about making *your* screen update faster no matter what CPU, hard disk, or video gear you have.

I admit that the faster your Mac, the less difference the techniques in this chapter will make to your overall performance. If you've got a Mac with a 68040, 68LC040, or PowerPC chip, try my suggestions out for a while and see if you think they're worth it. Because your Mac has relatively high performance, screen updating is relatively speedy, even with some of the options mentioned in this chapter turned on.

You be the judge.

Depending on your video card or internal video, you will be able to choose from black & white, 4 colors, 16 colors, 256 colors, thousands of colors, or millions of colors.

You choose the number of colors that you want your screen to display in the Monitors control panel, which is shown Figure 11-3.

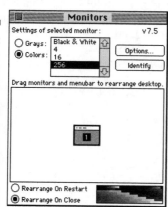

Figure 11-3: The Monitors control panel, where you choose how many colors you want to see on-screen.

The Quadra 605 (whose Monitors control panel is displayed in Figure 11-3) has built-in video and doesn't require a video card; it can display a maximum of 256 colors at once.

Most Macs today can display a maximum of 256 colors on a 14" monitor using built-in video circuitry. And many of these Macintosh models can be upgraded to display thousands or millions of colors by adding an inexpensive VRAM (video RAM) chip. For example, the Quadra 605 in Figure 11-3 can be upgraded from 256 colors to thousands of colors (on a 14" monitor) by adding a VRAM chip.

If you want more colors than your Mac model supports (even with additional VRAM) or want to use a larger monitor, you'll need to purchase a video card that supports that combination of colors and size. Video cards range from a low of a couple of hundred dollars to several thousand dollars. For the big bucks, you can get a super-fast, accelerated video card capable of powering a 21" monitor set to display millions of colors with bells and whistles such as virtual desktops, hardware zoom and pan, and resolution switching.

If you choose the Black & White option, each pixel on the screen has only two options: to be black or white. If you choose 256 colors, each pixel on-screen can be any of 256 possible colors. If you choose millions of colors, each pixel on-screen can be any one of millions of possible colors.

As you might expect, the more choices each pixel has, the more processing time your Mac requires to update the screen. So the more colors you choose in the Monitors control panel, the more sluggish your Mac will feel. Scrolling in many programs is much faster if you choose the Black & White option.

So here's my advice: Unless your application requires color, set your monitor to black & white for maximum performance. When you're using your word processor or spreadsheet, you probably don't need color anyway. Why make your Mac slower if you don't have to?

In your More Automated Tasks folder are three useful scripts that set your monitor to 1-bit (black & white), 8-bit (256 colors), or the maximum pixel depth that your Mac supports. (In the case of my Quadra 605, the maximum pixel depth is 256 colors unless I install the VRAM upgrade, which would increase the maximum to thousands of colors.) Just choose one of these scripts from the Automated Tasks submenu in the Apple menu (shown in Figure 11-4) to avoid time-consuming trips to the Monitors control panel.

Use 1-bit color for speed and 8-bit color for games. The three scripts in your Apple menu make it convenient. Try it for a while.

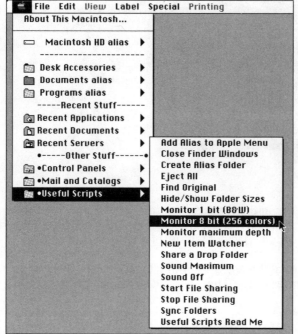

Figure 11-4:
The three
bit-depth
scripts are
indeed
useful.

In computerese, the number of colors that your monitor displays is often referred to as *bit depth* (or sometimes, *pixel depth*). In a nutshell, bit is short for Binary digIT, the smallest unit of information that the computer can understand. The bit depth describes how many bits of information can be sent to each pixel.

Here are the English translations for the most common bit depths:

- 1-bit means black & white.
- 8-bit means 256 colors.
- 24-bit means 16.7 million colors.

Window color considerations

If you choose to display colors on your monitor, the window color, as chosen in the Color control panel (shown in Figure 11-5), has a slight impact on your Mac's apparent speed.

Figure 11-5:
The Color
control
panel. Set
the Window
color to
Black &
White for
better
performance.

The Window color setting manages the color of your window borders, scroll boxes, and scroll arrows. For all the same reasons mentioned previously, the Black & White option is faster than any of the colors.

I have to admit that this adjustment won't make much difference in your Mac's speed, but it makes a little. The older and slower your Mac, the more it'll help.

A Mac with a view

The Views control panel (shown in Figure 11-6) is another place where your choices affect how quickly your screen updates in the Finder.

Geneva: It's not just a city in Switzerland anymore

Using the Geneva 9 font in the Finder will be slightly faster than using most other fonts, as Geneva 9 is one of the fonts that your Macintosh stores in its ROM (Read-Only Memory).

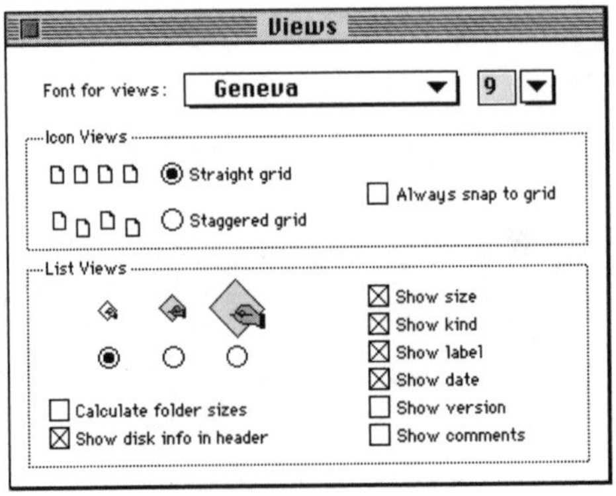

Figure 11-6:
Your
choices in
the Views
control
panel can
make your
Mac feel
faster.

When bigger isn't better

The smaller the icon, the faster the screen will refresh. In the List Views section of the Views control panel, the little tiny icon on the left is the fastest; the big, horsy-looking icon on the right is the slowest. (The one in the middle is, of course, in the middle.)

It doesn't pay to calculate folder sizes

I recommend that you deactivate Calculate folder sizes (that is, uncheck or clear its check box) to make the screen redraw faster in the Finder — or at least, to me, the screen feels like it redraws faster with this feature off.

Actually, the Finder is kind of smart about the Calculate folder sizes option. If you try to do anything in the Finder — make a menu selection, open an icon, move a window, and so on — while folder sizes are calculating, the Finder will interrupt the calculation and let you complete your task before it resumes calculating. So in theory, you should never notice a delay when Calculate folder sizes is on.

Try the Calculate folder sizes option both on and off. I don't know about you, but I find any noticeable delay unacceptable, and I notice a delay when it's turned on, even on very fast Macs. Maybe this feature is just annoying and not actually slowing things down, but I can't stand having it on. If I want to know how big a folder is, I select it and select the Get Info command from the File menu (Command-I).

Getting ahead-er and other stuff

The rest of the check boxes in the List Views section of the Views control panel — Show disk info in header and Show size, kind, label, date, version, and comments — have a slight impact on screen update speed when you open a Finder window in any list view. The fewer items you have checked, the fewer items there are for the Finder to draw. As a result, the Finder updates windows faster.

The impact of these seven items on screen updating is pretty small, so your choice should be made based on what information you want to see in Finder windows, not whether choosing them will slow your Mac down. Play around with these options if you like, but unless your Mac is very slow, you probably won't notice much difference whether they're on or off.

If you don't need it, turn it off or toss it out

A whole forthcoming chapter is devoted to showing you how to turn off or eliminate System 7.5 features that you don't need or want. Read it carefully. Features like AppleTalk, File Sharing, and PowerTalk use prodigious amounts of memory and can also slow down your Mac's CPU. If you don't need 'em, don't let 'em clog up your Mac. Read Chapter 15 carefully and then fine-tune your Mac for the best performance.

What Else Can I Do?

If you've tried every trick in the book (or at least in this chapter) and still think that your Mac is too slow, what can you do? Here are four suggestions:

✔ Get a new, faster model or upgrade yours. Apple keeps putting out faster and faster Macs at lower and lower prices. From time to time, Apple offers reasonably priced upgrades that can transform your older, slower Mac into a speedy new one.

✔ Get an accelerator. I only offer this suggestion because one of you out there is considering it. I beg you, *don't do it.* I've rarely known an accelerator owner who hasn't discovered an incompatibility somewhere along the line.

✔ Get an accelerated graphics card. Rather than attempt to accelerate your CPU, an accelerated graphics card is designed specifically to speed up one thing: the screen update rate. These things work, blasting pixels onto your screen at amazing speeds. They're extremely popular with graphic arts professionals who would otherwise suffer agonizingly slow screen redraws when working with 24-bit graphics.

✔ Get a new hard disk. Depending on the speed of your Mac, a faster disk may provide a substantial speedup.

Chapter 12
Advanced Techniques for Beginners

● ●

In This Chapter

▶ Modifying your Apple menu

▶ Startup items

● ●

In the last chapter, you learned how to make your Mac faster. In this one, I'll show you ways to make it better. Indeed, if you haven't guessed already, this chapter is about ways to make your Mac do the work instead of you.

Souping Up Your Apple Menu

A customized Apple menu is an absolute must in my book. It's the fastest, easiest, most happening way to manage your Mac. If you don't put your Apple menu to work for you, you're missing out on one of the best things Apple's done for you lately, especially with the new hierarchical folders.

The items in your Apple menu are sorted alphabetically by your Mac, so they appear in alphabetical order in the Apple menu. If you understand how the Macintosh sorts items in a list, you can use this knowledge to your advantage.

Remember, everything in your Apple Menu Items folder will appear in your Apple menu.

If you want an item to appear at the top of the Apple menu, precede its name with a number (or a space).

In Figure 12-1, I force the first four items on the menu to be Macintosh HD alias, Documents alias, Programs alias, and Desk Accessories, and I preceded each one's name with a number. Because the Macintosh sorting algorithm sorts numbers before letters, these items now appear before the first alphabetical entry (Apple Menu Items alias) in numerical order.

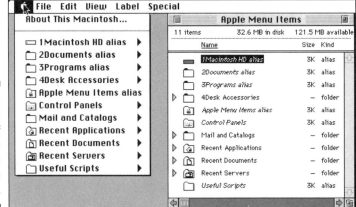

Figure 12-1:
Controlling the order of items in the Apple menu with numbers.

Space cowboy

A second, slightly prettier way to accomplish the same sort is to precede the item names with one or more spaces instead of numbers, as demonstrated in Figure 12-2.

In Figure 12-2, Macintosh HD alias has four spaces before its name; Documents alias has three spaces before its name; Programs alias has two spaces before its name; and Desk Accessories has a single space before its name.

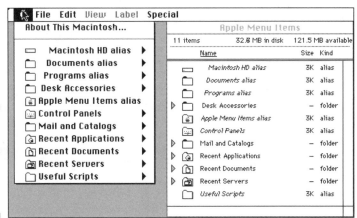

Figure 12-2:
Controlling the order of items in the Apple menu with spaces.

Divide and conquer

You can create dividers in your Apple menu using the same principle. Say I want a dividing line after Desk Accessories. I just use the principles of Macintosh sorting to create a divider line of dashes using an empty folder (see Figure 12-3).

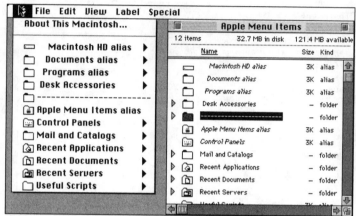

Figure 12-3: An empty folder becomes a divider in the Apple menu.

The divider appears between Desk Accessories and Apple Menu Items alias because the hyphens (the empty folder's name) sort after spaces but before letters (or numbers).

Instead of using an empty folder, make an alias of the Clipboard in your System Folder and use it for dividers instead. Using Clipboard aliases makes dividers at least somewhat useful, as you can choose one instead of using the Finder's Show Clipboard command. Just create an alias of the Clipboard, rename it "------------," and toss it in your Apple Menu Items folder.

There are plenty of interesting characters on your Mac keyboard that you can use instead of spaces to force a specific sorting order. The bullet (•, which you create by typing Option-8) sorts after the Z, so items with names preceded by a bullet will sort at the bottom of the list after items starting with a Z (see Figure 12-4).

Notice in Figure 12-4 that all the folder aliases in the Apple menu have hierarchical submenus. This feature is what makes all of my organizational tips so great. You can organize your Apple menu so that you can quickly get to any file on your hard disk.

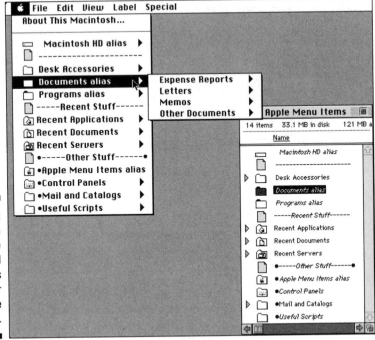

Figure 12-4:
You can
even use
unusual
characters
to reorder
your Apple
menu.

Look, ma, no dividers!

If you want your dividers to look even spiffier, you can make them appear
without an icon at all, just like what's shown in Figure 12-5. This trick is strictly
cosmetic, but I think it looks cool.

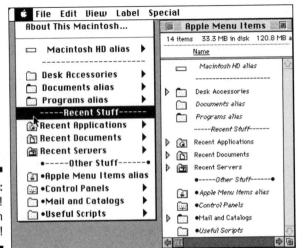

Figure 12-5:
Look, ma!
No icons on
my dividers!

Here's how to make icon-less dividers:

1. Open any graphics program and use its selection tool to select a patch of white about 1-inch square. Choose Edit⇨Copy to copy the white square to the Clipboard (see Figure 12-6).

Figure 12-6:
Copy a
white
square
to the
Clipboard.

2. Jump back to the Apple Menu Items folder and select the divider's icon.

3. Choose File⇨Get Info (Command-I).

   The Get Info window for that icon appears.

4. Click on the icon in the Get Info window.

   A border appears around it.

5. Choose Edit⇨Paste (Command-V).

   The patch of white, which is invisible on the Desktop and in the Apple menu, becomes the icon for the divider (see Figure 12-7).

Figure 12-7:
The white
square
becomes
the divider's
icon.

Neat, huh?

All of these sorting and organizing tricks are easy once you get the hang of the way the Mac sorts items in folders. And the principles you learn here work in any window.

I use my sorting tricks in most of my folders. In Figure 12-8, I force the most frequently used item (S7.5fD.Ch12.Adv Tech f...) to the top of the list by preceding its name with a space, and I force less important items to the bottom by preceding their names with an accent (`).

Figure 12-8:
Use a space or tilde key before a file's name to force it to the top or bottom of the list.

Name	Size	Kin
□ S7.5fD.Ch12.Adv Tech f...	14K	
□ S7.5fD.Ch00.Frontal.BL	14K	
□ S7.5fD.Ch15.Stay & Go	8K	
□ S7.5fD.PX3.Companies.BL	6K	
▶ ⌂ `S7.5fD.as sent	—	
▶ ⌂ `S7.5fD.Back from IDG	—	
□ `S7.5fD.Chapter Template	4K	
□ "S7.5fD.Chapter Outline....	22K	

S7.5fD.Chapters — 8 items — 42.5 MB in disk — 75.5 MB avai

When you press the tilde key (usually found in the upper-left corner of the keyboard), your Mac types an accent (`) if the Shift key isn't down; it types a tilde (~) if the Shift key is held down. The tilde sorts after the Z in the Macintosh sorting scheme. (To be perfectly precise, the tilde sorts after the accent, which sorts after the Z.) Figure 12-9 shows other characters that sort after the tilde; these include ™ (Option-2) and • (Option-8). But the accent/tilde is handy, being right there in the corner of my keyboard.

S7.5fD.Chapters — 11 items — 42.4 MB in disk — 75.6 MB available

Name	Size	Kind
□ S7.5fD.Ch12.Adv Tech f...	12K	Microsoft Word
□ S7.5fD.Ch00.Frontal.BL	14K	Microsoft Word
□ S7.5fD.Ch15.Stay & Go	8K	Microsoft Word
□ S7.5fD.PX3.Companies.BL	6K	Microsoft Word
▶ ⌂ `S7.5fD.as sent	—	folder
▶ ⌂ `S7.5fD.Back from IDG	—	folder
□ `S7.5fD.Chapter Template	4K	Microsoft Word
□ "S7.5fD.Chapter Outline....	22K	Inspiration™ 4.0
▶ ⌂ •	—	folder
▶ ⌂ ™	—	folder
▶ ⌂ º	—	folder

Figure 12-9:
Option characters sort after Z and after the tilde.

Rather than have me tell you about file sorting, why don't you give it a try for yourself? So go to your Mac right now (unless you've been there all along) and try all the tips you just learned.

If the stuff you've read so far in this chapter is not making sense or not working for you, make sure that the By Name command is selected in the View menu. These sorting tips only work in the View by Name view.

Start Up Your Mornings Right

This section presents a pair of techniques for making your Mac start up better. The Startup Items folder tip is the most useful, but the other one, which closes all open windows automatically at startup, can be convenient as well. Both are techniques worth knowing.

On becoming a (startup) item

Don't overlook the convenience of the Startup Items folder in your System Folder. Everything in this special folder will launch automatically at startup.

Think about that for a second. What's the first thing you do after you turn on your Mac and the Desktop appears? If your answer begins with the word "Open" or "Launch," you can save yourself some effort by putting an alias of the launched or opened item in the Startup Items folder. It will then launch automatically at startup.

If you work with a single database or spreadsheet file every day, why not put an alias of it in the Startup Items folder? When you turn on your Mac, that document automatically appears on the screen? Or if the first thing you do each morning is check your e-mail, put an alias of your e-mail program in the Startup Items folder.

You can even put a sound in the Startup Items folder. Thereafter, that sound will play as the Finder appears.

For this trick to work, the sound must be stored in the System 7 sound format. You can tell if a sound is in this common format by opening the sound file. If the sound is a System 7 sound, you will hear it play when you open it. Other sound file formats (such as AIFF, WAV, and so on) will do nothing or display an "application can't be found" error message when you open them.

Most sounds floating around Mac circles these days are in the System 7 format.

The new Stickies feature is neat to have around all the time. If you put an alias of Stickies in the Startup Items folder, your sticky memos will always be available (see Figure 12-10).

Stickies knows that you're likely to want to use it all the time, so it's got a preference setting that not only puts an alias of it in the Startup Items folder, but it also makes sure that it launches into the background, making the Finder the active application at startup.

To use this feature, launch Stickies, choose Edit⇨Preferences, and check both the Launch at system startup and ... in the background check boxes (see Figure 12-11).

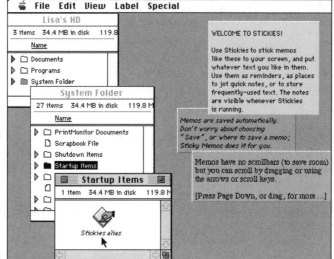

Figure 12-10:
When I start up my Mac, Stickies will launch automatically.

Figure 12-11:
Stickies launch preferences.

☒ Launch at system startup
  ☒ ...in the background

Not all programs are as considerate as Stickies, as the items in the Startup Items folder launch alphabetically, using that same Macintosh sorting order that I talked about in the previous section. And under ordinary circumstances, the last item to launch would be the active application at the end of the startup sequence.

Stickies can launch itself and then make the Finder the active application.

So if you want the Finder to be the active application at startup and you've got several items in your Startup Items folder, just make sure that Stickies loads last and that you've checked the ...in the background check box in Stickies' preferences.

In other words, precede Stickies' name with a few Zs (or a tilde or bullet) to make it the last item in the list when you view the Startup Items window by name.

Chapter 13

Control Tweaks

•••

In This Chapter

▶ Instructions on tweaking every single control panel

▶ Lots of pictures

•••

*T*he Control Panels folder contains (what else?) your control panels. What exactly are control panels? They're usually little mini-programs that control a single aspect of your Mac's operation.

I've talked about some of the control panels (Memory, Sharing Setup) earlier in this book, but because System 7.5 includes about 40 control panels for most Macs, in this chapter I'll go through them one at a time, in alphabetical order, describing and suggesting settings for each and every one.

After a brief AppleScript interlude in Chapter 14, I'll continue this discussion in Chapter 15, "What Can Stay and What Can Go," with a full disclosure of how much memory and disk space each control panel uses and how to remove or temporarily disable ones that you don't need. I even explain why you might want to do this stuff.

I've included *no-brainer* settings at the end of most sections for those of you who just want to know how to set the thing and don't care what it does or why. These no-brainer settings are not the gospel, but they're a good place to start. (You can always come back and change them later after you figure out what they are and what they do!)

Apple Menu Options

The Apple Menu Options control panel has two functions:

▮ ✔ Turns the hierarchical submenus on or off.

▮ ✔ Lets you specify *how many* Recent Documents, Applications, and Servers your Mac should track.

The first function controls whether or not folders (and aliases of folders as well as disks) in the Apple menu display their contents when you highlight them. Put another way, the submenus on/off switch (actually, a pair of radio buttons) turns the little triangles on and off.

The second function requires that you check the Remember recently used items check box. When you do so, your Mac will remember the specified number of documents, applications, and servers for you. You'll find the remembered items in the similarly named folders in the Apple menu (see Figure 13-1).

The Mac remembers these items by creating aliases and putting them in the appropriate Recent Items folder. All three Recent Items folders are in the Apple Menu Items folder.

The Mac uses FIFO (First In First Out) to limit the number of items in each folder according to your choices in the Apple Menu Options control panel. Say you set the number of documents to 20. When you open document number 21, document 1 is forgotten. More long-windedly, when you open document number 21, your Mac creates an alias for document 21. It then deletes the alias for document number 1 so that there are again only 20 items in the folder, as you requested.

All of this stuff is done invisibly, without your knowledge or intervention.

Figure 13-1:
The Apple
Menu
Options
control
panel and
its two
offspring —
hierarchical
submenus in
the Apple
menu and
the three
Recent
Items
folders in
the Apple
menu.

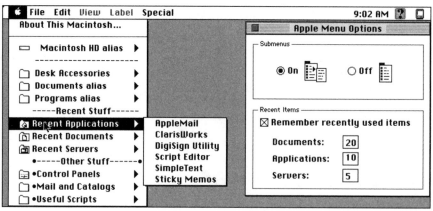

Apple Menu Options no-brainer setting

Submenus: On. Documents: 15. Applications: 15. Servers: 5.

ATM GX

ATM GX is Adobe Type Manager, adapted to run under QuickDraw GX. ATM eliminates the jaggies in Type 1 fonts on-screen. And, if your printer doesn't have PostScript, it eliminates jaggies in your printed output.

ATM has been available from Adobe as an extra-cost add-on product for years; System 7.5 is the first time Apple's included it in the box for free.

You only need ATM GX if you meet the following two criteria:

1. You are running QuickDraw GX.

   and

2. You are using Type 1 fonts.

If you don't meet both criteria, click the Off button and be done with it.

ATM GX no-brainer setting

(Assumes you're running QuickDraw GX and using Type 1 fonts.) Font Cache: 96K. Preserve Line Spacing: On (see Figure 13-2).

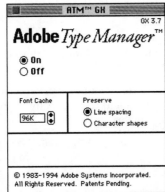

Figure 13-2: ATM GX. Not much to look at, eh?

If you use many Type 1 fonts, or screen updating seems unusually sluggish, try increasing the Font Cache until the sluggishness goes away. But like the Disk Cache in the Memory control panel, don't forget that this cache uses RAM. The higher you set the Font Cache, the less RAM will be available for applications.

AutoRemounter (PowerBooks Only)

This control panel deals with what happens to shared disks that you have mounted on your PowerBook's Desktop when you shut down or put your PowerBook to sleep. It's shown in Figure 13-3. Sleeping, restarting, and shutting down all have the same effect on shared disks: the network connection is broken. With AutoRemounter, you have some control over what happens when you wake up or start up. Without it, you'd have to manually reestablish the network connection to each shared disk.

Figure 13-3:
Auto-
Remounter
can remount
remote
volumes
automatically
after shut
down or
sleep.

The Remount Shared Disks choices are mutually exclusive (you can select only one of the three choices at a time):

- ✔ **After Sleep:** This option will automatically remount any shared disks on your Desktop when you put your Mac to sleep.

- ✔ **Always:** This option will automatically remount any shared disks on your Desktop when you put your Mac to sleep and remount any shared disks on the Desktop when you shut down or restart.

- ✔ **Off:** This option disables the AutoRemounter control panel completely.

The Connect to Disks By choices are

✔ **Automatically Remounting:** This option will automatically remount any shared disks on your Desktop after you shut down, restart, or sleep (based on your selection in the Remount Shared Disks section) but will not require a password for the disk to be remounted.

✔ **Always Entering Passwords:** This option will automatically remount any shared disks on your Desktop after you shut down, restart, or sleep (based on your selection in the Remount Shared Disks section) but *will* require a password before the disk is remounted.

Don't choose the Automatically Remounting option if the contents of shared disks are confidential. Someone else could awaken or restart your computer; selecting this option gives that person access to files on the remote disks. Choose the Always Entering Password option instead so that other users will only gain access to remote disks if they know the password.

Just a reminder that choices are, by their nature, mutually exclusive when you see a set of *radio buttons*. Radio buttons always signify that only one choice may be active at any time.

AutoRemounter no-brainer setting

If you don't use File Sharing, click the Off button and forget it. If you use File Sharing, click Always and Automatically Remounting. (Choose Always Entering Passwords if your office is secure and you don't want to have to type your password each time a disk is remounted.)

Brightness

This control panel lets you adjust the brightness of some monitors, mostly PowerBook and Duo models. The System 7.5 Installer is smart and usually doesn't install this control panel unless your monitor supports it (most don't).

If the Brightness control panel was installed inadvertently on a Mac that doesn't support it and you try to open it, an error message like the one in Figure 13-4 will tell you that your Mac can't use this control panel. No big deal. Just trash it and forget it.

Figure 13-4:
You get this
message if
your Mac
can't
use the
Brightness
control
panel.

The control panel "Brightness" cannot be
used with this Macintosh.

OK

For those of you who can use the Brightness control panel, all I can say is that
very few people have ever cast their gaze upon it and lived to tell the tale.
Suffice it to say that this control panel has a slider bar to control screen
brightness, and it gives you the option of setting up a keyboard shortcut to do
the same thing. So few Mac users need to worry about this control panel that I
won't expose them to the curse by presenting a screen shot.

Cache Switch (Macs with 68040 Processors Only)

The Cache Switch control panel (shown in Figure 13-5) enables or disables the
68040's (the Mac's CPU chip) built-in, on-chip caches. These caches make Macs
with the 68040 chip run faster.

Figure 13-5:
Faster is
usually
better.

Cache Switch

040 Processor Cache :   v 7.5

◉ Faster (Caches Enabled)
○ More Compatible (Caches Disabled)

Some applications will not work correctly
when the processor's caches are enabled.

The on-chip case has nothing to do with the Disk Cache in the Memory control
panel, and it has nothing to do with disk performance. This cache is actually
part of the 68040 chip inside your Mac.

Macs that use the 68040 chip include Centris series, the Quadra series, 500-series PowerBooks, and high-end Performas. See the Poguemeister's _Macs For Dummies_ for a comprehensive description of the Mac product line.

Under most circumstances, you want this control panel set to Faster (Caches Enabled). If you discover a program that bombs or freezes when you launch or use it, try switching to More Compatible (Caches Disabled).

CPU Energy Saver (Energy Star-Compliant Macs Only)

Some recent Mac models, which are said to be _Energy Star-compliant_, can turn themselves off at a specific time or after a specified idle period. If your Mac supports this feature, the CPU Energy Saver control panel will be installed when you install System 7.5. (If your Mac doesn't support this control panel but it was somehow installed and you try to open it, you'll see an error message haughtily informing you that your Mac can't use it. No problemo. Trash it.)

In the top part of the dialog box, you can choose to have your computer shut down automatically after so many minutes of idle time (kind of like a killer screen saver). To turn this feature on, click the Idle Time check box at the top left of the window. To set the idle time, click on the slider next to it, as shown in Figure 13-6, and move the slider until the appropriate time displays beneath it.

Figure 13-6:
To set the idle time before your Mac automatically shuts down, click the slider and drag.

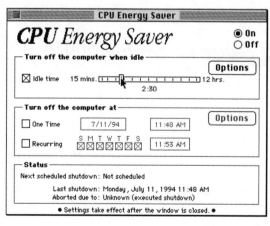

Click the Options button and you'll see four check boxes representing conditions when you don't want the shutdown to occur. You can instruct your Mac not to shut down automatically if one, some, or all of the following conditions apply:

- ✔ You are connected to a shared disk.
- ✔ A serial port is being used.
- ✔ The "busy" cursor (the wristwatch or spinning beachball) is on the screen.
- ✔ A sound is playing.

Check whichever options you want to apply to unattended, idle time shutdowns.

In the middle part of the window, you can choose to have your Mac shut down once at a specific time, or you can set up a recurring shutdown (for example, every day at 11:29 p.m., just in time for Dave). The Options button here gives the same choices as the Idle Time options button with an additional option for "Notify __ minutes before Shut Down." Type in a number if you want to be warned of impending automatic shutdowns.

The bottom part of the window shows the status of all current and pending automatic shutdowns.

If you're not around when one of these shutdowns occurs and you have unsaved work in any application, you'll see a dialog box asking if you want to save your changes. The Mac won't shut down until you click a button in this dialog box. In fact, if you click the Cancel button in this dialog box, the shutdown is canceled along with the Save dialog box.

CPU Energy Saver no-brainer settings

Click the Off button in the upper right-hand corner; then remember to turn your Mac off manually when you're not going to need it for a while.

CloseView

CloseView is a control panel that makes the screen easier to see. Though it's designed primarily for visually impaired users, you may find a use for it someday.

CloseView is not ordinarily installed with System 7.5. You have to install it with the Custom Install option that the System 7.5 Installer offers.

CloseView is described in Chapter 16.

Color

The Color control panel governs the highlight color (the color of selected text), the window highlight color, and the color of accents in scroll bars and title bars. The options in this control panel are purely cosmetic.

There's an Easter egg in the Color control panel. To see it, click repeatedly on the sample text below the word Highlight Color. Dean Yu and Vincent Lo are apparently the programmers of the Color control panel.

Color no-brainer settings

Whatever you like. Black and white is slightly faster for window highlights on some Macs, but it's not as pretty.

ColorSync System Profile

ColorSync is a color-matching technology that ensures color consistency between screen representation and color output. It is of no importance unless you are also using the ColorSync color-matching system on your printing devices and scanners.

I thought not.

So this control panel's settings are totally irrelevant. Nothing whatsoever will happen if you change them.

ColorSync System Profile no-brainer settings

Don't touch it.

Control Strip (PowerBooks Only)

Show or hide the Control Strip by choosing the appropriate radio button in this control panel. (The Control Strip is discussed in Chapter 6.)

Use the Control Strip's built-in hide and show feature (demonstrated in Figure 13-7) to collapse and expand the strip on-screen. Click the little nub to expand it again.

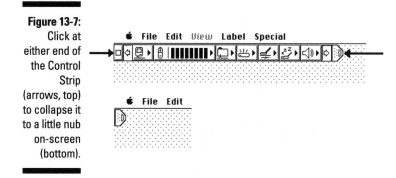

Figure 13-7:
Click at either end of the Control Strip (arrows, top) to collapse it to a little nub on-screen (bottom).

Control Strip no-brainer settings

Click the Show Control Strip radio button and then use the tip above to hide and show it.

Date & Time

The Date & Time control panel enables you to configure your Mac's internal clock, which many programs use, and configure the menubar clock (see Figure 13-8).

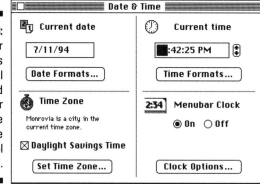

Figure 13-8:
Set your Mac's internal clock (and the menubar clock) in the Date & Time control panel.

To set the date or time

Click the number that you want to change in the Current Date or Current Time fields. The number will become highlighted when you click it, and a pair of arrows appear. Increase the selected number by clicking the up arrow; decrease it by clicking the down arrow. You can also use the arrow keys on the keyboard to increase or decrease the number. Or you can type a new number right over the selected number.

Use the Tab key to move from number to number. Month, day, year, hour, minute, second, and AM/PM will be selected in sequence when you press the Tab key. If you want to move backward through the sequence, press Shift-Tab. As long as you hold the Shift key down, you'll cycle through the numbers in reverse order as you press Tab.

Time and date formats

Your choices in the Date or Time Formats dialog boxes will be seen any place your Mac displays the date and time: in the menubar, in programs that date or time stamp documents, in the Finder (creation and modification dates), and so on.

To change formats, click the appropriate button. The Date Format dialog box (shown in Figure 13-9) lets you change the punctuation marks in the long date and the dividers in the short date.

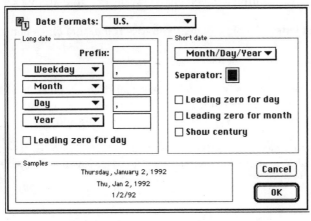

Figure 13-9: The Date Format dialog box. Apple thinks of everything, doesn't it?

You can change the display order of both long and short dates. Use the Week-day, Month, Day, or Year pop-up menus to change the order of the long date; click the Month/Day/Year pop-up menu to choose a different order for the short date.

The Time Format dialog box lets you choose a 12- or 24-hour clock and a bunch of other stuff, as Figure 13-10 shows.

Figure 13-10:
The Time
Format
dialog,
which
probably
doesn't
need
changing.

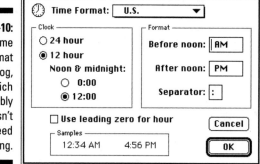

The rest of it

The Daylight Savings Time check box sets the clock forward one hour (checked) or backward one hour (unchecked).

The Set Time Zone button lets you choose your time zone from a scrolling list.

Type the first letter of a big city near you to scroll to that city's name in the list.

Is this thrilling or what?

Finally, the Clock Options button lets you do all kinds of fun stuff with your menubar clock (shown in Figure 13-11). You can set the clock to chime on the hour or quarter-hour, and you can select custom fonts and colors.

Apple's menubar clock is based on Steve Christensen's popular freeware menubar clock, SuperClock, which many Mac users loved and revered long before the advent of System 7.5.

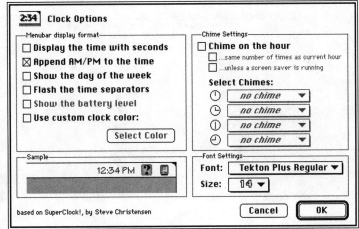

Figure 13-11:
If you're a
tweak freak,
you'll have a
field day
with all of
the menubar
clock's
options.

Desktop Patterns

This control panel, shown in Figure 13-12, lets you select a decorative pattern for your Desktop. To choose from the 56 available patterns, click the left- and right-arrow buttons on the Desktop Pattern window (or the left-arrow and right-arrow keys on the keyboard). When a pleasing one appears, click the Set Desktop Pattern button.

I lied: Desktop Patterns is an application, not a control panel. If you don't believe me, view the Control Panels folder's window by kind. Why did Apple choose to place it in the Control Panels folder? I don't know, but it seems like as good a place for it as any.

Desktop Patterns is a vast improvement over earlier versions of the System, which offered only a handful of ugly patterns with a maximum of 8 colors. The Desktop Patterns control panel, er, application offers up to 256 colors and looks great in thousands or millions of colors as well.

This functionality was previously available in third-party programs like Wall-paper and Screenscapes, so it's nice that Apple is throwing in this utility for free.

Easy Access

Easy Access lets you control the cursor using the numeric keypad instead of a mouse, and it provides other options for people with impaired dexterity. Though primarily for the handicapped, it provides a useful function, and you might want to install it.

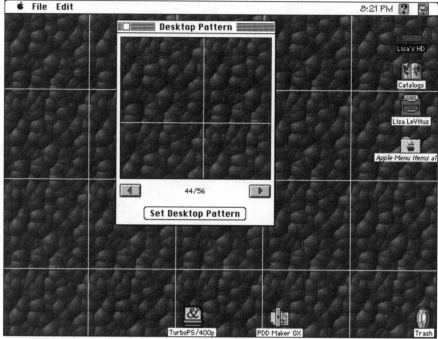

Figure 13-12:
Desktop
Patterns
gives you a
choice of 56
fancy
Desktop
patterns.

Easy Access is not ordinarily installed with System 7.5 — you have to install it with the Custom Install option that the System 7.5 Installer offers.

Easy Access is described in detail in Chapter 16.

Extensions Manager

Extensions Manager is another program that's been around for years as freeware but makes its first appearance as an Apple product in System 7.5. Extensions Manager allows you to turn extensions and control panels on and off easily.

There's a longer, more technical discussion of why you need Extensions Manager and some tips in Chapter 15. For now, here's how you use it.

Extensions and control panels load into memory if they're in the Extensions or Control Panels folders at startup. Without Extensions Manager (or one of its third-party counterparts such as Now Software's Startup Manager, Inline

Software's INITPicker, or Casady & Greene's Conflict Catcher II), you would have to move an extension or control panel out of its special folder manually and then restart your Mac to disable it, which, as you might guess, isn't much fun.

You still have to restart your Mac, but you can use Extensions Manager to turn individual control panels and extensions on and off without moving them manually.

You can work with Extensions Manager in the Finder by opening its icon or choosing Apple menu⇨Control Panels⇨Extensions Manager. Or you can work with it at startup, before any control panels or extensions load.

To open Extensions Manager at startup, hold down the spacebar on your keyboard until the Extensions Manager window appears (see Figure 13-13).

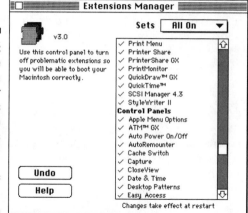

Figure 13-13:
The
Extension
Manager
window lets
you turn
extensions
and control
panels on
and off
individually.

Regardless of which way you open it, choose which items you want to turn on or off by clicking them (a check mark before an item means that it's turned on). Your choices remain in effect until you change them in the Extensions Manager window.

You can create *Sets* with Extension Manager, groups of extensions and control panels that you want to use simultaneously. To create a set, click items in the list until the ones that you want on have check marks and the ones that you want off don't. When everything is just the way you like it, choose Save Set from the Sets pop-up menu (see Figure 13-14).

You'll be asked to name the set. After you do, the set will appear in the Sets menu as a custom set along with the preinstalled sets — All On, All Off, and System 7.5 Only. Sets can be quite convenient, as you'll see in Chapter 15.

Figure 13-14:
Get the
check marks
just the way
you like
them and
then create
a Set.

When you finish making your selections or creating sets, close the Extensions Manager window. If you used the spacebar to open Extensions Manager at start up, your Mac will start up with only the checked items loaded; if you're in the Finder, you'll have to restart for your selections to take effect.

The System 7.5 Only set turns on only the most essential control panels and extensions, turning off memory hogs like PowerTalk and QuickDraw GX (see Chapter 15 for details).

File Sharing Monitor

The File Sharing Monitor control panel tells you which items on your local disk are currently being shared, how much network activity there is, and who is currently connected to your hard disk. It's shown in Figure 13-15.

Figure 13-15:
The File
Sharing
Monitor
control
panel tells
what's being
shared as
well as
who is
connected.

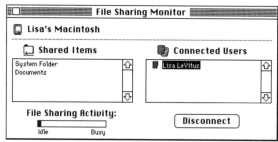

The only thing you can actually *do* with the File Sharing Monitor control panel is to disconnect connected users, which you do by clicking them so that they're selected and then clicking the Disconnect button.

General Controls

This is the big fellow, the granddaddy of all control panels. Figure 13-16 doesn't do it justice.

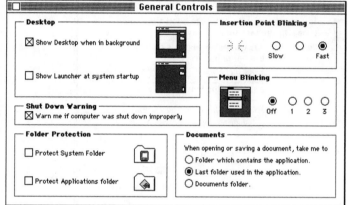

A whopping six different options are managed by General Controls.

Desktop options

The Show Desktop when in background check box determines whether the Finder shows through in the background when you've got another application open. Unchecking this option makes Finder windows and icons disappear when other programs are active, which means that the only way to switch to the Finder is to choose it from the Application menu. In other words, if you click outside of a word processor window, you don't pop into the Finder.

Checking the Show Desktop when in background option makes it more convenient to return to the Finder from other programs by clicking the Desktop or a Finder window, but this feature may be more confusing for beginners.

The Show Launcher at system startup check box governs whether the Launcher is active. I ranted about Launcher in Chapter 7, so I won't bore you with my vitriol. Suffice it to say that I don't find it very useful, but beginners might.

Shut Down Warning

If this check box is checked, you'll see a warning like the one in Figure 13-17 when you restart your computer after a crash, freeze, power interruption, or improper shutdown.

Figure 13-17:
Your Mac
will scold
you if you
shut down
improperly.

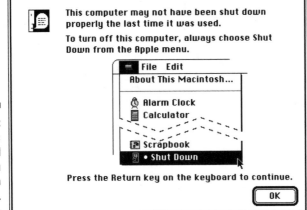

Folder Protection

If the Folder Protection check boxes are checked, items in those folders (System or Applications or both) can't be renamed or deleted.

Insertion Point Blinking

This option sets the speed at which the text insertion point, a flashing vertical line, blinks in documents. Your choices are Slow, Medium, or Fast. I like Fast because I find it easiest to see.

Menu Blinking

This option controls whether or not menu items flash when you select them, and if they flash, how many times.

Off is the fastest setting.

Documents

This set of radio buttons determines what folder will be active in Open and Save dialog boxes:

- **Folder which contains the application:** This option brings up the Open or Save dialog box ready to save or open files in the folder that contains the program you're using. So if you're using ClarisWorks and you choose File⇨Save or File⇨Open, the list of files you see in the Open or Save dialog box will be the contents of the ClarisWorks folder.

- **Last folder used in the application:** This option brings up the Open or Save dialog box ready to save or open a file in the last folder you saved to or opened a document from. In other words, your Mac remembers for you.

- **Documents folder:** This option will bring up the Open or Save dialog box ready to save or open a document in the Documents folder.

General Controls no-brainer settings

For beginners

Show Desktop when in background: Off. Show Launcher at system startup: On. Shut Down Warning: On. Folder Protection: On for both. Insertion Point Blinking: Fast. Menu Blinking: 3 times. Documents: Documents folder.

For more advanced users

Show Desktop when in background: On. Show Launcher at System Startup: Off. Shut Down Warning: Your call. Folder Protection: Off for both. Insertion Point Blinking: Fast. Menu Blinking: Off. Documents: Last folder used.

Keyboard

The Keyboard control panel modifies how your keyboard responds to your keystrokes. It's shown in Figure 13-18.

The Key Repeat Rate sets how fast a key will repeat when you hold it down. This feature comes in to play when you hold down the dash key to make a line or the * key to make a divider.

The Delay Until Repeat option sets how long you have to hold down a key before it starts repeating.

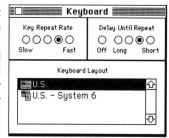

Figure 13-18:
The
Keyboard
control
panel
governs how
your
keyboard
responds.

The Keyboard Layout section allows you to choose a different keyboard layout for languages other than United States English.

Because changes to the Keyboard control panel take place immediately, you can open it and a word processor and experiment with its settings until you are comfortable.

Keyboard no-brainer settings

Look at Figure 13-18. Duplicate its settings. If you live somewhere other than the U.S. and see a familiar-sounding keyboard layout in the lower part of the window, select it.

Labels

The Labels control panel (shown in Figure 13-19) lets you change the names and colors of the labels in the Label menu.

Figure 13-19:
The Label
menu
reflects your
choices in
the Labels
control
panel.

To change a label's name, select the old name and then type the new one.

To change a label's color, click directly on the color and then choose a new one in the color picker, which is shown more or less in Figure 13-20.

Figure 13-20:
The color picker appears when you click a color in the Labels control panel.

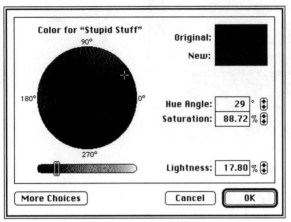

I know that all the colors on the color picker look gray in the picture, but on a color monitor, they are in color, I promise. To select a new color, just click in the color wheel or change the Hue Angle, Saturation, and/or Lightness settings.

Launcher

Launcher is Apple's cheesy little file launcher. It lets you open items in its window with a single click, which saves you the trouble of rummaging through folders.

The Launcher window's buttons reflect the contents of the Launcher Items folder in your System Folder (see Figure 13-21).

Whatever is in the Launcher Items folder will appear as a button in the Launcher window. A single-click on the button opens the item, which can be a file, a folder, a document, or a control panel, or (better idea) an *alias* of a file, a folder, a document, or a control panel.

If you want Launcher to start up automatically, there's an option for that very thing in the General Controls control panel.

Figure 13-21:
The Launcher window contains single-click launch buttons for each item in the Launcher Items folder.

Macintosh Easy Open Setup

Macintosh Easy Open (MEO) is the enabling technology that lets you choose another application to open a document when you don't have the actual application that created it. Figure 13-22 provides a demonstration.

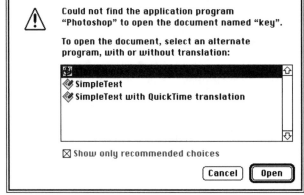

Figure 13-22:
This translation dialog box is part of Macintosh Easy Open.

If MEO isn't turned on or isn't installed, instead of this dialog box, you see an error message telling you that an application couldn't be found for this document.

The two check boxes in this control panel manage how the translation dialog box works (see Figure 13-23).

Figure 13-23:
The MEO
Setup
control
panel.

```
≣□≣  Macintosh Easy Open Setup  ≣
  ☐□≣
      📄   Macintosh Easy Open v.1.1     ⦿ On
           © Apple Computer, Inc.        ○ Off

      ☐ Always Show Choices
      ☐ Include Choices from Servers

      ( Delete Preferences... )
```

If you check the Always Show Choices option, you must confirm your translation preference every time you open a document. In other words, if this item is checked, you see the dialog box shown back in Figure 13-22 every time you open a Photoshop file. If you uncheck this option, the second time (and every time thereafter) that you open a Photoshop file, it will automatically launch into the selected alternate program, in this example, ClarisWorks.

If you check the Include Choices from Servers option, MEO will look on all network volumes currently mounted for an application that can open the document.

If you don't have a high-speed network (such as EtherNet or Token Ring), launching a remote program can take a long, long time. You might want to consider leaving this option off unless you really, really need it.

The Delete Preferences button deletes any links that you've created between documents and applications. Why would you need to delete preferences? If the Always Show Choices option isn't checked and a document always launches the wrong application, click Delete Preferences. The next time you try to open that document, you'll get a dialog box allowing you to choose a different application. In other words, the Delete Preferences button makes MEO forget any connections between documents and applications previously created in a translation dialog box.

Macintosh Easy Open Setup no-brainer settings

MEO: On. Always Show Choices: Unchecked. Include Choices from Server: Unchecked.

MacTCP

MacTCP is the control panel that allows your Mac to connect to industry-standard TCP networks. MacTCP is what lets you use cool Mac software to deal with the so-called information superhighway, the Internet.

MacTCP is not ordinarily installed with System 7.5 — you have to install it with the Custom Install option the System 7.5 Installer offers.

MacTCP is described in Chapter 16.

Map

A lame little control panel that's virtually useless. I'm not gonna waste your time with it. Figure 13-24 shows a picture, just for kicks.

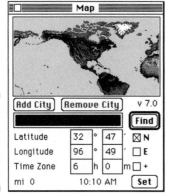

Figure 13-24:
The lame and useless Map control panel.

If you want a prettier Map like mine, open the Scrapbook DA and find the color map picture. Copy it to the Clipboard. Open the Map control panel and paste. A warning will appear. Click OK. It's done. Your Map control panel has a pretty color picture instead of the ugly black-and-white one.

This tip doesn't make the Map control panel any more useful, but it definitely makes it prettier.

Memory

See Chapter 10, which covers nothing else.

Memory no-brainer settings

Cache Size: 32K. Virtual Memory: Off. 32-bit Addressing: Off (unless you have 9 or more megabytes of RAM, in which case it should be On). Ram Disk: Off.

Monitors

The Monitors control panel (shown in Figure 13-25) lets you specify the number of colors or grays that you want your monitor to display.

Figure 13-25:
The
Monitors
control
panel lets
you decide
how many
colors or
grays you
want to see.

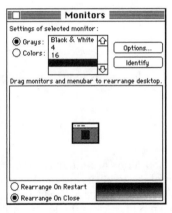

If you have more than one monitor, you can also choose which one contains the menubar and which one displays the Welcome to Macintosh message at startup. You can also determine their relative positioning.

Macs with one monitor only

Click the number of colors in the scrolling list and then click the Grays or Colors radio button. The Identify and Rearrange options don't apply to single monitors. The Options button presents some stuff that you don't need to worry about.

Macs with two or more monitors

If you have multiple monitors, first click one of the monitor icons to select it (see Figure 13-26). Click the number of colors in the scrolling list and then click the Grays or Colors radio button. Repeat this process for each monitor — first click the monitor's icon and then make your selections.

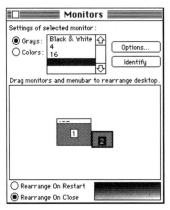

Figure 13-26:
If you have more than one monitor, click the icon of the one that you want to configure.

In Figure 13-26, I've selected monitor 2 by clicking its icon; I've configured it to display 256 grays.

The Identify button will flash a large number on each monitor, telling you which is monitor 1, which is monitor 2, and so on.

To rearrange multiple monitors, drag their icons around in the Monitors control panel window. The spatial relationship of the icons in the window should match their physical proximity on your desk. In other words, if the little monitor is to the right and slightly lower than the big monitor, drag the icons until they look like Figure 13-26.

If the Rearrange On Close option is selected, the monitors will reflect the changes when you close the Monitors window. If the Rearrange On Restart option is selected, the changes won't occur until you restart.

The new Rearrange options are a nice touch. Under previous versions of the operating system, you had to restart for changes to take effect.

To move the menubar from one monitor to another, click the menubar icon and drag it to the new monitor (see Figure 13-27).

Figure 13-27:
When I
release the
mouse
button (and
after I restart
my Mac),
Monitor 2
will display
the menubar
instead of
Monitor 1.

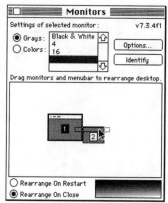

Sigh. You still have to restart to change which monitor has the menu bar.

To change the startup monitor, the one on which the Welcome to Macintosh startup message displays (and at the bottom of which the control panel and extension icons appear at startup), hold down the Option key. A smiling Mac icon will appear on the current startup monitor. Drag it to the monitor that you want to be the new startup monitor and then restart. Figure 13-28 demonstrates.

Figure 13-28:
To change
startup
monitors,
hold down
the Option
key and drag
the smiling
Mac icon
to the
appropriate
monitor.

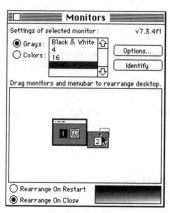

Finally, the Options button doesn't do anything worth knowing about and may confuse you. Unless someone smarter than me tells you otherwise, leave it alone.

Mouse

This control panel, shown in Figure 13-29, sets the mouse tracking and double-click speeds.

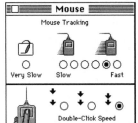

Figure 13-29:
The Mouse control panel, where speed is king.

The Mouse Tracking setting governs the relationship between hand movement on the mouse and cursor movement on the screen. Fast mouse tracking settings will send the cursor squirting across the screen with a mere flick of the wrist; slow mouse tracking settings will make the cursor crawl across in seemingly slow motion even when your hand is flying. Set it as fast as you can stand it. I like the second-fastest speed, as shown in Figure 13-29. Try it. You may like it.

The Double-Click Speed setting determines how close together two clicks must be for the Mac to interpret them as a double-click and not two separate clicks. The leftmost button is the slow setting. It lets you double-click at an almost-leisurely pace. The rightmost is the fast setting (which I prefer). The middle button, of course, represents a double-click speed somewhere in the middle.

Changes in the Mouse control panel take place immediately, so you should definitely play around a little and see what settings feel best for you.

Mouse no-brainer settings

Mouse Tracking: Moderately fast. Double-click speed: Middle setting.

Network

Select your network connection here. I've only got one connection available, LocalTalk, so it's selected in my Network control panel (see Figure 13-30).

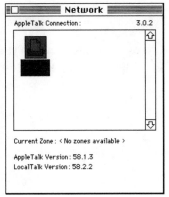

Figure 13-30:
Select your
network
connection
in the aptly
named
Network
control
panel.

If I had an EtherNet or Token Ring network connected to my Mac, the Network control panel would allow me to choose it instead of the built-in LocalTalk connection.

Numbers

Use this control panel to change the decimal and thousands separators (the period and comma in $1,000,000.00) as well as the symbol used to denote currency ($ in the U.S.A., £ in England, and so on). Figure 13-31 shows the Numbers control panel.

Figure 13-31:
You'll
probably
never see
your own, so
here's a
picture of my
Numbers
control
panel.

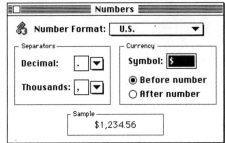

You could go through your entire life without ever needing to open the Numbers control panel.

PC Exchange

PC Exchange manages which Macintosh program launches when you open documents created on that other kind of computer, running that other operating system, MS-DOS (see Figure 13-32).

Figure 13-32:
If I open
a DOS
document
that has
the .TXT
suffix, PC
Exchange
tells
SimpleText
to launch
and
open the
document.

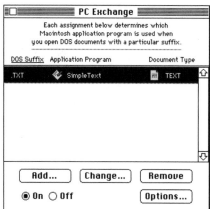

Apple throws in this application assignment — .TXT documents open in SimpleText — for free. If you'd prefer to read DOS files in a program other than SimpleText, click the application assignment to select it and then click the Change button (see Figure 13-33).

Figure 13-33:
ClarisWorks
will now
launch
when I open
a DOS
document
with the
.TXT suffix.

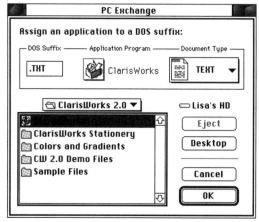

In the Change dialog box, you can change the three-letter suffix, the application program that you want to use to open that type of document, and the type of document.

If you click the Document Type pop-up and nothing happens, the type is set already for that document and you can't change it.

To remove an application assignment, select it by clicking and then click the Remove button.

Double-clicking an application assignment opens the dialog box, the same as selecting it and then clicking the Change button.

The Add button in the PC Exchange control panel brings up the same dialog box shown in Figure 13-33. To create a new application assignment, make your choices in the dialog box and then click OK.

PowerBook (PowerBooks Only, but You Knew That)

Less filling. Tastes great. Better Conservation. Better Performance. While you might find the first two in a bottle of beer, you won't find the next two on your PowerBook, at least not both at the same time. Using a PowerBook is a trade-off (more of a battle) between battery life and overall performance.

In Figure 13-34, if you move the slider toward Better Performance, your PowerBook will speed up but will use up batteries faster. If you move the slider toward Better Conservation, your batteries will last longer but your PowerBook will slow down.

Figure 13-34:
Better
Conservation
or Better
Performance?
You make
the call.

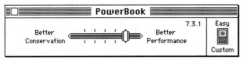

Simple enough. What's that you say? You want to know about the Easy/Custom switch? Don't ask.

You had to ask. OK, here goes. If you move the switch to Custom, a bunch of new controls appear, as shown in Figure 13-35.

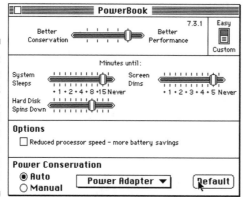

Figure 13-35:
The Custom
PowerBook
controls.
Think of all
the time you
can waste
playing with
these!

The Custom controls give you individual control over all the things that drain your battery. The number of combinations is endless.

I told you not to ask. Now don't blame me if you spend weeks playing with the Custom settings, using a stopwatch to see how long each battery lasts. Don't laugh. I've known people like that.

Me? I've got too much to do to fret over how many more minutes I can squeeze out of a battery. I don't care that much. I've got one of those big, fat PowerPlate 3X batteries from Technöggin that attaches to the bottom of your PowerBook with Velcro-like stuff. I keep the slider in the PowerBook control panel a little to the right of center, and the PowerPlate (plus the Apple battery in the PowerBook) is good for at least 5 or 6 hours, which is plenty long enough for me to find an outlet and recharge.

You can open the PowerBook control panel or choose from two arbitrary settings on the Performance/Conservation scale from the PowerBook Control Strip. Just press and hold on the icon as shown in Figure 13-36.

Figure 13-36:
Open the
PowerBook
control panel
or choose a
setting for it
right from
the Control
Strip.

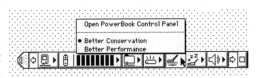

PowerBook Setup (PowerBooks Only, of Course)

PowerBook Setup (shown in Figure 13-37) does two things and two things only:

- Chooses an internal or external modem.

    and

- Chooses a SCSI ID number for your hard disk to use if you plug it into another Mac using "SCSI Disk Mode."

Figure 13-37:
The dual-
purpose
PowerBook
Setup
control
panel.

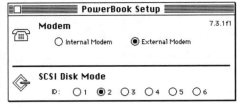

What is this SCSI Disk Mode (a.k.a. SCSI docking) stuff? Most PowerBooks can, with the proper cable, be hooked up to a desktop Mac's SCSI chain as though the PowerBook were a hard disk. This feature is neat. The PowerBook's hard disk mounts on the desktop Mac's Desktop just like any other hard disk would.

Anyway, because every SCSI device must have a unique ID number, you need a way to change the ID number of your PowerBook when you hook it up to your desktop Mac. Why? Internal hard disks are always numbered 0 at the factory.

Your desktop Mac probably has an internal drive with the ID number 0. And your PowerBook's internal drive came from the factory with the SCSI ID set to 0. Without PowerBook Setup, there would be a SCSI ID conflict and your Mac wouldn't boot.

So use PowerBook Setup to change your PowerBook's ID to one that isn't already being used on your SCSI chain before you try to dock it, OK?

PowerTalk Setup

As you might expect, this thing's only in your Control Panels folder if you install PowerTalk, the collaboration portion of System 7.5. You can turn PowerTalk on or off here; you can password protect your Key Chain after a set amount of inactivity; you can turn password protection at startup on or off; and you can open your PowerTalk Key Chain by clicking a button. Figure 13-38 shows you what I mean.

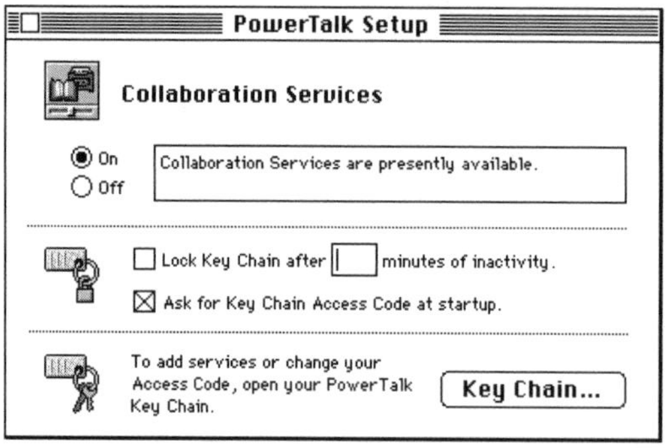

Figure 13-38:
The
PowerTalk
Setup
control
panel isn't
very
exciting,
is it?

That's what it does. You'll have to read Chapter 16 to find out what all this PowerTalk stuff is about.

Sharing Setup

Been there. Done that. Chapter 9, in case you've forgotten.

Sound

Use the Sound control panel to select the alert sound (the *beep* sound you hear a zillion times a day) and perform a few other audio-related tasks.

If your beep is still set to Simple Beep, try one of the others for a while.

To select a new beep, merely click its name in the sound list on the right side of the Sound control panel (see Figure 13-39).

Figure 13-39:
A Quack or
Droplet is
better than a
(Simple)
beep.

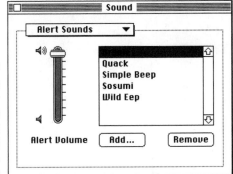

Or you can record your own sound if you have a microphone attached to your Mac. It's easy.

1. Click the Add button.

   A recording box appears, just like the one in Figure 13-40.

Figure 13:40:
Click the
record
button to
make your
own sounds.

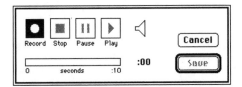

2. Click the Record button.

3. Make your noise or sound.

4. Click the Stop button.

5. Name the sound.

Bingo. That's it. Your new sound appears in the list of sounds. Select it now as your beep sound if you like. See. Told you it was a piece of cake (as long as you have the microphone).

The pop-up menu in the Sound control panel (it says Alert Sounds) contains three other choices: Sound In, where you choose an alternative to the built-in microphone if such a device is connected; Sound Out, where you can choose an alternative to the built-in speaker for playback; and Volumes, where you can set the master volume level for your computer (and the volume level for built-in headphones, for those lucky enough to own a Macintosh AV model). The Volumes options are shown in Figure 13-41.

Figure 13-41:
Some Macintosh AV models have a built-in headphone jack; these options enable you to control its volume level and that of the speaker.

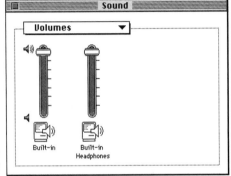

If you have an internal CD-ROM drive and want to listen to audio CDs through the built-in speaker or headphones, click the Options button in the Sound In window. Then click Internal CD and Playthrough.

Startup Disk

With this control panel, you choose which hard disk or hard disk volume (if you've partitioned your hard disk) should act as the startup disk when more than one drive with a System Folder is connected to the Mac (see Figure 13-42).

Figure 13-42:
This Mac
has six hard
disks
attached.
Das Boot
will be the
startup disk,
even if one
of the others
contains a
System
Folder.

Text

Another control panel you'll never need. Unless, of course, you have a version of System 7.5 other than the U.S. version. If you use more than one language on your Macintosh, you can choose between them in this control panel, which is shown in Figure 13-43.

Figure 13-43:
You'll
probably
never need
to touch the
Text control
panel.
Here's what
it looks like.

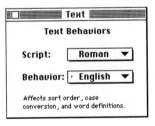

Users and Groups

I'm sorry if I sound like a broken record, but I covered this one in great detail back in Chapter 9. If you need to know, that's where to go.

Views

I've mentioned the Views control panel more than once, most recently in Chapter 11, but what the heck. A pop-up menu lets you select a font to be used in the Finder (see Figure 13-44).

Figure 13-44:
The Views control panel. Configure it properly and your Mac will feel faster.

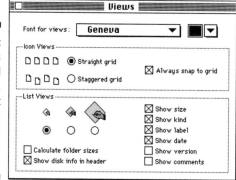

Geneva, which is in your Mac's ROM, is the fastest font. Fancy fonts can make the Finder feel sluggish.

The Icon Views section lets you turn on an invisible grid in windows using Icon views (view by Icon, view by Small Icon) and on the Desktop. Icons snap to the invisible grid, so your icons always line up in rows and columns, even without the Clean-Up command.

In the Finder, holding down the Command key while dragging an icon temporarily reverses the grid setting. In other words, if Always Snap To Grid is checked, holding down the Command key turns the grid off temporarily; if Always Snap To Grid is unchecked, holding down the Command key turns the grid on.

A Staggered grid nudges every other icon up or down a few pixels. A straight grid lines up all the rows.

The List Views section manages the appearance of Finder windows when they're in any of the list views. The three icons represent the size of icons in the list views. The small icon is the fastest of the three and also the least visually descriptive. The medium icon is a good compromise — it's more colorful and not terribly large. The large icon is all but useless, as it's so big in the lists that you can only see a few items at a time.

Calculate folder sizes puts the size (in K) next to each folder. It's discussed in Chapter 3 and Chapter 11 (I still say it makes your Mac feel more sluggish if it's turned on).

Show disk info in header tells you how much space has been used and how much space is remaining on the parent disk. It also tells you how many items are in a window (see Figure 13-45).

Figure 13-45:
The header tells me that there are 24 items using 34MB on my hard disk and that there are 120.2MB remaining.

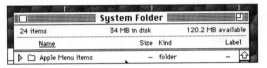

This header information is good to know, so I leave this option enabled on my Mac.

The six check boxes in the lower right of the Views control panel control what information is displayed in list views. Check the check boxes of ones that you want to see in the Finder.

Views no-brainer settings

See Figure 13-44. Make yours look like that.

WindowShade

WindowShade is a nifty little gadget that lets you roll up windows (like a window shade, get it?) at will. Figures 13-46 and 13-47 demonstrate.

Figure 13-46:
A double-
click in the
title bar will
hide the
window.

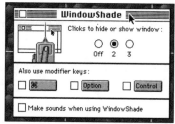
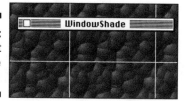

Figure 13-47:
All that's left
is the title
bar. See!

It works in any application, with almost every kind of window.

If you don't like rolling up your windows with a double-click, you can click one of the modifier-key check boxes. If I were to click the check box for the Command key, I would have to Command-double-click to roll up windows. You can use any combination of the Command, Option, and Control keys along with two or three clicks.

Finally, the sound check box provides a whooshing sound when you roll up a window.

The freeware version of WindowShade has been popular for years. Kudos to Apple for adopting this wonderful and useful little piece of code.

Chapter 14

How to Write an AppleScript in 21 Minutes

(The chapter title is, of course, a take-off on Viki King's wonderful book about that other kind of script writing, *How to Write a Movie in 21 Days.*)

AppleScript is like a tape recorder for your Mac. It can record and play back things that you do, such as opening an icon or clicking a button.

Describing AppleScript to a Mac beginner is a bit like three blind men describing an elephant. One man might describe it as the Macintosh's built-in automation tool. Another might describe it as an interesting but often overlooked piece of enabling technology. The third might liken it to a cassette recorder, recording and playing back your actions at the keyboard. A fourth (if there were a fourth in the story) would assure you it looked like computer code written in a high-level language.

They would all be correct. AppleScript is the Mac's built-in automation tool (at least in System 7.5 it is built in). It is a little-known (at least up to now) enabling technology. It is like a cassette recorder (for programs that support AppleScript recording). And scripts do look like computer programs (which could be because they are computer programs).

I call AppleScript a *time and effort enhancer*. AppleScript, if you just spend the time and effort it takes to learn it, will save you oodles of time and effort.

Therein lies the rub. This stuff isn't simple. There's no way in heaven I'm going to teach you how to use AppleScript in the next 15 pages. Entire books have been written on the topic, for gosh sake!

And don't kid yourself. AppleScript is complicated and will take some effort to master. So rather than try to teach you how to use it, I'll try to show you what AppleScript can do for you, and I'll get you to the point where you can write a simple script of your own, all in about 21 minutes.

What the Heck Is an AppleScript Anyway?

In the broadest sense, AppleScript is an enabling technology that lets you record and playback complex sequences of Macintosh events occurring in the Finder, programs, or any combination of the Finder and programs. In a narrower sense, AppleScript now makes it possible to automate multistep sequences, such as changing the bit depth of your monitor. What used to take at least three steps...

1. Open the Monitors control panel

2. Click a Number of Colors

3. Close the Monitors control panel

...can now be performed instantly and effortlessly with one script. This feature may not sound like much, but it can sure save you time and effort. The more often you perform a task each day, the more you should consider automating it (if, of course, it can be automated — not all programs can be automated, as you'll soon see).

The AppleScript components are installed automatically when you install System 7.5. (I'll discuss the components one-by-one after a brief rant.)

AppleScript has been around for a couple of years, but it was never included in System software. It always came in separate Scripter and Developer packages at additional cost. So it never really caught on with the masses.

In the meantime, many forward-thinking developers have incorporated AppleScript support in their programs. Better still, that number is growing faster now that AppleScript is part of the System software.

Power users have been clamoring for this stuff for years. It's finally here and it's only going to get better and more powerful as time goes on and more people get copies for free.

I encourage you, if you really want to master your Macintosh, to learn at least a bit of basic scripting. This chapter is a start, but your investment of time spent learning AppleScript will be repaid tenfold in time you save performing your daily tasks.

The Script Editor requires at least 700K of free memory (Largest Unused Block in About the Finder). If you're running QuickDraw GX and PowerTalk, you may not have enough free memory to launch Script Editor. You can free up over 3,000K if you turn PowerTalk and QuickDraw GX off. The easiest way is to open the Extensions Manager control panel, select the System 7.5 Only option from the pop-up menu, and then restart your Mac. (Don't forget to turn PowerTalk and QuickDraw GX back on later if you need them.)

Tools of the Trade: What the System 7.5 Installer Installs and Where It Installs It

System 7.5 includes a bevy of AppleScript-related items in various places on your hard disk. Some are essential to AppleScript's operation; the rest are merely convenient. Before you learn how to use them, here are your tools.

The AppleScript extension (in the Extensions folder, which is in the System Folder)

This extension is installed in the Extensions folder (in the System folder). It's the engine that makes AppleScript work. If it's not in the Extensions folder at startup, AppleScript won't work. It requires no other care or maintenance.

Scripting Additions folder (in the Extensions folder, which is in the System Folder)

This folder contains add-on parts of the AppleScript system. AppleScript is modular, so new commands can be added to AppleScript by merely dropping a new item into the Scripting Additions folder. Leave it be.

AppleScript Guide (in the AppleScript folder, which is in the Apple Extras folder)

This item consists of a pair of SimpleText documents, AppleScript Guide and AppleScript Guide part 2.

Why is AppleScript Guide in two parts? Because there's a limit to the size of SimpleText documents, and there's more stuff you need to know than can fit in a single document file. That's why. I think.

It doesn't matter why there are two of them. If you want to learn AppleScript, you're going to have to read them. They're dry but not as boring as they look once you get started.

Script Editor (in the AppleScript folder, which is in the Apple Extras folder)

Script Editor is the program with which you edit scripts. Duh. We'll play with it in a minute.

Automated Tasks folder (in the AppleScript folder, which is in the Apple Extras folder)

The Automated Tasks folder contains several useful scripts. Open and read the About Automated Tasks Read Me document at your earliest convenience.

There's an alias of the Automated Tasks folder in your Apple Menu Items folder (System 7.5 put it there for you; isn't it thoughtful?), so you can select any of these useful scripts right from the Apple menu.

Please note that Apple may have changed the names of some of the scripts before this book went to press. Also note that Apple will probably add and remove some scripts that the Installer installs as time goes by. So if you can't seem to find on your hard drive some of the scripts that I mention on the next few pages, there's nothing wrong with your System. Apple just changed the software.

Add Alias to Apple Menu

Creates aliases of items and places them in the Apple Menu Items folder. You can select the item and then run the script (via the Apple menu), or you can drag an item onto the icon of Add Alias to Apple Menu. Either way, an alias of the item will be created and stashed in the Apple menu.

Because of this drag-and-drop capability, you might want to keep a copy of this script (or better still, an alias of it) on your Desktop. A winner if you like adding stuff to your Apple menu.

Close Finder Windows

This script closes all of the open windows in the Finder. Big stupid deal. Command-Option-W or Option-clicking the close box of any window does the same thing.

It's not even a very interesting script — all it says is "Tell the Finder to close every window." A turkey.

Create Alias Folder

There are two ways to use this script, although I've yet to figure out what I'd use it for in real life. Here's what it does, anyway: It finds all items with a certain name and then creates aliases of them. The certain name is the name of a folder. Confused? Here, here are two ways to use it:

✔ **Way 1:** Create a folder (File⇨New Folder or Command-N) and name it the certain name you want your Mac to search for and make aliases of. In Figure 14-1, the word is "off." When I drop the "off" folder on the Create Alias Folder icon, an alias of every file on my hard disk that has the word "off" in its name will be placed in the "off" folder (see Figure 14-2).

Figure 14-1:
Dragging the "off" folder onto the Create Alias Folder script.

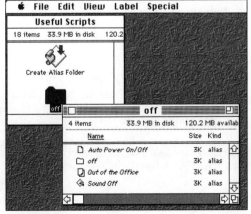

Figure 14-2:
The contents of the "off" folder after the Create Alias Folder script runs.

✔ **Way 2:** Open Create Alias Folder by choosing Apple menu⇨Automated Tasks⇨Create Alias Folder or by opening its icon. You will be prompted to enter a string of text to find (see Figure 14-3). If a folder of that name does not exist at the root level of your startup disk, it will be created. Aliases of all matching files whose name contains the string you entered will be placed inside this folder. In other words, it will look like the folder in Figure 14-2.

Figure 14-3:
The other way to fill a folder called "off" with aliases of every file whose name contains "off."

Find:

off

[Cancel] [OK]

Eject All

This script ejects all CDs, SyQuest, Bernoulli, or optical cartridges, and floppy disks. If File Sharing is on, it stops File Sharing, ejects the disks and then restarts File Sharing. This one is a winner. Sometimes, when you try to eject a CD, SyQuest, Bernoulli, or optical cartridge, your Mac will complain that it can't do that because File Sharing is on. The ordinary solution is to open the Sharing Setup control panel, turn File Sharing off, eject the disk or cartridge, turn File Sharing on, and then close Sharing Setup.

The script does not check to see if there are any connected users before turning off File Sharing, so if you want to be a good citizen, open your File Sharing Monitor control panel and see if anyone is connected before you use it.

Find Original from Alias

This script shows the original item (the parent) of an alias or aliases. Select the alias in the Finder and then run the script by choosing Apple menu⇨Automated Tasks⇨Find Original. You can also run the script by dragging any alias on top of the Find Original icon or an alias of it.

The other way to find the originator of an alias is to select the alias and choose File⇨Get Info (Command-I). Then click the Find Original button.

Hide/Show Folder Sizes

This script toggles the Calculate folders sizes check box in the Views control panel on and off. It's a little easier than opening the Views control panel. Each time you run the script, the setting is toggled. If Calculate folder sizes is currently on, running the script will turn it off, and vice versa.

Monitor 1 bit (B&W)

This script changes the setting in the Monitors control panel to black and white (2 colors/grays). This script and the next two are extremely handy.

Monitor 8 bit (256 colors)

This script changes the setting in the Monitors control panel to 256 colors/grays (bit depth of 8). If your monitor does not support 256 colors/grays, you'll be given the option to set the monitor to the maximum supported depth.

New Item Watcher

To use this script, you must first specify a single folder that you wish to watch. You can specify the folder by dragging a folder on top of the application or by launching the application and selecting a folder in the dialog box. The New Item Watcher script will then run in the background while you perform other tasks. If any new items are added to the watched folder, an alert will appear.

This process is easier to do than explain, so drop a folder on New Item Watcher (or select a folder in its dialog box) and then add an item to it. Within a few minutes, your Mac will let you know that a new item has arrived in the watched folder.

Neat exhibition of what AppleScript can do, but I've still never used it in real life. Maybe if I were in an office on a network, I could use it as a way of monitoring incoming documents in a shared folder.

Share a Drop Folder

This script checks to see if there is a folder named Drop Folder at the root level of the startup disk. If there is not one, the script creates one. If File Sharing is off, it turns File Sharing on. It then sets full guest access privileges for Drop Folder.

I guess if you're going to create a drop folder (which many people go through their entire existence without even considering), this script is a pretty nifty way to do it.

Sound Off

This script sets the volume in the Sound control panel to off. Good to have when the boss calls and you don't want him to hear the Disney screen saver rendition of "Beauty and the Beast."

When the sound is set to 0, the menubar will blink when your Mac would normally beep.

Start File Sharing

This script turns on File Sharing. It's much easier and faster than the old way. Two thumbs up.

Stop File Sharing

This script turns off File Sharing.

Sync Folders

This script compares the contents of two folders and synchronizes their contents. For example, let's say you have two folders, Folder A and Folder B. Folder A contains a document named "Document 1" and Folder B contains a document named "Document 2." The script copies "Document 1" to Folder B and "Document 2" to Folder A so that both folders contain both files (then they're said to be *synchronized,* thus the name of the script). To run the script, either drag two folders onto its icon or select two folders in the Finder and then choose Apple menu⇨Automated Tasks⇨Sync Folders.

If there are files of the same name in the folders, then the file with the latest modification date (the "newest" version) is copied to the other folder.

If you have a PowerBook, this script is very handy for keeping folders synchronized between the PowerBook and your regular Mac. Use File Sharing to mount the PowerBook's drive on your regular Mac's Desktop (or vice versa) and then Sync one folder from the PowerBook with one folder from the desktop Mac.

But wait, there's more

If you want to use AppleScript with programs other than the Finder, they have to be AppleScript enabled, which means that they have to be adapted by their developers to work with AppleScript.

There are three levels of AppleScript support found in applications: Scriptability, Recordability, and Attachability. Programs can support one, two, or all three levels.

Unfortunately, there is no easy way of telling whether a program is AppleScript enabled at all, much less if it's recordable or attachable. For what it's worth, the Finder supports all three levels.

Here are brief descriptions of the three levels of AppleScript support that you may find in third-party programs:

Scriptable programs

Scriptable means that the program can follow instructions sent by AppleScript scripts. Scriptable apps are the most common kind. If a program proclaims that it supports AppleScript, it's at this level, at least.

Unfortunately, it's up to the developer to decide how much of the program is actually scriptable, so some programs are more scriptable than others. Microsoft Excel, FileMaker Pro, PageMaker (limited support), and Now Up-to-Date/Now Contact are a few scriptable programs I know of.

Recordable programs

Recordable programs go scriptable programs one better. Recordable means that you can record your actions in the program and automatically create an AppleScript script for future playback based on what you did within the program. Few programs are recordable yet.

Attachable programs

Attachable programs are even rarer than recordable ones. Attachable means that the program will let you attach a script to an item or element in a document, such as a cell in a spreadsheet, a button in a database, or a rectangle in a drawing. The Finder is attachable because you can attach a script to an icon.

What it all means

At this point, you should know at least this much:

- AppleScript is a kind of recording and playback mechanism for repetitive tasks on your Mac.
- Some programs, most notably System 7.5's Finder, can be scripted to do some things under script control.
- A few programs can record and attach scripts.

Notice I didn't say "understand" up there, I said "know." To develop true understanding would require more pages than I've got. But I had to mention this stuff so that when you try to use a script with a non-scriptable (or non-recordable or non-attachable) program, you have at least a vague idea of why it's not working.

Writing a Simple Script

I agonized for a long time over this section. I want to teach you something useful, but it had to be easy enough to show in just a few pages.

I've realized that it can't be done. If a script is useful, it's going to require more explaining than I have space for. (And most of the easy, useful scripts are already done for you and thoughtfully placed in the Useful Scripts folder.) So instead, I'm going to show how to write a script that's totally dumb but fun to watch.

If you want to see smart scripts, open any of the ones in the Useful Scripts folder in Script Editor and examine it closely.

1. Launch the Script Editor application.

   A new, untitled script appears on the screen.

2. Type **My first stupid script** in the description field at the top of the document window.

3. Click the Record button.

   After a brief pause, your screen should look more or less like Figure 14-4. Notice the cassette tape where the Apple menu used to be. It flashes to let you know that you're recording.

4. Make the Finder active by clicking the Desktop or any open windows or choosing Finder in the Application menu.

5. Close all open windows (Option-Click on any window's close box, hold the Option key and choose File⇨Close All, or use the keyboard shortcut Command-Option-W). If there are no open windows on your screen, ignore this step.

6. Create a new folder on the Desktop (File⇨New Folder or Command-N).

7. Open the new, untitled folder and then click on its title bar and drag it to a new location. The farther you drag it, the better.

8. Option-click the zoom box (on the far-right side of the title bar) of the untitled folder window.

9. Drag the folder to a new location.

10. Return to the Script Editor application and click the Stop button.

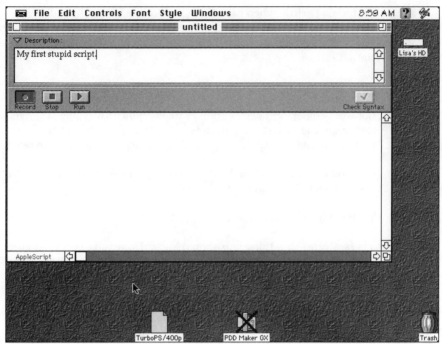

Figure 14-4:
Ready to
record a
script.

That's it! You've written your first script. It should look something like Figure 14-5. Don't save it yet. (As you'll see in a moment, there are choices yet to make about *how* to save your script.)

To see how your script works, click the Run button. Watch closely, as it happens fast. If you miss it, run the script again. It switches to the Finder, closes all open windows, creates a new folder, moves it, grows it, and then moves it again.

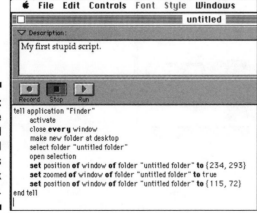

Figure 14-5:
The
completed
stupid
script. Yours
should look
similar.

```
tell application "Finder"
    activate
    close every window
    make new folder at desktop
    select folder "untitled folder"
    open selection
    set position of window of folder "untitled folder" to {234, 293}
    set zoomed of window of folder "untitled folder" to true
    set position of window of folder "untitled folder" to {115, 72}
end tell
```

I'm fudging a little when I say that you wrote a script. Actually, you recorded a script. If you had *written* it, you would have typed all the stuff between "tell application Finder" and "end tell" from memory, without actually performing the actions.

In fact, the most effective way to use AppleScript is a combination of recording and writing. First record your actions, analyze the script, and then try to figure out ways to perform each action more efficiently by typing in different commands and trying them. To reach this level of scripting mastery, you'll need to know a lot more about the AppleScript language than this chapter can teach you.

OK. You can return to the Finder and trash those untitled folders (one was created each time you ran the script).

So that's how to record a script.

There is one more thing you should know: Unfortunately, most control panels are not scriptable (Monitors and Sharing Setup are special cases).

If Your Script Is Any Good, It Should Be Saved

There are a three different ways to save a script. If you choose Save or Save As from the File menu in the Script Editor, a pop-up menu in the Save dialog box gives you your choices (see Figure 14-6).

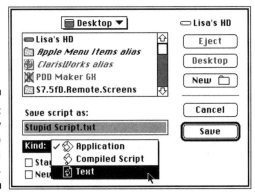

Figure 14-6:
So many
ways to
save a
script.

✔ The Text option creates a text file of your script. This script can be opened in any text editor for editing or reopened by Script Editor.

✔ The Compiled Script option creates a Script Editor file. You can open, run, or modify the file with the Script Editor program.

✔ The Application option creates a self-running script.

The files in the Useful Scripts folder are scripts saved as applications.

If the Never Show Startup Screen check box is unchecked in the Save dialog box, your script will display a startup screen with a Run button before it executes, as shown in Figure 14-7.

Figure 14-7:
Eliminate
this startup
screen by
checking the
Never Show
Startup
Screen
check box in
the Save
dialog box.

If you check the Stay Open check box, the script application remains open until you quit it. Scripts saved with this option usually look for something to happen and then perform an action. The New Item Watcher script in the Useful Scripts folder is one of these "stay-open-and-watch" applications.

Run Only means the saved file can't be edited. You would use the Save As Run Only command (in the File menu) if you had a spiffy script that you didn't want others to see or modify. Anyway, a Run Only script can never be modified. If you choose Save As Run Only instead of Save or Save As, the resulting file will be a Run Only application or compiled script (you can't save a Run Only text file). This script can never be modified or changed.

Chapter 15

What Can Stay and What Can Go

This chapter is by far the most useful chapter in the book. In this chapter, I go through the entire System Folder one item at a time. I show you how much RAM each item uses, how much disk space it occupies, and what (if any) side effects will occur if you delete or disable it.

There are no substitutes for RAM or hard disk space. But no matter how much you have, there will come a day when you need more of one or the other or both.

Yes there are band-aids like Virtual Memory or RAM Doubler (for making your Mac think it has more RAM than it does) or Stacker or AutoDoubler or other compression software (for making your hard disk think it's bigger than it is). And yes, I think you can use programs like this safely most of the time.

Most of the time. RAM Doubler doesn't pose much threat, as it doesn't really deal with files or the file system. Compression software, on the other hand, adds another layer of complexity to your Mac. It's always expanding and compressing files in the background, reading and writing from the hard disk. So there's more chance for errors to occur. And all compression software extracts a noticeable performance penalty, slowing down your Mac anywhere from a little to a lot, depending on the compression software, your Mac model, and the speed of your hard disk.

My advice: Resort to those devices if you must, but *real* RAM and hard disk space are much better.

Reclamation Theory

RAM and hard disks are expensive. Thus, I created this chapter, a first, I believe, in System software book history, a chapter dedicated to telling you how to get rid of the deadweight among the 20 megabytes of files in your System Folder by deleting or disabling.

Let's face it: System 7.5's Easy Install option puts a lot of files on your hard disk. (If you install both QuickDraw GX and PowerTalk, that's 187 files and folders, give or take a few.) Not everybody needs every single one of these files. These files can be deleted to free up (reclaim) hard disk space.

Many control panels and extensions load into RAM at startup. So not only do they take up disk space, extensions and control panels can use up your valuable RAM.

I'll go through the System Folder and see what each item costs you in terms of RAM and disk space, and what, if any, repercussions will be felt if you Trash or disable the item.

Life After Death: The Truth About Restoring Deleted Files

Before I can show you how to save RAM and disk space, I need to briefly cover a couple of important topics, backing up and reinstalling.

Other benefits of a lean, mean System Folder

There are a bunch of other benefits to keeping your System Folder lean and mean:

- The Apple menu submenu for the Control Panels folder will be shorter.

- The Control Panels folder will contain fewer items and thus be easier to manage.

- The Chooser will be less cluttered when you get rid of printer drivers you'll never need.

- Your Mac may start up and run faster if you don't load unneeded extensions and control panels.

Back up first

If you don't have a backup and you don't have a set of System 7.5 install disks, DO NOT DELETE ANY FILES! I repeat: If you don't have a backup and a set of System 7.5 install disks, DON'T TRASH ANYTHING.

That said, if you're faithful about making backups (you should be, as you've heard me harp about it enough times by now), you can delete files with relative impunity. If you decide you miss them, restore them from your backup.

Beware if you only have one backup set of disks or cartridges. Your backup software may keep a *mirror image* of your hard disk on the backup media. In other words, when you delete a file from your hard disk, the backup software may delete it from the backup disk(s).

The Installer: restorer of lost items

Any System software file you delete can be restored if you have a set of System 7.5 install disks. The degree of difficulty you'll encounter (and the amount of time it will take you) depends on what you need to restore.

For example, the System 7.5 Installer's Custom Install can install control panels and Apple menu items individually, but it won't, for some strange reason, install extensions individually (see Figure 15-1).

Figure 15-1:
The Custom Install Option. Strangely, you can't install individual extensions, only individual control panels and Apple menu items (not shown).

To reinstall any extensions you delete, you have to perform an Easy Install, which will reinstall anything and everything in one fell swoop.

Certain other files, such as printer drivers and some multimedia and networking files, can also be installed individually. Explore the Custom Install feature and you'll see what's what.

I still want to know why I can't install just the Find File extension (or any other single extension) using the Custom Install option. Apple?

Anyway, that's all you need to know at this time. It's OK to trash any piece of System 7.5 as long as you have a set of Install disks so that you can reinstall it if you discover you need or want it. Now let's move on and discover...

What, Exactly, Are Extensions and Control Panels?

Control Panels and Extensions appear first and second in the chapter because they make the most difference in reclaiming disk space and RAM. (I'll cover the rest of the System Folder later in the chapter.)

Extensions and control panels are a type of System software file with a special property: If they are not in the Control Panels or Extensions folder at startup, they do not load and will not function. (Or at least most won't. Some control panels can be used even if they aren't in the Control Panels folder at startup.)

Apple isn't the only one to make extensions and control panels. Many popular third-party programs, including famous names like After Dark, QuicKeys, and Now Utilities, are extensions or control panels.

Most extensions and control panels grab a certain amount of RAM when they load at startup. If you choose Apple menu⇨About this Macintosh right now, you'll see how much RAM they're using by looking at the bar for your System software, which includes the RAM used by all loaded extensions and control panels.

Some control panels can be run from a floppy disk. In other words, if you're really tight on hard disk space, you can copy certain control panels, such as Color or Date & Time, to a floppy disk and open the copy on the floppy if you need to change color, date, or time. Alas, this feature is only available with a handful of control panels. The rest must be in the System Folder at startup or they won't work. When in doubt, try it out.

Disabling 'em all with the Shift Key

You can disable *all* control panels and extensions by holding down the Shift key during startup until you see the "No Extensions" message appear beneath the "Welcome to Macintosh" greeting. That's what I've done in Figure 15-2. So my naked System software uses 1,376K of RAM, leaving me 6,774K available for running applications (the Largest Unused Block in Figure 15-2).

Figure 15-2:
No extensions
or control
panels loaded
= 6,774K of
RAM available
for my
programs.

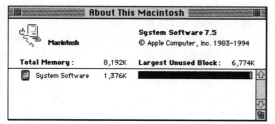

Discriminating disabling with Extensions Manager

When I use the Extensions Manager control panel to turn on all the Extensions, including PowerTalk and QuickDraw GX (both of which, you remember, have to be installed separately and are not part of the Easy Install), the System software uses 5,220K of RAM, leaving me only 2,623K for programs (the Largest Unused Block in Figure 15-3).

System 7.5 (finally) includes an extension manager that lets you enable and disable extensions and control panels quickly and easily to make better use of your precious RAM.

Figure 15-3:
With
everything
loaded, there's
a lot less RAM
available for
my programs
(4,000K less,
give or take
a few).

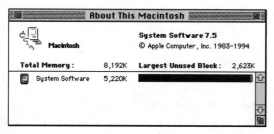

In the bad old days, disabling extensions and control panels was a messy affair that entailed moving them out of the Extensions or Control Panels folders manually and rebooting. It wasn't long before a wide variety of third-party extension/control panel managers appeared on the market. Prior to System 7.5, almost everyone I know used one.

Here's an example of why you might want to: You can reclaim more than 3 megabytes of RAM by just disabling the PowerTalk and QuickDraw GX extensions and control panels!

In the rest of the chapter, when I say how much RAM you'll save by disabling an extension or control panel, I mean that's how much RAM you'll save by turning it off (that is, unchecking it) in the Extensions Manager control panel. (Of course, you'll also save that amount of RAM if you delete the file totally.)

The disk space measurement for each file is the size shown in list view in the Finder. The Quadra 605 I used had a 160 megabyte hard disk. If you have a much larger disk, the files may occupy slightly more space on your disk than the numbers shown in this chapter due to something called File Allocation Blocks, which is complicated and not important.

In other words, your mileage may vary and my disk-size figures are just estimates provided for your convenience.

The same goes for my RAM measurements. Your mileage may vary slightly. I measured RAM usage with a wonderful shareware extension/control panel manager called Symbionts, of which I'm proud to be a registered owner. If you use other software to measure RAM usage, your numbers may be slightly higher or lower.

One final thing: I performed all the testing for this chapter using a freshly installed copy of System 7.5. If you have other files in your System Folder, they're not part of System 7.5.

In your System Folder, you'll see several folders with "(disabled)" after their names, such as Control Panels (disabled) and Extensions (disabled). Leave them alone. They are used by the Extensions Manager to disable control panels and extensions by moving them into these folders. *Remember, if the control panel or extension isn't in the Control Panels or Extensions folder at startup, it doesn't load.*

Control Panels

These control panels were covered in depth in Chapter 13. If you don't understand the cryptic comments or side effects, try re-reading that control panel's entry in Chapter 13.

Apple Menu Options

Disk Space: 60K

RAM Used: 47K

Side effects if disabled or deleted: Lose Apple menu submenus and Recent Item tracking.

Comments: I'd keep it. I love submenus and Recent Item tracking. Unless I were terribly RAM-constrained (using a 4 or 5MB Mac), I would never even consider disabling it, much less deleting it.

ATM GX

Disk Space: 408K

RAM Used: 436K

Side effects if disabled or deleted: Jaggies on-screen and on output from non-PostScript printers if you use Type 1 fonts.

Comments: You only need ATM GX if you meet the following two criteria:

1. You are running QuickDraw GX.

    and

2. You are using Type 1 fonts.

(Reprinted from Chapter 13 with permission.)

With its whopping memory and disk requirements, if you don't need it, trash it. 408K is a lot of disk space and 436K is a lot of RAM to waste. If you think you may someday need it, at least disable it with Extensions Manager until then.

Cache Switch (68040 Macs)

Disk Space: 8K

RAM Used: 0

Side effects if disabled or deleted: Lose capability to turn 68040 internal cache on and off.

Comments: Keep it. You'll probably need it some day.

Color

Disk Space: 13K

RAM Used: 0

Side effects if disabled or deleted: Lose capability to change window and text highlight color.

Comments: Keep it or you'll be stuck with same window and text highlight color for the rest of your life. (Gasp.)

ColorSync System Profile

Disk Space: 23K

RAM Used: 0

Side effects if disabled or deleted: Lose capability to use ColorSync.

Comments: Get rid of it unless you use ColorSync on all your monitors, printers, and scanners.

Date & Time

Disk Space: 68K

RAM Used: 5K

Side effects if disabled or deleted: Lose capability to set Macintosh internal clock.

Comments: Keep it. If your hard disk is horribly crowded, this is one of the control panels that you can copy to a floppy disk and use, even if it wasn't in the Control Panels folder at startup.

Desktop Patterns

Disk Space: 190K

RAM Used: 0

Side effects if disabled or deleted: Lose capability to change Desktop pattern.

Comments: Can be run from a floppy if you must.

Extensions Manager

Disk Space: 130K

RAM Used: 0

Side effects if disabled or deleted: Lose capability to enable and disable individual control panels and extensions.

Comments: You need it. Keep it.

File Sharing Monitor

Disk Space: 5K

RAM Used: 0

Side effects if disabled or deleted: Lose capability to monitor network traffic or disconnect users from your disk.

Comments: If you don't use File Sharing, you don't need it.

General Controls

Disk Space: 63K

RAM Used: 18K

Side effects if disabled or deleted: Too numerous to mention.

Comments: Keep it. If 63K of hard disk space or 18K of RAM makes a difference to you, you've got big problems, and disabling or trashing the General Controls control panel isn't going to help you.

You can get along without General Controls, but you won't be able to change any of its settings without first putting it back in the Control Panels folder and restarting your Mac. It won't run if you try to launch it from a floppy; it has to be in the Control Panels folder when you start up or it won't work.

Keyboard

Disk Space: 10K

RAM Used: 0

Side effects if disabled or deleted: Lose capability to specify key repeat speed and rate or choose foreign language keyboard layouts.

Comments: Keep it.

Labels

Disk Space: 5K

RAM Used: 0

Side effects if disabled or deleted: Lose capability to change names or colors of labels (as seen in the Finder's Label menu).

Comments: Your call. I never use it. But at a mere 5K of disk space, there's not much to be gained by deleting it, and you might miss it some day.

Launcher

Disk Space: 130K

RAM Used: 0

Side effects if disabled or deleted: Loss of Launcher window.

Comments: You've already heard what I think about Launcher (Chapter 7, if you've forgotten already). I trashed mine.

Macintosh Easy Open Setup

Disk Space: 10K

RAM Used: 0

Side effects if disabled or deleted: Lose capability to configure Macintosh Easy Open (see Chapter 13).

Comments: Keep it.

Map

Disk Space: 33K

RAM Used: 0

Side effects if disabled or deleted: Loss of map.

Comments: Big deal. Trash it.

Memory

Disk Space: 40K

RAM Used: 0

Side effects if disabled or deleted: Too numerous to mention (see Chapter 10 for details).

Comments: Do not delete!

Monitors

Disk Space: 130K

RAM Used: 0

Side effects if disabled or deleted: Lose capability to switch monitor color depths. Lose other capabilities if you have more than one monitor.

Comments: Keep it.

Mouse

Disk Space: 20K

RAM Used: 0

Side effects if disabled or deleted: Lose capability to change mouse tracking or double-click speed.

Comments: Keep it.

Network

Disk Space: 43K

RAM Used: 0

Side effects if disabled or deleted: Lose capability to choose a network connection.

Comments: You don't need it if you're not on a network.

Numbers

Disk Space: 18K

RAM Used: 0

Side effects if disabled or deleted: Lose capability to change thousands separators, decimal separators, and symbols for currency.

Comments: I've never used it.

PC Exchange

Disk Space: 358K

RAM Used: 18K

Side effects if disabled or deleted: Lose capability to mount PC- (DOS) formatted floppy disks.

Comments: If you never get or use DOS disks, you can safely delete it. If you occasionally have to deal with DOS disks, disable it with Extensions Manager and save 18K of RAM.

PowerTalk Setup

Disk Space: 18K

RAM Used: 1K

Side effects if disabled or deleted: Lose capability to configure PowerTalk and your Key Chain.

Comments: If you use PowerTalk, you need it; if you don't, you don't.

Sharing Setup

Disk Space: 5K

RAM Used: 0

Side effects if disabled or deleted: Lose capability to turn File Sharing (and Program Linking) on or off.

Comments: You only need it if you use File Sharing. If you never use File Sharing, make sure it's turned off before you delete it.

Sound

Disk Space: 5K

RAM Used: 0

Side effects if disabled or deleted: Lose control over speaker and microphone volumes; lose choice of beep sound; lose capability to record sounds.

Comments: Keep it.

Startup Disk

Disk Space: 8K

RAM Used: 0

Side effects if disabled or deleted: Lose capability to choose a startup disk if more than one disk with a System folder is connected at startup.

Comments: You may need it someday, especially if you're going to add an additional storage device — external hard disk, SyQuest, Bernoulli, or magneto-optical disk drive, or whatever. I say keep it.

Text

Disk Space: 15K

RAM Used: 0

Side effects if disabled or deleted: Lose capability to choose Text Behaviors.

Comments: If you only run the American version of System 7.5, you'll probably never need it.

Users & Groups

Disk Space: 5K

RAM Used: 0

Side effects if disabled or deleted: Lose capability to create users and groups for File Sharing.

Comments: If you don't use File Sharing, you don't need it.

Views

Disk Space: 5K

RAM Used: 0

Side effects if disabled or deleted: Lose capability to configure Finder views.

Comments: Keep it.

WindowShade

Disk Space: 28K

RAM Used: 7K

Side effects if disabled or deleted: Lose capability to roll up windows.

Comments: I love it. I'm keeping mine.

Control panels by RAM used

Table 15-1 is a quick-reference chart of the control panels in descending order of RAM usage.

Table 15-1	Control Panel RAM Usage
Control Panel	*RAM Used*
ATM GX	436K
Apple Menu Options	47K
PC Exchange	18K
General Controls	18K
WindowShade	7K
Date & Time	5K
PowerTalk Setup	1K

Cache Switch (68040 Macs), Color, ColorSync System Profile, Desktop Patterns, Extensions Manager, File Sharing Monitor, Keyboard, Labels, Launcher, Macintosh Easy Open Setup, Map, Memory, Monitors, Mouse, Network, Numbers, Sharing Setup, Sound, Startup Disk, Text, Users & Groups, and Views use no RAM, even if they're in the Control Panels folder at startup.

Control panels by disk space used

Table 15-2 is a quick-reference chart of the control panels in descending order of disk space they consume.

Table 15-2	Control Panel Disk Space Usage
Control Panel	*Disk Space*
ATM GX	408K
PC Exchange	358K

(continued)

Table 15-2 (continued)

Control Panel	Disk Space
Desktop Patterns	190K
Extensions Manager	130K
Launcher	130K
Monitors	130K
Date & Time	68K
General Controls	63K
Apple Menu Options	60K
Network	43K
Memory	40K
Map	33K
WindowShade	28K
ColorSync System Profile	23K
Mouse	20K
Numbers	18K
PowerTalk Setup	18K
Text	15K
Color	13K
Keyboard	10K
Macintosh Easy Open Setup	10K
Cache Switch (68040 Macs)	8K
Startup Disk	8K

File Sharing Monitor, Labels, Sharing Setup, Sound, Users & Groups, and Views use 5K each.

Extensions

There are three main types of extensions among the approximately 60 items in your Extensions folder:

- ✔ System extensions
- ✔ Chooser extensions
- ✔ AppleGuide documents

AppleGuide documents use no RAM, nor do most Chooser extensions. System extensions, on the other hand, almost always grab a bit of RAM at startup. There are also a couple of other kinds of files in the Extensions folder; I'll talk about them after I finish with the big three.

Let's start with the most important extensions, the ones that can save you lots of precious RAM if you disable or delete them (if, of course, you don't need them). I'm talking about your System extensions.

System extensions

EM Extension

Disk Space: 5K

RAM Used: 1K

Side effects if disabled or deleted: Lose use of Extensions Manager control panel.

Why is EM Extension first in an alphabetical list? Because Apple ships it with a space before the E so that it is first in alphabetical lists. Extensions load alphabetically, and because this is the extension that gives Extensions Manager its powers, it must load before other extensions in order to turn them on or off.

Hold down the spacebar just after you power up your Mac to use Extensions Manager *before* other extensions begin to load.

Comments: Keep it.

Apple CD-ROM

Disk Space: 40K

RAM Used: 0

Side effects if disabled or deleted: Lose use of CD-ROM drives.

Comments: If you have a CD-ROM drive, keep it.

Apple Guide

Disk Space: 523K

RAM Used: 43K

Side effects if disabled or deleted: Lose AppleGuide (interactive help).

Comments: Tough call. It uses a great deal of disk space and a significant amount of RAM, but I think it's worth keeping. Delete or disable it only if you must.

Apple Photo Access

Disk Space: 160K

RAM Used: 0

Side effects if disabled or deleted: Lose capability to open PhotoCD files.

Comments: PhotoCD is the Kodak format for high-resolution image storage. They mostly come on CD-ROM disks. If you're likely to encounter PhotoCD files, keep it. If you don't have a CD-ROM drive, you probably don't need it.

AppleScript

Disk Space: 298K

RAM Used: 40K

Side effects if disabled or deleted: Lose use of AppleScript scripts and Script Editor program.

Comments: You read Chapter 14, right? You know if you want to keep AppleScript. (I would.)

Audio CD Access

Disk Space: 10K

RAM Used: 0

Side effects if disabled or deleted: Lose capability to play audio CDs (that is, your Pearl Jam and Elvis Costello CDs, or at least *my* Pearl Jam and Elvis CDs).

Comments: If you don't have a CD-ROM drive, you don't need it. If you have a CD-ROM drive, you should probably keep it around, just in case.

Catalogs Extension

Disk Space: 405K

RAM Used: 0

Side effects if disabled or deleted: Lose use of PowerTalk features.

Comments: Don't delete it if you use PowerTalk.

Clipping Extension

Disk Space: 28K

RAM Used: 0

Side effects if disabled or deleted: Lose Macintosh Drag and Drop features.

Comments: Keep it.

Color Picker

Disk Space: 120K

RAM Used: 2K

Side effects if disabled or deleted: Loss of the new Color Picker 2.0 (shown in Figure 15-4).

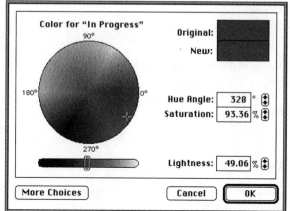

Figure 15-4:
The new Color Picker 2.0.

Comments: This whole shebang refers to which Color Picker you'll see in programs that use a color picker to choose among colors (most graphics programs). To see it yourself, open the Labels control panel and click on any of the colors.

The new Color Picker is, in my humble opinion, prettier than the old one (which is shown in Figure 15-5) and probably easier to use. The gray-scale picture doesn't do it justice, but trust me: the new one looks better.

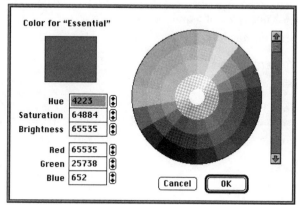

Figure 15-5:
The old-style Color Picker.

ColorSync

Disk Space: 80K

RAM Used: 33K

Side effects if disabled or deleted: Lose use of ColorSync (Apple's color matching system for monitors, printing devices, and scanners).

Comments: You probably don't need it unless you scan or print color images.

File Sharing Extension

Disk Space: 173K

RAM Used: 4K

Side effects if disabled or deleted: Lose File Sharing capability.

Comments: If you don't use File Sharing, you can safely delete it.

File System Extensions

Disk Space: 43K

RAM Used: 9K

Side effects if disabled or deleted: Lose several file system bug fixes and support for volumes between 2 and 4 gigabytes.

Comments: Keep it. It fixes bugs.

Find File Extension

Disk Space: 23K

RAM Used: 20K

Side effects if disabled or deleted: Lose use of the new Find File feature (see Figure 15-6).

Comments: The System 7.5 Find File is much better than older versions. It's faster. It displays its results in a window (the old one takes you to your file in the Finder, which is much slower), and it can search on multiple criteria (that is, name and size, or date and label, and so on). The old Find File (see Figure 15-7) can only search for one thing at a time.

I wouldn't delete or disable it.

Finder Scripting Extension

Disk Space: 183K

RAM Used: 1K

Side effects if disabled or deleted: Lose use of AppleScript in the Finder.

Comments: If you use AppleScript, don't delete or disable it.

Foreign File Access

Disk Space: 35K

RAM Used: 126K

Side effects if disabled or deleted: Lose capability to mount some CD-ROM disks.

Comments: If you have a CD-ROM drive, you need it; if you don't, you don't.

High Sierra File Access

Disk Space: 18K

RAM Used: 0

Side effects if disabled or deleted: Lose capability to mount some CD-ROM disks.

Comments: If you have a CD-ROM drive, you need it; if you don't, you don't.

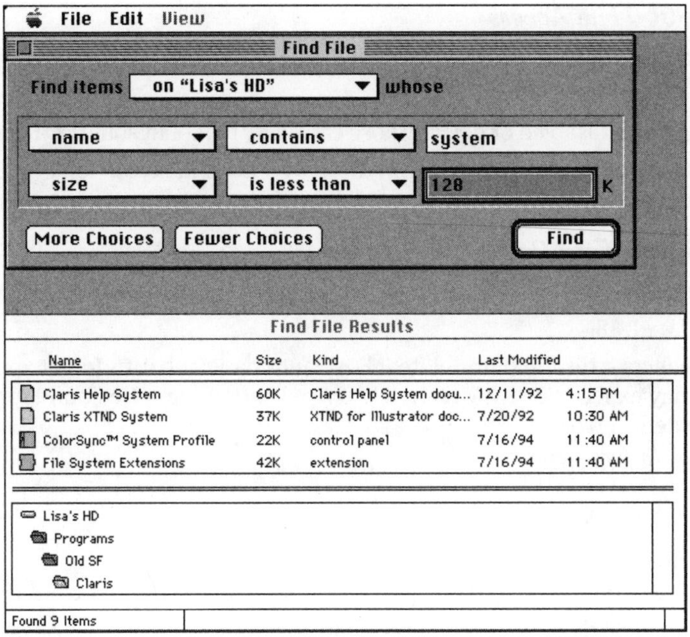

Figure 15-6:
The System
7.5 Find File.
Compare it
to Figure
15-7, the
old-style
Find File
(System 7.0).

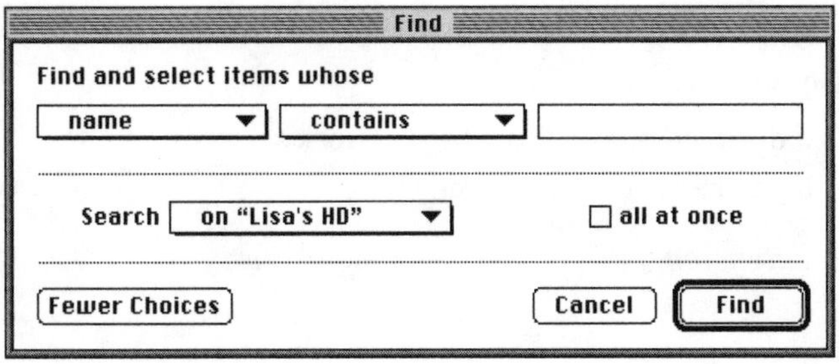

Figure 15-7:
The old-
style Find
File. This is
what you'll
see if you
disable
or delete the
Find File
Extension.

InlineFilter (non-U.S. Systems only)

Disk Space: 3K

RAM Used: 1K

Side effects if disabled or deleted: Lose use of AppleScript in double-byte foreign languages.

Comments: If it's in your Extensions folder, you need it. If you have the U.S. version of System 7.5, you don't have it, nor do you need to worry about it.

ISO 9660 File Access

Disk Space: 20K

RAM Used: 0

Side effects if disabled or deleted: Lose capability to mount some CD-ROM disks.

Comments: If you have a CD-ROM drive, you need it; if you don't, you don't. (I'm sorry if I sound like a broken record, but that's my advice.)

Macintosh Easy Open

Disk Space: 135K

RAM Used: 18K

Side effects if disabled or deleted: Lose automatic substitution of applications. You may experience the dreaded "An Application Can't Be Found for This Document" error.

Comments: Keep it.

Mailbox Extension

Disk Space: 148K

RAM Used: 0

Side effects if disabled or deleted: Lose PowerTalk mailbox services.

Comments: If you use PowerTalk, keep it.

Network Extension

Disk Space: 80K

RAM Used: 0

Side effects if disabled or deleted: Lose network services.

Comments: If you're on a network, keep it.

PowerTalk Extension

Disk Space: 625K

RAM Used: 65K

Side effects if disabled or deleted: Lose use of PowerTalk.

Comments: If you use PowerTalk, keep it.

PowerTalk Manager

Disk Space: 553K

RAM Used: 8K

Side effects if disabled or deleted: Lose use of PowerTalk.

Comments: If you use PowerTalk, keep it.

Printer Share

Disk Space: 80K

RAM Used: 12K

Side effects if disabled or deleted: Lose capability to share certain devices such as plotters that could not be shared previously. Also lose the capability to password-protect color printers that use expensive printing materials as well as services.

Comments: If you're on a network, ask your network administrator before deleting or disabling.

PrinterShare GX

Disk Space: 33K

RAM Used: 0

Side effects if disabled or deleted: Lose capability to share certain devices such as plotters that could not be shared previously. Also lose the capability to password-protect color printers that use expensive printing materials as well as services

Comments: Only required if you're using QuickDraw GX. Check with your network administrator before deleting or disabling it, though.

Quadra (or PowerBook or Power Macintosh or Performa) Monitors Extension

Disk Space: approximately 8K

RAM Used: 0

Side effects if disabled or deleted: Lose monitor options usually seen if you Option-click the Options button in the Monitors control panel, including (but not limited to) special gamma settings.

Gamma refers to the balance between colors on your screen. Depending on your monitor and video card, you may be able to change the gamma setting for your monitor.

The Quadra 605's internal video gives me two preset choices when I Option-click the Options button in the Monitors control panel: Mac Std Gamma or Uncorrected Gamma. Other monitors and video cards may offer no choices or three or more preset choices. To my eye, on my monitor, Mac Std Gamma is clearly brighter and clearer than Uncorrected Gamma, which is darker and muddier.

Unless you're involved in color prepress or other work where the absolute correctness of colors on-screen is a must, there is no reason not to choose the setting that most pleases your eye.

Comments: Keep it (even though you'll probably never use it).

QuickDraw GX

Disk Space: 1,600K

RAM Used: 1,130K

Side effects if disabled or deleted: Lose use of QuickDraw GX features (see Chapter 8).

Comments: It's a pig — over a megabyte of RAM and more than 1.5 megabytes of disk space. You should carefully consider whether the new features of QuickDraw GX are worth the RAM and disk space they consume. (See also the ATM GX control panel, described earlier in this chapter.)

QuickTime

Disk Space: 825K

RAM Used: 40K

Side effects if disabled or deleted: Lose capability to play QuickTime movies or use QuickTime applications.

Comments: Can be turned off until needed to reclaim 40K of RAM. I leave mine enabled all the time, but I probably have more stuff that requires QuickTime than you do.

SCSI Manager 4.3

Disk Space: 50K

RAM Used: 67K

Side effects if disabled or deleted: Slower hard disk access.

Comments: Keep it.

Shortcuts

Disk Space: 183K

RAM Used: 0

Side effects if disabled or deleted: Lose Finder Shortcuts in the Help menu.

Comments: Read the Shortcuts at least once. After that, it's your call.

Chooser extensions

Chooser extensions are extensions that appear in the Chooser desk accessory when you open it. AppleShare is one of them; all the others are *printer drivers*, the software that your Mac requires to talk to a printer.

AppleShare

Disk Space: 78K

RAM Used: 32K

Side effects if disabled or deleted: Lose use of File Sharing.

Comments: If you use File Sharing, you need it; if you don't, you don't.

Printer Drivers

The Installer puts several printer drivers into your Extensions folder for you:

Apple Color Printer, AppleTalk ImageWriter, ImageWriter, ImageWriter GX, ImageWriter LQ GX, LaserWriter, LaserWriter 300, LaserWriter 300 GX, LaserWriter 8, LaserWriter GX, LaserWriter IISC GX, LQ AppleTalk ImageWriter, LQ ImageWriter, LW Select 310, Personal LaserWriter SC, Portable StyleWriter, StyleWriter GX, and StyleWriter II.

Disk Space: Between 38K (LaserWriter IISC GX) and 500K (LaserWriter 8) each

RAM Used: 0

Side effects if disabled or deleted: None, as long as you leave the driver for *your* printer(s) (that is, the printer(s) that you use) in the Extensions folder.

Comments: You only need the driver or drivers that match the printer(s) you use. If you never use an Apple Color Printer, for example, get rid of the Apple Color Printer Chooser extension. If you never use an ImageWriter, get rid of all the ImageWriter Chooser extensions. And so on.

PDD Maker GX

Disk Space: 23K

RAM Used: 0

Side effects if disabled or deleted: Lose capability to make PDD files (see Chapter 8 for details).

Comments: I'm keeping mine.

AppleGuide documents

There are four AppleGuide documents in the Extensions folder: About Help Guide (5K), Macintosh Guide (1,788K), PowerTalk Guide (325K), and Shortcuts (183K).

Disk Space: 5K to 1,778K

RAM Used: 0

Side effects if disabled or deleted: Lose use of AppleGuide interactive help.

Comments: If you don't use PowerTalk, you can safely delete PowerTalk Guide. I'd leave the other four alone. You never know when you'll need help, and if you delete these files, help won't be available when you need it.

Other items in the Extensions folder

AppleTalk Service

Disk Space: 20K

RAM Used: 0

Side effects if disabled or deleted: Lose use of AppleTalk connections for PowerTalk.

Comments: If you use PowerTalk, you need it. If you don't, you don't.

PrintMonitor

Disk Space: 65K

RAM Used: 160K

Side effects if disabled or deleted: Lose capability to print in background.

Comments: Keep it.

PrintMonitor is not an extension, though it lives in the Extensions folder. It is an application. Thus, it only uses 160K of RAM when background printing is taking place.

If you have problems with background printing, try increasing PrintMonitor's Preferred Memory Size (in its Get Info window).

Finder Help

Disk Space: 65K

RAM Used: 0

Side effects if disabled or deleted: Loss of certain Balloon Help balloons in the Finder.

Comments: Keep it.

Printer Descriptions Folder

This folder in your Extensions folder contains printer description files for 21 Apple printers. Each requires 15K of disk space and uses no RAM. You can delete all but the one (or ones) that match your printer or printers.

Scripting Additions Folder

Contains components of AppleScript. Removing any of the files in this folder may cause AppleScript to behave erratically. If you use AppleScript, leave this folder alone. If you don't use AppleScript and never plan to, you can delete it.

Business Card Templates

Disk Space: 18K

RAM Used: 0K

Side effects if disabled or deleted: Lose use of business card templates when using PowerTalk.

Comments: If you use PowerTalk, you should probably keep it.

Extensions by RAM used

Table 15-3 is a quick-reference chart of the extensions sorted in descending order by RAM usage.

Table 15-3	Extension RAM Usage
Extension	*RAM Used*
QuickDraw GX	1,130K
Foreign File Access	126K
SCSI Manager 4.3	67K
PowerTalk Extension	65K
Apple Guide	43K
QuickTime	40K
AppleScript	40K
ColorSync	33K
AppleShare	32K
Find File Extension	20K
Macintosh Easy Open	18K
Printer Share	12K
File System Extensions	9K
PowerTalk Manager	8K

The following extensions use 5K of RAM or less: About Help Guide, Apple CD-ROM, Apple Photo Access, AppleTalk Service, Audio CD Access, Business Card Templates, Catalogs Extension, Clipping Extension, Color Picker, EM Extension, File Sharing Extension, Finder Help, Finder Scripting Extension, High Sierra File Access, InlineFilter, ISO 9660 File Access, Macintosh Guide, Mailbox Extension, Network Extension, PDD Maker GX, PowerTalk Guide, PrinterShare GX, Quadra Monitors Extension, and Shortcuts.

Extensions by disk space used

Table 15-4 is a quick-reference chart of the extensions sorted in descending order by the amount of disk space they require.

Table 15-4	Extension Disk Space Usage
Extension	*Disk Space*
Macintosh Guide	1,788K
QuickDraw GX	1,600K
QuickTime	825K

(continued)

Table 15-4 *(continued)*

Extension	Disk Space
PowerTalk Extension	625K
PowerTalk Manager	553K
Apple Guide	523K
Catalogs Extension	405K
PowerTalk Guide	325K
AppleScript	298K
Finder Scripting Extension	183K
Shortcuts	183K
File Sharing Extension	173K
Apple Photo Access	160K
Mailbox Extension	148K
Macintosh Easy Open	135K
Color Picker	120K
ColorSync	80K
Network Extension	80K
Printer Share	80K
AppleShare	78K
PrintMonitor	65K
Finder Help	65K
SCSI Manager 4.3	50K
File System Extensions	43K
Apple CD-ROM	40K
Foreign File Access	35K
PrinterShare GX	33K
Clipping Extension	28K
Find File Extension	23K
PDD Maker GX	23K

The following extensions use 20K of disk space or less: About Help Guide, AppleTalk Service, Audio CD Access, Business Card Templates, EM Extension, High Sierra File Access, InlineFilter, ISO 9660 File Access, and Quadra Monitors Extension.

Don't forget printer drivers! Though they're not listed individually, you may be able to free up a couple of megabytes of disk space by deleting the ones that you don't need.

The Rest of the Stuff in Your System Folder

The installer installed more than just control panels and extensions. Here's what the rest of it does:

Apple Menu Items

The Apple Menu Items folder, covered extensively in Chapter 4, contains some folders, some desk accessories, and some applications.

The items in your Apple Menu Items folder only use RAM after you open them. So don't get rid of them to save RAM. If you're really short on disk space, Table 15-5 shows how much each Apple Menu Item uses.

Table 15-5	Apple Menu Items Disk Space Usage
Item	*Disk Space*
Find File	168K
AppleCD Audio Player	138K
Jigsaw Puzzle	105K
Stickies	100K
Note Pad	63K
Scrapbook	50K
Chooser	38K
Key Caps	13K
Calculator	8K
Key Chain	5K
• Shut Down	5K

The only one that's an easy call is Jigsaw Puzzle, which is totally useless. (Wife Lisa chimes in: "Don't tell them that! I like the Mac jigsaw puzzle — the kids can't hide the pieces.") The other items are all useful in some way, and I'd recommend keeping them around.

The difference between applications and desk accessories

I promised back in Chapter 4 that I'd explain the difference between an application and a desk accessory (DA) here in Chapter 15. Being a man of my word, here goes:

Desk accessories are a throwback to System 4 and earlier, when there was no multitasking, and there was no way to run more than one program at a time. Desk accessories were mini-programs that could be used even while other programs were open.

These days, now that opening multiple programs is the norm, desk accessories are the same as other programs — with three little differences:

1. In list views, under the Kind category, desk accessories are listed as desk accessories (duh), not applications.

2. You can't change a desk accessory's Minimum or Preferred Memory Requirements.

3. Every desk accessory uses 20K of RAM (in About This Macintosh).

For all intents and purposes, a desk accessory is the same as an application program.

Clipboard

Disk Space: 10K

RAM Used: 0

Side effects if disabled or deleted: Lose Clipboard contents at the moment of deletion.

Comments: This file is like a chameleon's tail — it regenerates if it's damaged or destroyed. So don't bother deleting it, it'll just grow back. Besides, why would you want to?

Finder

Disk Space: 445K

RAM Used: About 400K

Side effects if disabled or deleted: Lose use of Mac.

Comments: Don't even think about it. Your Mac won't boot without a Finder.

MEO Database

Disk Space: varies

RAM Used: 0

Side effects if disabled or deleted: Lose all Macintosh Easy Open application/ document assignments.

Comments: Don't delete it if you use Macintosh Easy Open.

PowerTalk Data (folder)

Contains all your important PowerTalk stuff. Don't delete it if you use PowerTalk.

Preferences

The Preferences folder is where all programs, extensions, control panels, and desk accessories store their preferences files. These files store information that the program (or extension, control panel, or desk accessory) needs to remember between uses.

Most preference files regenerate themselves when deleted, so trashing them is usually a waste of time.

When you get rid of a program, extension, control panel, or desk accessory, there's a good chance that it's left behind a preference file in the Preferences folder. It's not a bad idea to go into your Preferences folder every so often and trash any files that appear to belong to software no longer on your hard disk.

For example, if you decide that you never want to use the Launcher control panel again, you can delete the Launcher Preferences. Though Launcher Preferences only uses a few K of disk space, after a while, your Preferences folder may become quite crowded with preference files that belong to software you don't even have on your hard disk any longer.

Ack! I just looked at the Preferences folder on my main Mac and discovered almost 200 preference files, at least half from programs that I no longer have or use.

I'll be right back — I'm going to practice what I preach and clean it up by trashing unneeded and unwanted prefs files.

I'm back. While I was doing my spring cleaning, I remembered another good tip having to do with preference files: Trashing a program's preference file can sometimes fix problems with the program itself.

If you have a program, extension, control panel, or desk accessory that's acting strange in any way, crashing, freezing, or quitting unexpectedly, look in the Preferences folder and see if it's got a preference file. If it does, try deleting it. Then restart your Mac.

This tip doesn't always work, but it's worth a try if a program that used to work starts acting funky.

By the way, some programs, such as Word 5, store all of your customized settings (key combinations, menu items, window positions, and so on) in their preference files. If you delete these files, you may have to reset some of your customized settings in these programs. In most cases, that's no big deal, but in the case of my Word preferences, I'd have to spend about three hours recustomizing all of my menus and keyboard shortcuts. Not fun. In fact, I keep a backup copy of my Word prefs on a floppy just in case the file gets corrupted or somebody comes along and changes things when I'm not around.

ColorSync Profiles (in Preferences folder)

Disk Space: 70K

RAM Used: 0

Side effects if disabled or deleted: Lose use of ColorSync.

Comments: If you don't use ColorSync, you can delete it.

System

Disk Space: 2,503K

RAM Used: About 1,200K

Side effects if disabled or deleted: Lose use of Mac.

Comments: Don't even think of it. Your Mac won't boot if this file isn't in the System Folder.

System 7.5 Update

This file is installed when you upgrade to System 7.5.1. For more information on the System 7.5 Update and System 7.5.1, see the Appendix.

Part IV

Beyond the Lunatic Fringe:
The Infamous Part of Tens

The 5th Wave   **By Rich Tennant**

IF BOB DYLAN HAD PURSUED A CAREER IN COMPUTERS.

"PUT HIM IN FRONT OF A TERMINAL AND HE'S A GENIUS, BUT OTHER-WISE THE GUY IS SUCH A BROODING, GLOOMY GUS HE'LL NEVER BREAK INTO MANAGEMENT."

In this part...

We're in the home stretch now. Just three more chapters and you're outta here.

These last three are a little different — they're kind of like long top ten lists. I'd like you to believe that it's because I'm a big fan of Dave, but the truth is, IDG Books has always put "Part of Tens" in books with *Dummies* in their titles, and this book must continue the tradition. Because IDG pays me, I'm doing these chapters their way. (Actually, it's kind of fun.)

First, I'll briefly describe ten items that weren't installed with System 7.5 (but you might need someday). I'll show you what they do, how to install them, and why you might need them. A couple of them might actually be useful to you someday.

I'll then move on to a subject near and dear to my heart: Ten awesome things for your Mac that are worth spending money on.

Finally, you'll take a tour of Dr. Mac's top ten troubleshooting tips, for those times when good System software goes bad.

Chapter 16

Ten Optional Pieces of System Software You Might Someday Need

● ●

In This Chapter

▶ MacTCP

▶ Easy Access

▶ TokenTalk

▶ Close View

▶ PlainTalk (AV models only)

▶ PowerTalk

▶ QuickDraw GX

● ●

*T*here's a bunch of stuff that's not installed when you perform an Easy Install of System 7.5, and it's all covered in this chapter. Maybe you won't need it, maybe you will, but there's no way to tell until you know what it is, what it does, and how to install it.

As they say in the Hokey Pokey, that's what it's all about.

You can use the Custom Remove option in the Installer pop-up menu to remove any of these items after you've installed them.

MacTCP

MacTCP is the control panel that allows Macs to connect to industry-standard TCP/IP (the industry-standard five-letter acronym [FLA] for Transmission Control Protocol/Internet Protocol) networks.

If you're interested in the Internet, you've surely heard about the wonderful graphical user interface (GUI, pronounced "gooey") software that's available for Mac users, such as Eudora, TurboGopher, and Mosaic. Well, you'll need MacTCP if you plan to run any of this cool stuff.

You'll also need SLIP (FLA for Serial Line Internet Protocol) or PPP (TLA for Point to Point Protocol), but neither of these two programs (they are actually control panels) comes from Apple, so you'll have to find them yourself.

In other words, you need MacTCP to connect to any TCP/IP network (that is, most large businesses' networks and/or the Internet). If you want to use neat software like Eudora or Mosaic, you'll also need to get SLIP or PPP software.

Installing MacTCP

If you're planning to communicate over a TCP/IP network, here's how to install MacTCP:

1. Insert Install Disk 1 (or, if your System software came on a CD-ROM, insert the CD), launch the Installer, and click the Continue button on the Welcome to System 7.5 screen.

2. Choose Custom Install from the pop-up menu at the top left of the Installer window (see Figure 16-1).

Figure 16-1:
To get to the Custom Install screen, choose Custom Install from the pop-up menu.

3. Click the triangle to the left of Networking Software to expand it. Then click the MacTCP check box (see Figure 16-2).

4. Click the Install button.

Figure 16-2:
First, click
the triangle
to the
left of
Networking
Software (to
expand it);
then click
the MacTCP
check box.

5. Insert disks as requested.

(If you're installing from CD-ROM, you don't need to insert disks; the Installer pulls what it needs from the CD.)

When it's done, you'll see a dialog box telling you the software was installed successfully and you must restart your Mac to use your new software.

6. Click the Restart button.

The little "i" button to the far right of each item in the Installer reveals a screen full of information about the item. You'd think it might tell you something useful, but it doesn't.

What? You want to see for yourself? OK. Look at Figure 16-3.

Figure 16-3:
The little "i"
button
doesn't
provide
much
information,
does it?

And don't get your hopes up for the Help button. It's a little more informative, but not much (see Figure 16-4). Balloon Help isn't any better. Fortunately, as you can see, using the Installer program is relatively straightforward.

This is Apple's spiffy new Installer program?

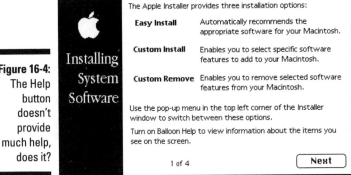

Figure 16-4:
The Help button doesn't provide much help, does it?

> ### Help
>
> The Apple Installer provides three installation options:
>
> **Easy Install** Automatically recommends the appropriate software for your Macintosh.
>
> **Custom Install** Enables you to select specific software features to add to your Macintosh.
>
> **Custom Remove** Enables you to remove selected software features from your Macintosh.
>
> Use the pop-up menu in the top left corner of the Installer window to switch between these options.
>
> Turn on Balloon Help to view information about the items you see on the screen.
>
> 1 of 4   Next

Installing System Software

Aren't you glad you bought *Macintosh System 7.5 For Dummies?*

I'm not going to even *try* to tell you how to configure MacTCP. And I'm not weaseling out. Figure 16-5 shows you what I mean.

Figure 16-5:
The configuration dialog box for MacTCP.

> Obtain Address:
> ○ **Manually**
> ● **Server**
> ○ **Dynamically**
>
> IP Address:
> Class: **A** Address: 0.0.0.0
> Subnet Mask: 255.0.0.0
>
> Net | Subnet | Node
> Bits: 8   0   24
>
> Net: 0   □ Lock
> Subnet: 0   □ Lock
> Node: 0   □ Lock
>
> Routing Information:
> Gateway Address:
> 0.0.0.0
>
> Domain Name Server Information:
> Domain   IP Address Default
>
> OK   Cancel

The reason I'm not going to tell you how is that I don't know how — it's different for every network. You'll have to contact your network administrator or Internet service provider to find out how to configure MacTCP.

Disk Space: 118K

RAM Used: 93K

Side effects if not installed: Can't connect to TCP/IP networks.

Comments: Don't run it if you don't need it. Don't even install it. For most of you, this chapter is just to let you know that this stuff is available if you ever need it.

Easy Access

Easy Access (shown in Figure 16-6) is a control panel designed primarily for people with impaired mobility. That doesn't mean it might not come in handy for you.

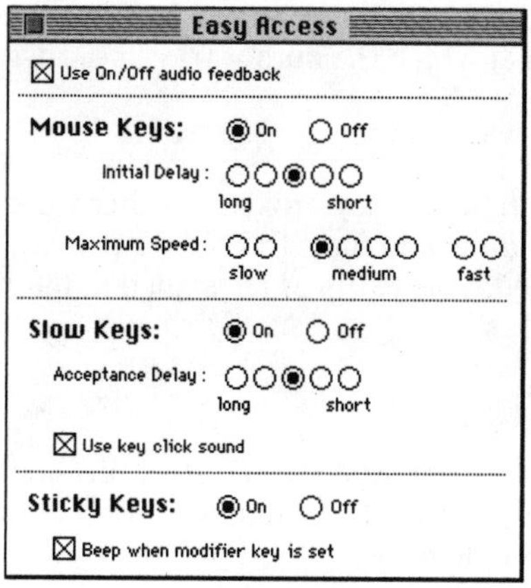

Figure 16-6:
The Easy
Access
control
panel may
come in
handy for
any user.

Easy Access lets you do three things:

✔ Use the numeric keypad on your keyboard (instead of the mouse) to control the cursor on the screen.

✔ Type keyboard shortcuts without having to press both keys at the same time.

✔ Type very slowly.

Mouse Keys

When you turn on Mouse Keys, the numeric keypad controls the cursor instead of the mouse. The 5 key is the mouse button; the 0 key is the click and hold button. The rest of the numbers control the cursor direction (see Figure 16-7).

Figure 16-7: The numeric keypad controls the cursor. The 5 key is a click; the 0 key is a click and hold.

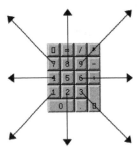

The keyboard shortcut Command-Shift-Clear toggles Mouse Keys on and off. If you have the audio feedback option checked, you'll hear a whoop when Mouse Keys is turned on and another when it's turned off.

The Mouse Keys radio buttons control the delay before movement occurs (after you press the key) and the speed at which the cursor travels across the screen.

Slow Keys

Slow Keys delays the Mac's recognition of keystrokes. In other words, if the acceptance delay is set to Long, you would have to hold down a key for almost two seconds for it to be recognized. This feature is designed to filter out inadvertent and accidental key presses.

Sticky Keys

Sticky Keys lets you type keyboard shortcuts one key at a time. In other words, to open on an icon, you'd ordinarily press the Command and O keys simultaneously. Sticky Keys makes it possible to press the Command key first and then the O key after it.

The keyboard shortcut for turning Sticky Keys on and off is to press the Shift key five times in rapid succession. To lock the modifier key down, press it twice in rapid succession.

As illustrated in Figure 16-8, when you press the modifier key, you'll see a little icon in the upper-right corner of your menubar that gives you visual feedback on the state of Sticky Keys.

Figure 16-8:
Sticky Keys
On (left);
modifier key
pressed and
waiting for
keystroke
(middle);
and modifier
key locked
(right).

Installing Easy Access

Follow the steps for installing MacTCP but substitute Control Panels for Networking Software and Easy Access for MacTCP.

Disk Space: 13K

RAM Used: 18K

Side effects if not installed: Can't use keypad instead of mouse, type slow, or type using Sticky Keys.

Comments: It can come in handy. For example, in programs that don't have a nudge command for moving objects one pixel at a time using the arrow keys, Easy Access' Mouse Keys makes a decent substitute. It might be worth installing for this feature alone.

TokenTalk

If you're on a Token Ring network, you need to install this software. If you need to install this puppy, there's probably someone with a title like "network administrator," "computer guy," or "boss" who can help you configure it.

Choosing this option will install a total of five files: A/ROSE, TokenTalk Phase 2, TokenTalk Prep, and MacTCP Token Ring Extension (all System extensions), and the Token Ring control panel.

A/ROSE stands for Apple Realtime Operating System Extension. I don't know what that means, but that's what it stands for. I don't really know what any of this stuff does, just that you need it if you're on a TokenTalk network.

Because the A/ROSE extension requires 75K of RAM, I strongly recommend you not install the TokenTalk software unless you're on a Token Ring network.

Installing TokenTalk

TokenTalk is installed exactly like MacTCP — just substitute TokenTalk for MacTCP in Step 3.

Disk Space: Way too much if you're not on a TokenTalk web.

RAM Used: At least 75K.

Side effects if not installed: Can't connect to TokenTalk.

Comments: Don't even install it unless you need it.

Close View

Close View blows up your screen. No, it doesn't make it explode; it enlarges the image, and it can all be done with keyboard shortcuts!

The Close View control panel appears in Figure 16-9. The black frame around it is the area that will be displayed when I turn Magnification on (in Figure 16-10).

Installing Close View

Follow the steps for installing MacTCP but substitute Control Panels for Networking Software and Easy Access for MacTCP.

Disk Space: 33K

RAM Used: 333K

Side effects if not installed: Lose magnification of screen.

Comments: Close View uses a lot of memory. If you can afford the RAM, it's a useful little doohicky to have around. It can give you a zoom feature in programs that don't allow zooming. On the other hand, 333K is a lot of RAM to waste if you don't use Close View often.

Install it, but turn it off using Extensions Manager. If you need it, enable it in Extensions Manager and restart.

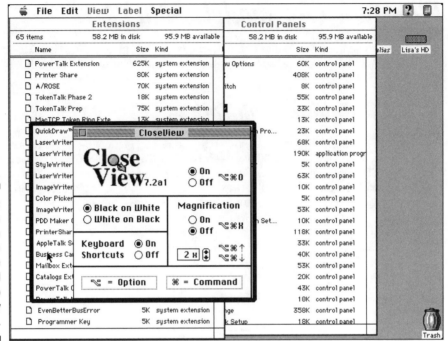

Figure 16-9:
If I turn on
Magnification
now, the
area in the
frame will
be blown up
to fill my
screen.

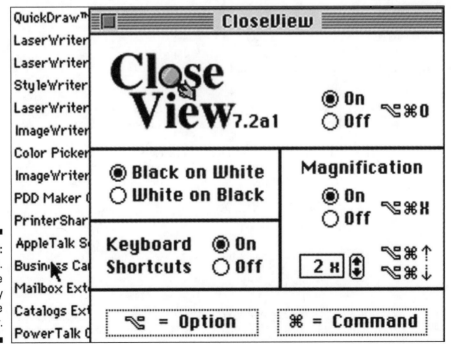

Figure 16-10:
Like this.
This image
fills my
entire
monitor.

PlainTalk (AV models only)

If you have any Macintosh with the letters AV in its name, your Mac can talk. And listen. And respond to voice commands. Not well, but not that badly either.

Installing PlainTalk

The PlainTalk software (shown in Figure 16-11) must be installed for talking to take place. To install it, insert the PlainTalk Install 1 disk (or insert the CD-ROM), open the Installer, and perform an Easy Install, just like you would with System 7.5 or QuickDraw GX or PowerTalk. This installs several files including the Speech Setup control panel shown in Figure 16-11.

Figure 16-11:
The Speech
Setup
control
panel.

I had a Power Macintosh 7100/66 AV for a while and found that PlainTalk was fun to show visitors but not quite useful in everyday work.

When you turn Speech Recognition on, a small windoid appears on your screen with your selected character. Her ear 'glows' when she's listening as shown in Figure 16-12. If she doesn't understand you, she'll say "Pardon me?"

Unfortunately, the computer doesn't understand you far too often for PlainTalk to be truly useful.

Disk Space: Over 5 megabytes

RAM Used: More than 55K

Side effects if not installed: Your Mac won't understand you when you speak to it (not that it does with PlainTalk installed), and your Mac won't talk back.

Comments: Install it, play with it for a while, and then turn it off using Extensions Manager.

Turn off the Speech Manager, SR Monitor, and Speech Recognition extensions, as they're the ones that use up all the RAM.

Five megs is a lot of space on your hard disk. You might want to remove the whole mess once you've played with it. Because it's made up of almost half a dozen extensions and control panels, the easiest way is to use the Installer's Uninstall option. Just hold down the Option key when you see the Custom Install screen.

PowerTalk

PowerTalk, the collaboration software I told you about in Chapter 6, is not installed when you install System 7.5. It uses a separate installer program on a separate set of disks.

Installing PowerTalk

To install PowerTalk, insert the disk called Install (or the CD-ROM) and open the icon called Install PowerTalk (see Figure 16-13). Click the Continue button on the splash screen and then click the Install button in the Install PowerTalk window. Feed disks as needed. Restart.

You may have noticed there are no tutorials for using PowerTalk in this book. That's because I think that not many people are going to use it. At least not right away. And, to tell the truth, I thought that the pages could be put to better use explaining other things, things you were more likely to need to know.

Figure 16-13:
The Install disk is the same for PowerTalk and Quick-Draw GX.

I could be wrong. If you would have liked to have seen a PowerTalk chapter with tutorials in this book, please send IDG Books or me a note or e-mail. If enough people say so, I'll add a chapter to the second edition.

PowerTalk consists of many files and folders including: PowerTalk Setup, Catalogs Extension, Mailbox Extension, PowerTalk Extension, PowerTalk Manager, and PowerTalk Guide, plus templates and folders.

Disk Space: 2,000+K

RAM Used: 74K

Side effects if disabled or deleted: Lose use of PowerTalk.

Comments: If you use PowerTalk, keep it all.

QuickDraw GX

Another puppy that's not installed with System 7.5.

Installing QuickDraw GX

If you want it, perform its installation the same way you install PowerTalk. Substitute the word QuickDraw GX for PowerTalk in the PowerTalk hands-on section and you'll be set.

I'm not going to say much about QuickDraw GX here except that it's optional and belongs in this chapter. Anything else I have to say I said already in Chapter 8.

OK. I'll say one more thing: I think that for most people, the benefits of QuickDraw GX, at least today, aren't worth the RAM it uses (almost 1.5 megs of RAM if you use ATM GX!).

Reread Chapter 8 if you can't remember what the benefits are. (I can't. I just had to reread it myself!)

The next three items neatly round off this particular Part of Tens. They are installed along with QuickDraw GX. Look for them in your Programs folder.

Because all three items are application programs, you can copy them to a floppy disk after they're installed on your hard disk. Then delete them from your hard disk. Run them from the floppy when you need them.

LaserWriter Utility

LaserWriter Utility is a multipurpose program for configuring your Apple laser printer. It won't work with third-party printers, so don't even try it.

Figure 16-14 shows its File and Utilities menus, which contain all the things it can do. If you need to do any of these things, just launch LaserWriter Utility and choose the command from the appropriate menu.

Figure 16-14:
LaserWriter
Utility does
a lot for
one little
program.

File	
Download Fonts...	⌘D
Display Available Fonts...	⌘L
Initialize Printer's Disk...	
Page Setup...	
Print Font Catalog...	⌘P
Print Font Samples...	
Quit	⌘Q

Utilities
Name Printer...
Set Startup Page...
Get Page Count...
Imaging Options...
Calibrate Printer...
Configure Communication...
Print Configuration Page...
Download PostScript File...
Remove TrueType™...
Restart Printer...
Change Zone...
Print Density...
Paper Handling...
Power Saving...

Paper Type Editor

Paper Type Editor lets you create new paper descriptions that you can use with the new QuickDraw GX print dialog boxes (Chapter 8, remember?). This utility lets you specify paper with dimensions other than the ones that come with your Mac (letter, legal, and so on). Figure 16-15 shows what it looks like.

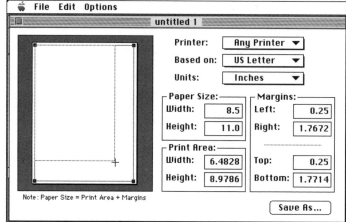

Figure 16-15:
The Paper
Type Editor
in action.

Type 1 Enabler

The Type 1 Enabler program converts Type 1 fonts to QuickDraw GX-compatible fonts, making them fully scalable so that they look better on-screen. Before conversion, you may only have one or two point sizes that look good on-screen. After conversion, the font will look good in any size you use, even odd numbers like 13 points.

It's a good idea to convert your Type 1 fonts if you're going to use QuickDraw GX.

To use Type 1 Enabler, launch it. You'll see a standard Open dialog box like the one in Figure 16-16. Choose a single font suitcase or a folder full of Type 1 fonts that you want converted. Another Open dialog box will appear. Choose the Fonts folder in your System Folder as the destination for the converted fonts. Type 1 Enabler does the rest.

Figure 16-16:
Just open
the font or
folder,
choose a
destination
folder, and
Type 1
Enabler
does the
rest.

Select Type 1 Fonts Source Folder or Suitcase

Printer Apps ▼   Lisa's HD

Eject

Desktop

Cancel

Open

Select "Printer Apps"

Chapter 17

Ten Ways To Make Your Mac Better by Throwing Money at It

In This Chapter

▶ Stuff I think you ought to buy

T his is my favorite part. As you've probably figured out by now, I love souping up my Mac. I live to find ways of working smarter, saving time, and saving hand motion. And I revel in tweaking my Mac and System 7.5. So it gives me great pleasure to share this chapter, my personal top ten things you can buy for your Mac to tweak it and make it faster, easier to use, and (I hope) more fun.

The items listed in this chapter are things I have, use every day, love dearly, and would buy again.

✔ **RAM:** It's worth every penny. If you have a four- or five-meg Mac, you'll like it a lot better if you upgrade to 8 (for under $150).

✔ **Big monitor:** You'll spend less time scrolling and rearranging windows. You'll spend more of your time getting actual work done, which is a good thing, right?

✔ **Modem:** You're capacity to communicate will increase ten-fold. Join an on-line service, surf the Internet, e-mail you friends, and much, much more.

✔ **Now Utilities:** It puts System 7.5 on steroids. Use it for a week and you'll wonder how you lived without it.

✔ **QuicKeys:** This utility creates macros, called *shortcuts,* that can perform a task or a series of tasks (a *sequence*) with a single command. It's like AppleScript, only better.

✔ **Retrieve It:** This little-known utility from Claris searches for text within documents. It's a great addition to Find File.

✔ **Back up software:** If your work means anything to you, get something that helps automate the task of backing up your files.

✔ **Games:** I just love Prince of Persia 2, Spectre Supreme, PGA Tour Golf II, Jewelbox, and MYST.

✔ **CD-ROM Drive:** Turn your boring Mac into a multimedia entertainment and education center. Just make sure that you at least get a double-speed drive. And then buy a few...

✔ **CDs:** There are some great games, references, and educational titles out there. You'll love 'em, and so will your kids.

So there you have it: ten awesome ways to spend a big chunk of change. So ladies and gentlemen, start your checkbooks. Go forth, throw money at it, but most of all, have fun.

Chapter 18

Troubleshooting: Ten Things to Try When Good System Software Goes Bad

● ●

In This Chapter

▶ The dreaded sad Mac

▶ The flashing question mark

▶ Startup crashes

▶ Reinstallation

● ●

I said Chapter 15 was "easily the most useful chapter in the book." It is. Unless you wake up one morning to find your Macintosh sick or dying. Then (and only then) is this chapter more useful because it's the one that is going to save your bacon.

As a bleeding-edge Mac enthusiast with almost ten years of Mac under my belt, I've had more than my share of Mac troubles. Over those years, I've developed an arsenal of tips and tricks that I believe can resolve more than 90 percent of Macintosh problems without a trip to the repair shop.

Disclaimer: Of course, if your hardware is dead, there's nothing you or I can do about it. But if your hardware is OK, there's a 90-percent chance that something (or a combination of things) in this chapter will get you up and running.

 I know that there are *more* than ten things in this chapter. My editor, Tim Gallan, says it doesn't matter, that the "Part of Tens" in *Dummies* books is sort of just for show, and I don't really have to have ten of anything as long as I use the word "ten" in the chapter name.

Think of this chapter as yet another occasion where I give you more than your money's worth.

Dem Ol' Sad Mac Chimes of Doom Blues

One thing we all dread seeing is the sad Mac icon (see Figure 18-1) and hearing that arpeggio in G minor better known as the Chimes of Doom.

Figure 18-1:
The sad
Mac icon.

The sad Mac usually indicates that something very bad has happened to your Mac, often that some hardware component has bitten the dust. But sad Macs are rather uncommon — many users go years without seeing one. If you've got one, don't despair. Yet. There is something you can try before you diagnose your Mac as terminal — something that just might bring it back to life! Try this:

1. Shut down your Mac.

2. Insert the Disk Tools disk.

3. Restart your Mac.

If you see the Welcome to Macintosh message when you booted off your Disk Tools disk, there's hope for your Mac. You're in like Flynn. The fact that you could boot from a floppy indicates that there's a problem with your hard disk or your System Folder. Whatever it is, it will more than likely respond to one of the techniques discussed throughout the rest of this chapter, so read on.

If the forthcoming techniques don't fix the problem, or you still see the sad Mac icon when you start up with Disk Tools, your Mac is beyond my help and needs to go in for repairs (usually to an Apple dealer).

Before you drag it down to the shop, you might try 1-800-SOS-APPL. They may well suggest something else you can try.

Flashing Question Mark Problems

Go through these steps in sequence. If one doesn't work, move on to the next.

Now would be a good time to reread the "Question Mark and the Mysterions" section of Chapter 1, which explains the flashing question mark and why Disk Tools is the ultimate startup disk. Both are things you need to know before you continue.

1-800-SOS-APPL

This is a very good number to know. It's Apple's technical support line and it's good for all Apple-branded products. If nothing in this chapter brings you relief, call them before you lug the box down to the repair shop. Maybe they know something I don't.

In the bad old days, Apple's stance on technical support was, "Ask your Apple dealer." That position, as you might guess, wasn't very satisfying, at least not to users. So a few years ago, Apple saw the light and instituted direct, toll-free technical support via the aforementioned 1-800-SOS-APPL, a big win for Macintosh users.

I have, since the line opened up several years ago, called a few times a year, often with an obscure problem. I have to say that they are very well informed at Apple tech support — they are batting close to 1000, believe it or not. These guys and gals do know their stuff.

There is a drawback to this service: You may have to wait a bit. Some days it takes 30 minutes to get a live person on the phone.

Call using a speakerphone. Enjoy the soothing music and continue with your work until you hear a live person.

On the other hand, I've often had my call answered on the first ring. I think it's easier to get through first thing in the morning; they're open from 6 to 6, Pacific time.

The Disk Tools disk is *soooo* important, so it's a good idea to have more than one copy. That way, if one copy gets misplaced, damaged, eaten by the dog, accidentally formatted, exposed to a strong magnetic field, or otherwise rendered useless, you won't be totally out of luck.

I keep a copy of Disk Tools in my middle desk drawer and the master disk(s) on the bookshelf.

It's a good idea to make copies of the rest of the System 7.5 master installer disks and then use the copies to install. But that's a lot of disk copying and I wouldn't blame you if you didn't bother. If a disk goes bad, you can easily get it replaced.

But if you don't have a working copy of Disk Tools, you can't do any of the stuff in the rest of the chapter. So make a copy of it right this minute before you forget. It's the most important floppy disk you own.

If you still see the flashing question mark after inserting the Disk Tools disk, it's possible your Disk Tools disk is damaged. As a last resort, try starting up your Mac with the Install Disk 1 inserted. If you see the Installer, your copy of Disk Tools isn't functional. Try your backup copy.

Start with something easy: rebuild the desktop

Before attempting more drastic measures, try rebuilding the desktop.

Actually, rebuilding the desktop should go under the heading of preventive maintenance. Apple recommends rebuilding the desktop once a month, and so do I.

Another good time to rebuild the desktop is if you notice icons disappearing, changing, or being replaced by generic icons (see Figure 18-2). This problem is usually a result of a desktop that needs rebuilding.

Figure 18-2:
If your formerly pretty icons turn generic, like these, try rebuilding the desktop.

The desktop (notice that I'm using a small "d" to differentiate it from the Desktop on your screen) is an invisible database that keeps track of every file on your hard disk, manages what icon goes with which file, and manages which program launches when you open a document.

More strictly speaking, the desktop is a pair of invisible files called Desktop DB and Desktop DF. They're stored at root level, but you can only see them with special software designed to work with invisible files. Leave them alone.

Another good time to rebuild the desktop is if you start getting "an application can't be found for this document" errors when you know that you have the application or have assigned a substitute using Macintosh Easy Open.

How to actually do it

Anyway, to rebuild the desktop, hold down the Command and Option keys during startup until you see the dialog box in Figure 18-3.

After you click OK, you'll see a thermometer window as the desktop is rebuilt. In a moment or two, it disappears and you're off and running.

Figure 18-3:
Yes, you
want to.
Click OK.

Are you sure you want to rebuild the
desktop file on the disk "Lisa's HD"?
Comments in info windows will be lost.

[Cancel]   [OK]

If you have more than one hard disk or hard disk partition, a dialog box like
Figure 18-3 will appear for each disk that mounts on the Desktop at startup.
Click OK for every disk.

Oh yeah. You don't need to rebuild the desktop of the Disk Tools disk, so you
can click Cancel for that one. You need to deal with your hard disk, and rebuilding the desktop on the Disk Tools disk won't do you any good.

Some of you may be wondering about the blurb in Figure 18-3 about the comments in info windows being lost. This statement means that anything you've
typed into the Comments field (see Figure 18-4) in the Get Info (Command-I)
window of an icon will be lost after the rebuild occurs.

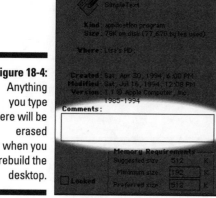

Figure 18-4:
Anything
you type
here will be
erased
when you
rebuild the
desktop.

Loosing comments in the info windows is the only side effect of rebuilding the
desktop, and it's no big deal because nobody types comments there anyway. So
just remember not to use the Comments field in Get Info windows. And remember to rebuild your desktop monthly to keep your Mac in tip-top shape. And
rebuild it again if you see the flashing question mark.

Try to boot from your hard disk now, so remove the Disk Tools disk from the
drive and restart.

If you still see the flashing question mark, it's time to...

Send for the ambulance: run Disk First Aid

The next step in the program is to run the Disk First Aid application on your Disk Tools disk.

The desktop isn't the only place where hard disks store information about themselves. There are BTrees, extent files, catalog files, and other creatively named invisible files involved in managing the data on your disks. Disk First Aid is a program that checks all these files and repairs ones that are damaged.

How to actually do it

If you haven't done so already, restart your Mac with the Disk Tools disk in the floppy drive.

1. Launch the Disk First Aid application (see Figure 18-5).

2. Click the icon for your hard disk at the top of the Disk First Aid window (see Figure 18-6).

3. Click the Repair button.

Your Mac will whir and hum for a few minutes, and the results window will tell you what's going on (see Figure 18-7).

Figure 18-5:
It's Disk First
Aid to the
rescue!

Disk First Aid

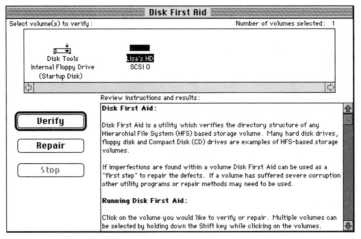

Figure 18-6:
Click your
hard disk's
icon and
then click
Repair; Disk
First Aid
does the
rest.

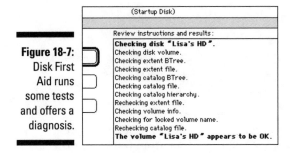

Figure 18-7:
Disk First
Aid runs
some tests
and offers a
diagnosis.

```
           (Startup Disk)

Review instructions and results :
Checking disk "Lisa's HD".
Checking disk volume.
Checking extent BTree.
Checking extent file.
Checking catalog BTree.
Checking catalog file.
Checking catalog hierarchy.
Rechecking extent file.
Checking volume info.
Checking for locked volume name.
Rechecking catalog file.
The volume "Lisa's HD" appears to be OK.
```

Ultimately, Disk First Aid will tell you (you hope) that the disk appears to be OK. If so, restart your Mac without the Disk Tools disk in the drive. If everything is OK, then go back to work.

If Disk First Aid finds damage that it's unable to fix, a commercial disk recovery tool such as Norton Utilities for the Macintosh or MacTools may be able to repair the damage.

If the software *can't* repair the damage, you'll have to initialize your disk. But that's OK, right? You have that backup software and you use it.

If everything checks out with Disk First Aid, try to boot from your hard disk again. If you still get the flashing question mark, try...

Installing new hard disk drivers

This section applies to Apple-brand hard disks only. If you have a third-party hard disk, the procedure will be different. Read your hard disk's manual before you continue. Sorry.

What you're going to attempt next is to install (update) your hard disk drivers.

Drivers are little invisible bits of code that tell your hard disk how to communicate with a Mac. They occasionally become damaged and need replacing. Done properly, the technique is completely harmless and can make the flashing question mark disappear.

How to actually do it

1. Restart your Mac using Disk Tools as your startup disk.

2. Launch the Apple HD SC Setup application.

3. Click the Update button. Do not click the Initialize button.

You should see the message "Driver update successfully completed."

Do not click Initialize! If you click Initialize, your hard disk will be erased completely and irrevocably.

You get a warning or two first, but if you're not paying attention, a few false clicks (or presses of the Return key) and your hard disk is blank.

So click Update, not Initialize, OK?

If that solution doesn't get you up and running and you're still seeing that danged flashing question mark when you try to boot from your hard disk, don't despair. There are still a few things you can try, such as...

The latest dance craze: zapping the PRAM

Sometimes your Parameter RAM (PRAM) becomes scrambled and needs to be reset.

The PRAM is a small piece of memory that's not erased or forgotten when you shut down. It monitors things like printer selection in the Chooser, sound level, and monitor settings.

Try zapping your PRAM if your Sound or Monitor control panels or your Chooser seem to forget their settings when you shut down or restart.

How to actually do it

Restart your Mac and hold down Command-Option-P-R (that's four keys — good luck; it's OK to use your nose) until your Mac restarts itself again. It's kind of like a hiccup. You see the smiling Mac or flashing question mark for a second, and then that icon disappears and your Mac restarts.

Zapping the PRAM returns some control panels to their default settings (but, interestingly, not the date or time), so you may have to do some tweaking after zapping the PRAM.

SCSI voodoo

It is said that connecting more than one SCSI device — an external hard disk, SyQuest, Bernoulli, optical disk, scanner, and so on — requires the luck of the gods.

The first bugaboo is SCSI termination. According to Apple, the first and last device on a SCSI chain must have a terminator. No devices in between should have termination. Internal hard drives are always terminated. And the total length of a SCSI chain can be no more than 22 feet.

But sometimes you can't get your SCSI chain to work by following the rules. Sometimes it requires terminating a drive in the middle of the chain as well as the first and last drives. Other times, a chain won't work if the last device *is* terminated. The physical order of devices matters. And, of course, there are those SCSI ID numbers.

So if you're seeing a flashing question mark still, and you have any external devices attached, shut down your Mac and unplug them. After they're all disconnected, try restarting your Mac using the Disk Tools disk.

Never plug or unplug SCSI devices with the power on. Turn both your Mac and the device off before you attempt to connect or disconnect any cables.

If your Mac starts up when no SCSI devices are connected, you've got a problem on the SCSI chain: a termination problem, a bad cable, or a SCSI ID conflict.

I'll be back: the terminator

A terminator is a plug that fits into the empty cable connector of the last device on your chain.

Some terminators are *pass-through* connectors, which can have a cable connected to them. Others block off that connector completely; these are known as block terminators.

If you see the flashing question mark and your last device isn't terminated, terminate it. If it is terminated, unterminate it. If you have more than one device and your terminator is a pass-through terminator, connect it to a device in the middle of the chain (instead of the end) and try to start your Mac.

If you have two terminators and two or more devices, try two terminators, one in the middle and one at the end. This trick isn't recommended, but sometimes that's what it takes to make it work.

If all this terminator juggling isn't working for you, try changing the physical order of the devices. If right now your Mac is connected to the hard disk, which is connected to the SyQuest, then try connecting the SyQuest to the Mac and the hard disk to the SyQuest.

I add and subtract SCSI devices more often in a year than most people do in two lifetimes. I'm always firing up some new storage device that someone wants me to check out. And I've had good luck since switching to a drive with Digital Active Termination.

Digital Active Termination senses how much termination your SCSI chain requires and then supplies it automatically. It's almost a miracle and it's an option on all new devices from APS Technologies. Just put any device with Digital Active Termination at the end of your chain, and you are virtually guaranteed perfect termination, regardless of the number of devices in the chain or the physical order of the devices.

Cables: cheap is bad

When troubleshooting SCSI problems, you should check your SCSI cables. If you can borrow others, try that option. Cheap cables, usually ones that are thin and flexible, are more prone to failure than heavy shielded cables. Again, APS has excellent cables at reasonable prices.

Gotta have some ID: unique SCSI ID numbers required

If you have multiple SCSI devices, don't forget that each must have a unique SCSI ID between 0 and 7. Your internal hard disk has ID 0, so external devices can have numbers from 1 to 6.

You usually select the ID number using a wheel or button on the back of the device. Just make sure that each drive in the chain has a unique number and you're all set.

Try again to restart without the Disk Tools disk.

If nothing so far has cured the flashing question mark, you have to suspect damage to the System software on your hard disk.

So now you're going to try to replace your old System software with fresh, new System software.

Reinstalling the System software

The reason that this procedure comes last in this section is that it takes the longest. The procedure is detailed at great length in the section of Chapter 1 known as "Anyone Can Install System 7.5."

Read it and follow the instructions.

If nothing has worked so far

If none of my suggestions have worked, if you've rebuilt the desktop, run Disk First Aid, installed new hard disk drivers, zapped your PRAM, disconnected all SCSI devices, and reinstalled your System software, and you're still seeing the flashing question mark, then you've got big trouble.

You may have any one of the following problems:

✔ Your hard disk is dead and so is your floppy drive.

✔ Your hard disk is dead but your floppy drive is OK.

✔ Some other type of hardware failure.

✔ Both your Disk Tools and Install Disk 1 disks are defective (unlikely).

The bottom line: If you're still seeing the flashing question mark after trying all the stuff in the previous pages, you need to have your Mac serviced by a qualified technician.

If You Crash at Startup

More of a hassle to solve than flashing question mark problems but rarely fatal, startup crashes are another bad thing that can happen to your Mac.

A *crash* is defined as a System Error dialog box, frozen cursor, frozen screen, or any other disabling event.

At startup is defined as any time between flicking the power key or switch (or restarting) and having full use of the Finder Desktop.

A startup crash may happen to you someday. If it does, here's what to do.

Restart without extensions and control panels

The first thing you need to do is establish whether an extension or control panel is causing the crash by starting up with all of them disabled.

How to actually do it

If your Mac is already on: Choose Special⇨Restart and then hold down the Shift key until you see "Extensions Off" in the Welcome to Macintosh dialog box. After you see "Extensions Off," you may release the Shift key.

If your Mac is off, power it up and hold down the Shift key until you see "Extensions Off" in the Welcome to Macintosh dialog box. Again, you can release the Shift key after "Extensions Off" appears.

If your Mac starts up successfully when you hold down the Shift key but crashes or freezes when you don't, you can deduce that one (or more) of your extensions or control panels is responsible for the crash. Read the section "Resolving extension and control panel conflicts" below.

If your Mac still crashes when you hold down the Shift key, you can deduce that something is wrong with your System or Finder. Read the section "How to perform a clean System reinstallation" a few pages hence.

Resolving extension and control panel conflicts

If you're reading this section, you have an extension or control panel that is causing your Mac to crash at startup. The trick now is to isolate which one (or, occasionally, more than one) is causing your troubles. Chances are, it's a third-party extension or control panel, but you can't rule out Apple extensions and control panels either. They too can conflict with other extensions or control panels or become corrupted and not function properly.

Because you know that your Mac will start up with the Shift key down, you use Extensions Manager to track down the rogue extension or control panel file.

I'm so happy Apple includes Extensions Manager as part of System 7.5 that I could turn back flips. You'll see why when I show you how to resolve your difficulties with Extensions Manager. Just imagine what a hassle it would be without EM.

How to actually do it

The first step is to establish whether any of the Apple System 7.5 extensions or control panels are causing problems.

1. Power up or restart your Mac and then press and hold the spacebar until the Extensions Manager window appears.

2. Choose System 7.5 Only from the pop-up menu (see Figure 18-8) and then click the Extensions Manager window's close box to begin the startup process.

Figure 18-8: Choose System 7.5 Only to load only the standard issue extensions and control panels. Then click the Close box to begin the startup process.

Situation 1: You can now boot successfully, which means that the culprit must be one of your third-party extensions or control panels.

Situation 2: You still crash at startup, which means that the culprit must be one of the System 7.5 extensions or control panels.

In Situation 1, repeat these steps until you crash again:

1. Power up or restart your Mac and then press and hold the spacebar until the Extensions Manager window appears.
2. Add one extension or control panel to the enabled list by clicking it so that a check mark appears.
3. Click the Extensions Manager's close box to begin the startup process.

If you start up successfully, you know that the extension or control panel that you just added is not the culprit. Repeat these three steps, enabling one new item each time you restart, until you crash. When you do, the last extension or control panel that you enabled is the culprit.

See the section called "Dealing with recalcitrant extensions and control panels" for possible solutions.

In Situation 2, repeat these steps until you stop crashing:

1. Power up or restart your Mac and then press and hold the spacebar until the Extensions Manager window appears.
2. Disable one of the currently enabled extensions or control panels by clicking it so that its check mark disappears.
3. Click the Extensions Manager's close box to begin the startup process.

Repeat these three steps, disabling one item each time you restart, until you stop crashing. When you do, the last extension or control panel that you disabled was the culprit.

See the section called "Dealing with recalcitrant extensions and control panels" for some things you can try.

Sometimes you can tell which extension or control panel is causing your crash by looking carefully at the little icons that appear on the bottom of your screen during startup. Each icon you see represents a control panel or extension loading into memory. If you can determine which icon was the last to appear before the crash, you can try disabling it before going through the iterative and frustrating process of determining the culprit as described above. You might get lucky and save yourself hours of boring detective work.

If you've got a good memory, you can enable or disable a few at a time in Step 2. Just keep track of what you're doing and you can reduce the number of restarts it takes to find your offender.

Dealing with recalcitrant extensions and control panels

In the previous section, you determined which particular extension or control panel was giving you fits. In this section, I've got a couple of suggestions — replace and reorder — that may let you use the offending item anyway.

How to replace a recalcitrant file

1. Delete the guilty control panel or extension from your hard disk by dragging it to the Trash.

2. Open the Preferences folder in your System Folder and delete any preference file with the same name as the guilty file.

3. Replace the guilty file with a fresh copy from a master disk.

If it's an Apple extension or control panel, use the Installer as described in Chapter 15. If it's a third-party product, follow the installation instructions in its manual.

Restart and see if the problem reoccurs.

If it does, you may *still* be able to use the recalcitrant extension or control panel by diddling with the loading order of extensions and control panels at startup.

How to reorder a recalcitrant file

To understand how to reorder, you must first understand why you need to reorder.

In some cases, extensions and control panels crash only if they load before or after another extension. Ergo, by diddling with the loading order, you can force one file to load before another.

How do you diddle the loading order, you ask? When extensions and control panels load at startup, they load in alphabetical order by folder. To wit:

1. The Extensions folder's contents, in alphabetical order

    and then

2. The Control Panels folder's contents, in alphabetical order

    followed by

3. Control panels or extensions loose in your System Folder (that is, not in the Extensions or Control Panels folders), in alphabetical order.

So, if you've got a recalcitrant extension or control panel, try forcing it to load either first or last. This trick works more often than not.

To force an offending control panel or extension (Now Toolbox in this example) to load first, precede its name by several spaces and move it to the Extensions folder. It should then appear first in both the Extensions Manager and the Extensions folder (see Figure 18-9).

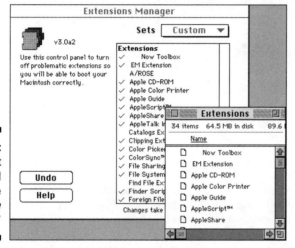

Figure 18-9:
The first item to load will be " Now Toolbox."

By putting Now Toolbox in the Extensions folder (so that it loads before items in the Control Panels folder or System Folder) and preceding its name with several spaces, I've ensured that this item is the first to load.

Going the other way, to force an extension or control panel (MacsBug in this example) to load last, precede its name with several tildes and move it out of the Extensions folder and into the System Folder itself (see Figure 18-10).

By preceding the item's name with several tildes and moving it out of the Extensions folder and into the System Folder itself, as shown, I've ensured that MacsBug will be the last extension or control panel to load.

More sophisticated startup managers, such as Now Utilities' Startup Manager and Casady & Greene's Conflict Catcher II, let you change the loading order of extensions and control panels by dragging them around, avoiding the inconvenience of renaming or moving them manually. I wish Extensions Manager had this capability.

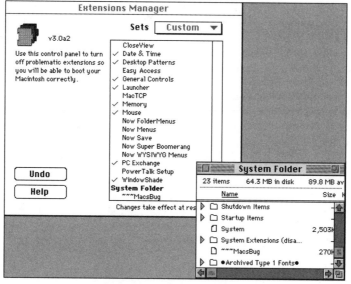

Both programs can also perform the conflict resolution three-step boogie automatically. You just restart, tell the software whether the problem is gone, and then restart again. The software does all of the enabling and disabling and keeps track automatically. At the end, it tells you which file is the culprit. If you have many of these conflicts, one of these two programs is a worthwhile upgrade to the bare-bones Extensions Manager.

If you're still reading and your problem hasn't been resolved, there's one last thing you can try, namely, a clean System software installation.

How to perform a clean System reinstallation

This is a drastic final step. If nothing so far has fixed your startup problems, a clean System reinstallation very well may. I saved this solution for last because it's the biggest hassle, and you don't want to go through the trouble if something easier can fix you up. So if you're doing a clean reinstall, it's more or less your last hope.

Don't worry. This solution will most likely get you back on your feet. This one will fix all but the most horrifying and malignant of problems. So let's get to it.

Clean versus regular installation

To understand why you need to do a Clean Install, or even what a Clean Install is, you have to understand a little about how the Installer works and what resources are.

Resources are the building blocks from which all programs, control panels, extensions, and so on, are built. The Installer is, technically, a resource installer. It installs the resources that become programs, control panels, extensions, and so on.

And the Installer is very smart about which resources it installs. It looks at your hard disk; then, if it sees a System Folder containing a System and a Finder, it installs only the resources it thinks you need. So, for example, if the Installer sees a System and Finder, it looks to see if they contain

the proper resources. If they do, it doesn't install anything, even if the resources are damaged.

Therein lies the rub. The Installer can sometimes outsmart itself. If the reason your Mac is crashing is that a resource inside the System, Finder, a control panel, or an extension has become damaged or corrupted, the Installer may not replace the defective resource if you perform a Regular Install.

A Clean Install, on the other hand, ensures that every single file and every single resource is replaced with a brand spanking new one. In fact, a Clean Install gives you a brand new System Folder.

The easy way to perform a Clean Install

Prior to System 7.5, Clean Installs were performed manually (see "The old and much harder way to perform a Clean Install" section, coming up in a second) and were much harder to explain.

Thankfully, there is now a hidden shortcut in System 7.5's Installer that lets you perform a Clean Install automatically, with no muss or fuss. Here's how:

1. Start up or restart your Mac with Install Disk 1 in your floppy drive (or the CD in your CD-ROM drive).

2. Click the Continue button on the splash screen.

3. When the main Installer window appears, type the keyboard shortcut for Clean Install, Command-Shift-K.

4. A dialog box will appear, as shown in Figure 18-11. Choose Install New System Folder and click OK.

5. The Easy Install button changes to the Clean Install button (see Figure 18-12). Click it and feed disks as requested.

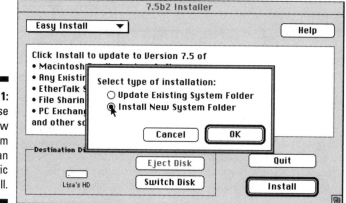

Figure 18-11: Choose Install New System Folder for an automatic Clean Install.

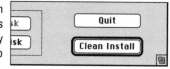

Figure 18-12: The button changes from Easy Install to Clean Install.

When the Installer is through, you'll have a brand spanking new System Folder on your hard disk. Your old System Folder has been renamed Previous System Folder. Nothing has been removed from it.

The folder called Previous System Folder contains all your old third-party extensions, control panels, and fonts. Because it's possible, even likely, that one of these items contributed to your problem, I recommend that you reinstall them one item at a time. In other words, move one extension or control panel from Previous System Folder onto the new System Folder's icon. Then restart and work for a while to see if any problems occur before reinstalling another.

It's a good idea to trash the System and Finder in the Previous System Folder as soon as possible after performing the Clean Install.

It's simply a bad idea to have two System Folders on one hard disk, and as long as Previous System Folder has a System and a Finder in it, your Mac could confuse Previous System Folder with the real System Folder, and that confusion could cause you major heartache.

So delete the old System and Finder files, the ones in the Previous System Folder, now. Just in case. Thanks.

Don't forget that the System Folder is smart. If you drag a control panel or extension onto its icon (but *not* into its open window), it will put the file in the proper folder for you.

The old and much harder way to perform a Clean Install

There is no reason to ever do a Clean Install the old-fashioned way anymore. It's presented here as an historical oddity, to show you the way things used to be.

Thanks, Apple, for the Clean Install option in the Installer. It makes things *so* much easier. (But why the obscure Command-Shift-K keyboard shortcut? Shouldn't it be in the pop-up menu like the Custom Install option?)

1. Drag your System and Finder files to the Trash.

2. Rename your System Folder "OldSys."

3. Restart your Mac (see Figure 18-13). When the flashing question mark appears, insert Install Disk 1.

4. Perform an Easy Install on your hard disk as detailed in the section of Chapter 1 called "Anyone Can Install System 7.5."

Figure 18-13:
This Mac is ready to perform a Clean Install the old-fashioned way.

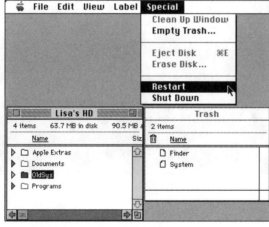

When the Installer is through, you'll have a brand spanking new System Folder on your hard disk.

Don't bother trying to empty the Trash after Step 1. It won't empty for obvious reasons. Don't sweat it, as you'll be able to empty it after you perform the Clean Install.

Appendix

Macintosh System 7.5 Update 1.0

What It Is, What It Does, and Why You Should Install It

So it's now six months after the original publication date of this book, and guess what? Apple has just released an update to System 7.5, cleverly named *Macintosh System 7.5 Update 1.0*. It makes System 7.5 better in many ways, and I recommend that you get and install it A.S.A.P.

Where To Get It

Macintosh System 7.5 Update 1.0 is available from all the major on-line services for the cost of the download. Unfortunately, it's a four disk-image set — over 4 megabytes — so you're probably better off ordering it on floppy disks from Apple. Just call 800–769–2775 extension 5794. The disks are free, but there's a $10 (plus applicable tax) charge for shipping and handling.

What It Is and What It Does

Macintosh System 7.5 Update 1.0 is a set of software enhancements that improves the performance and reliability of Macintosh computers running System 7.5. It provides enhancements to the system software — including the Launcher, system extensions, control panels, and applications — and provides solutions for problems encountered by some Macintosh computer users.

How to Install It

Insert Disk 1. Double-click the Installer. From here, it's just like installing System 7.5. Hint: Select the Easy Install option unless you have a compelling reason to choose Custom Install.

After you install the update, you're Mac won't be running System 7.5 anymore; it'll be running System 7.5.1. Sharing this kind of information makes computer people the life of any party.

Meet the System 7.5 Update File

The update installs a file called *System 7.5 Update* in your System Folder. This file improves system stability when memory is very low and fixes a bunch of bugs that Apple, in its wisdom, has decided to fix.

The Update file also lets you use the keyboard Power key to turn the computer off. To shut down your Mac, press the Power key. From the subsequent dialog box, you can shut down your Mac, restart your Mac, put it to sleep (if it supports sleep), or cancel the shutdown.)

The System 7.5 Update file is as important to the inner workings of your Mac as the System file and the Finder file. Don't move the it from your System Folder.

The Rest of the Cast

In addition to the ever-important System 7.5 Update file, the update installs the following:

- Launcher version 2.7
- File Sharing version 7.6.1
- Apple Guide version 1.2.5
- SCSI Manager version 4.3.1
- Speech Manager version 1.3
- General Controls version 7.5.3
- Apple Menu Options version 1.0.1
- Keyboard version 7.5.1
- WindowShade version 1.3.1
- MacTCP version 2.0.6
- Macintosh Easy Open version 1.1.1
- SimpleText version 1.2

- ✔ Find File version 1.1.1
- ✔ Stickies version 1.0.1
- ✔ Jigsaw version 1.0.1
- ✔ LaserWriter printer driver version 8.2

. . . plus other enhancements too numerous to mention.

All of the files in the preceding list are updated versions of the files you may have already installed. Unless Apple really screwed up, these new files ought to be better than the old ones.

Don't forget that the Update's installer replaces old System files with new ones, so you don't have to worry about deleting, say, your old WindowShade control panel before running the Installer. The Installer does all of your house cleaning for you.

If the Installer installs new versions of files you don't normally use, like the pathetic Launcher, you can just drag those new files to the Trash. Or you could do a Custom Install and exclude the files you don't need from the installation. Either method will keep the files off your System.

Index

IDG BOOKS WORLDWIDE REGISTRATION CARD

RETURN THIS REGISTRATION CARD FOR FREE CATALOG

Title of this book: Macintosh System 7.5 For Dummies

My overall rating of this book: ❑ Very good [1]   ❑ Good [2]   ❑ Satisfactory [3]   ❑ Fair [4]   ❑ Poor [5]

How I first heard about this book:

❑ Found in bookstore; name: [6]

❑ Advertisement: [8]

❑ Word of mouth; heard about book from friend, co-worker, etc.: [10]

❑ Book review: [7]

❑ Catalog: [9]

❑ Other: [11]

What I liked most about this book:

What I would change, add, delete, etc., in future editions of this book:

Other comments:

Number of computer books I purchase in a year: ❑ 1 [12]   ❑ 2-5 [13]   ❑ 6-10 [14]   ❑ More than 10 [15]

I would characterize my computer skills as: ❑ Beginner [16]   ❑ Intermediate [17]   ❑ Advanced [18]   ❑ Professional [19]

I use ❑ DOS [20]   ❑ Windows [21]   ❑ OS/2 [22]   ❑ Unix [23]   ❑ Macintosh [24]   ❑ Other: [25]_____

(please specify)

I would be interested in new books on the following subjects:
(please check all that apply, and use the spaces provided to identify specific software)

❑ Word processing: [26]

❑ Data bases: [28]

❑ File Utilities: [30]

❑ Networking: [32]

❑ Other: [34]

❑ Spreadsheets: [27]

❑ Desktop publishing: [29]

❑ Money management: [31]

❑ Programming languages: [33]

I use a PC at (please check all that apply): ❑ home [35]   ❑ work [36]   ❑ school [37]   ❑ other: [38] _____

The disks I prefer to use are ❑ 5.25 [39]   ❑ 3.5 [40]   ❑ other: [41]_____

I have a CD ROM: ❑ yes [42]   ❑ no [43]

I plan to buy or upgrade computer hardware this year: ❑ yes [44]   ❑ no [45]

I plan to buy or upgrade computer software this year: ❑ yes [46]   ❑ no [47]

Name: Business title: [48]   Type of Business: [49]

Address (❑ home [50] ❑ work [51]/Company name:)

Street/Suite#

City [52]/State [53]/Zipcode [54]:   Country [55]

❑ **I liked this book!** You may quote me by name in future
IDG Books Worldwide promotional materials.

My daytime phone number is _____

IDG BOOKS

THE WORLD OF
COMPUTER
KNOWLEDGE

 **YES!**
Please keep me informed about IDG's World of Computer Knowledge.
Send me the latest IDG Books catalog.